taste of home
farm
FRESH
favorites

taste of home
BOOKS

REIMAN MEDIA GROUP, LLC • GREENDALE, WI

tasteofhome

Reader's Digest

A TASTE OF HOME/READER'S DIGEST BOOK
©2012 Reiman Media Group, LLC
5400 S. 60th St., Greendale WI 53129
All rights reserved.

Taste of Home and Reader's Digest are registered
trademarks of The Reader's Digest Association, Inc.

Editor-in-Chief: Catherine Cassidy

Vice President, Executive Editor/Books:
Heidi Reuter Lloyd

Creative Director: Howard Greenberg

North American Chief Marketing Officer:
Lisa Karpinski

Food Director: Diane Werner, RD

Senior Editor/Retail Books: Faithann Stoner

Editor: Sara Rae Lancaster

Associate Creative Director: Edwin Robles Jr.

Art Director: Raeann Sundholm

Content Production Manager: Julie Wagner

Layout Designer: Kathy Crawford

Copy Chief: Deb Warlaumont Mulvey

Copy Editor: Alysse Gear

Recipe Asset System Manager: Coleen Martin

Recipe Testing & Editing: Taste of Home Test Kitchen

Food Photography: Taste of Home Photo Studio

Administrative Assistant: Barb Czysz

The Reader's Digest Association, Inc.
President and Chief Executive Officer: Robert E. Guth

President, North America: Dan Lagani

President/Publisher, Trade Publishing: Harold Clarke

Associate Publisher: Rosanne McManus

Vice President, Sales & Marketing: Stacey Ashton

"Cooking, Caring, Sharing" is a registered
trademark of Reiman Media Group, LLC.

For other Taste of Home books and products,
visit us at tasteofhome.com.

For more Reader's Digest products and information,
visit rd.com (in the United States)
or see rd.ca (in Canada).

International Standard Book Number
(10): 0-89821-961-2
International Standard Book Number
(13): 978-0-89821-961-6
Library of Congress Control Number: 2011940521

Cover Photography

Photographer: Lori Foy
Food Stylist: Shannon Roum
Set Stylist: Melissa Haberman

Pictured on front cover:
Pickled Peppers, page 226; Basil Jelly, page 215; Cinnamon
Plum Jam, page 218; Strawberry Salsa, page 235; Delicious
Tomato Pie, page 195

Pictured on back cover:
Swiss Chard Bean Soup, page 65;
Grilled Steak Bruschetta Salad, page 44;
Rhubarb Popover Pie, page 68

Printed in China.
1 3 5 7 9 10 8 6 4 2

table of CONTENTS

eating fresh is **BEST**

Mom knew a thing or two when she said, "Eat your veggies." And that old saying, "An apple a day keeps the doctor away"? There's a kernel of truth to that, too.

The nutritional benefits of fruits and veggies are no big secret. Why, then, do so many turn up their noses at the mere sight of a plate of broccoli or eagerly choose a candy bar over sun-ripened berries to calm a sweet tooth?

Because most people have never experienced the true flavor of a tomato or delighted in the simple pleasure of a juicy plum picked straight from the tree. But let's face it. Growing an extensive vegetable garden and orchard doesn't fit the average backyard or schedule.

WHY "PICK" THE FARMERS MARKET?

As any regular farmers market shopper will tell you, the benefits of buying local and eating with the seasons are without contest. First of all, the food tastes better. At the farmers market, produce is usually harvested less than 24 hours prior. Add to that the money-saving benefits, nutritional advantage and community-building aspect, and it's hard to imagine why someone wouldn't eat local. But where to begin?

Enter *Taste of Home Farm Fresh Favorites*. Think of this book as your **blueprint** for eating locally, whether that be your local farmers market, roadside stand or own backyard. *Farm Fresh Favorites* makes it easier than ever to experience the simple pleasures of eating close to the source.

With a **bounty of family-friendly** and **versatile recipes** (336 to be exact, each with a tempting full-color photo and handy section for cooking notes), *Farm Fresh Favorites* **guides the everyday cook through the seasons**, explaining what produce to look for and when, as well as **how to prepare mouthwatering, wholesome dishes** using simple, honest ingredients. Food just doesn't taste better, **it is better!**

Four **hefty chapters organized by season**—Spring, Early to Mid-Summer, Late Summer to Fall and Savor the Season—act as an easy-to-follow map for **eating seasonally, locally** and, of course, **deliciously**.

Peppered throughout are **55+ tips** to ensure every dish turns out just right, as well as information on **selecting and storing produce**, **handy reference charts**, a list of the **country's must-visit farmers markets** and a comprehensive chapter on **canning and preserving the harvest**.

At Taste of Home, we're all about **cooking, caring and sharing**. What better way to celebrate all three than with **whole, fresh foods prepared in your kitchen** from ingredients that are picked at the **peak of ripeness**.

Whether you want to use your **garden's bounty**, become a **locavore** for a week (or for life) or simply **eat better**, *Taste of Home Farm Fresh Favorites* brings you **336 seasonal dishes** made from **nature's freshest ingredients**.

WANT TO SHARE YOUR HOME-GROWN RECIPE?
We're looking for your garden's bounty recipes, from salads and sides to jams, jellies and wholesome entrees. Send them to: **tasteofhome.com/submit.**

step away from
THE SUPERMARKET

Go get your veggie fix at these top five cream-of-the-crop farmers markets.

For your convenience, we've scoped out five well-known markets. Just pack your canvas or recyclable shopping bag and get ready to thump cantaloupes and sniff tomatoes. You'll feel right at home.

1 PORTLAND FARMERS MARKET
Portland, Oregon

Open on Saturdays from late March through mid-December, this venerable feast for the senses, located on the Portland State University campus, appears on many lists of top farmers markets. Maybe that's because it offers great regional produce, live music, cooking demonstrations by top chefs and even a parcel pickup service for overeager shoppers. Four other affiliated markets run on weekdays in other neighborhoods. Go ahead and shop till you drop.
portlandfarmersmarket.org

2 SANTA MONICA SATURDAY ORGANIC FARMERS MARKET
Santa Monica, California

From master gardeners and dietitians to top chefs and free recipe samples, this Los Angeles-area standby is clearly more than just a produce paradise. Along with the entertainment, you'll find a year-round cornucopia of fresh fruits and veggies. Bonus points: Was that Brad Pitt standing behind the avocados? *smgov.net/farmers_market*

3 UNION SQUARE GREENMARKET
New York, New York

When in the Big Apple, do as the locals do: Go gourmet and shop at this urban oasis, where city slickers learn what produce really tastes like. Manhattan's rock-star chefs come here to sniff, squeeze and scrutinize a plethora of produce from upstate New York, Connecticut, New Jersey and beyond. The plentiful pluses include cheese, honey, jam and grass-fed beef. Dozens of other markets operate in New York City under the Greenmarket umbrella, but this is the group's flagship location. Take a bite and savor the flavor, baby. *grownyc.org*

4 DANE COUNTY FARMERS' MARKET
Madison, Wisconsin

About 150 regional vendors line the square around the state Capitol to sell mind-boggling mountains of fresh produce and, of course, cheese and other dairy products (don't miss the hot and spicy cheese bread!). Held rain or shine on Saturdays spring through fall, the market also features live music and arts-and-crafts booths. A stop here is a capital idea, for sure. *dcfm.org*

5 CRESCENT CITY FARMERS MARKET
New Orleans, Louisiana

Along with fresh produce, this colorful year-round market in the historic Warehouse District also offers baked goods and fresh seafood. Toss in live jazz and cooking demonstrations, and you've got a stew as sassy as a bowl of spicy, steamin' Cajun jambalaya. And leave it to the Big Easy to make shopping, well, easy. Vendors don't take plastic, but shoppers can convert credit- and debit-card allocations into Crescent coins, a sort of local currency accepted by all vendors. *Laissez les bon temps roulez! crescentcityfarmers market.org*

SHOP A MARKET NEAR YOU

Don't know where to start? To find organic markets, farms and other sources of sustainably grown food close to home, visit Agritourism World at *agritourismworld.com,* Local Harvest at *localharvest.org* or the USDA's *ams.usda.gov/ farmersmarkets.*

other top picks

Pike Place, Seattle, Washington *pikeplacemarket.org*

Ferry Plaza Farmers Market, San Francisco, California *ferrybuildingmarketplace.com*

Santa Fe Farmers Market, Santa Fe, New Mexico *santafefarmersmarket.com*

CitySeed Farmers' Market Wooster Square, New Haven, Connecticut *cityseed.org*

Green City Market, Chicago, Illinois *chicagogreencitymarket.org*

SPRING

USHER IN THE SEASON'S FRESHEST FLAVORS

Tender asparagus...sweet peas...aromatic herbs...
crisp greens...when these farm-fresh fruits and
veggies begin to appear, it's a sure sign that spring
has sprung and your local farmers markets are
officially open for business. Celebrate their arrival
with a tasty variety of market-to-table recipes.

ASPARAGUS

Asparagus, Brie & Parma Ham Crostini

Prep/Total Time: 25 min. • **Yield:** 1 dozen.
This special, filling appetizer is perfect to serve guests. The combination of crisp bread, rich melted cheese and fresh asparagus is out of this world.
—*Karla Johnson, East Helena, Montana*

- 12 fresh asparagus spears
- 2 tablespoons olive oil, *divided*
- 1/8 teaspoon salt
- 1/8 teaspoon pepper
- 12 slices French bread baguette (1/2 inch thick)
- 3 thin slices prosciutto *or* deli ham, cut into thin strips
- 6 ounces Brie cheese, cut into 12 slices

1. Cut asparagus tips into 2-in. lengths. (Discard stalks or save for another use.) Place asparagus tips in a 15-in. x 10-in. x 1-in. baking pan lined with foil. Drizzle with 1 teaspoon olive oil and toss to coat. Sprinkle with the salt and pepper. Bake at 425° for 10-15 minutes or until crisp-tender.

2. Brush baguette slices on both sides with remaining oil. Place on a baking sheet. Broil for 1-2 minutes on each side or until toasted.

3. Top each slice with asparagus, prosciutto and cheese. Broil 3-4 in. from the heat for 2-3 minutes or until cheese is melted.

Nutrition Facts: 1 piece equals 91 calories, 6 g fat (3 g saturated fat), 16 mg cholesterol, 191 mg sodium, 4 g carbohydrate, trace fiber, 4 g protein.

Its short growing season makes asparagus a coveted spring veggie. Versatile and nutritious, the superfood has edible, slender stalks with feathery tips and comes in two varieties: green and white.

SEASON: February through late June; peaks April-May.

AT THE MARKET: Select small, straight stalks with tightly closed, compact tips. Spears should be smooth and round. Green asparagus should have bright green stalks and tips with a slight lavender tint. White asparagus should have straight, firm stalks.

STORAGE: Refrigerate unwashed green asparagus in a sealed plastic bag for up to 4 days (2 days for white asparagus).

ASPARAGUS, BRIE & PARMA HAM
CROSTINI NOTES: _____
_____
_____
_____
_____

Fresh Asparagus with Pecans

Prep: 15 min. + marinating • **Yield:** 4 servings.
If it's a special occasion for my family, you can expect to see this simply elegant side. It tastes so good, you forget it's healthy, too!
—*Jennifer Clark, Blacksburg, Virginia*

1	pound fresh asparagus, trimmed	2	tablespoons sugar
1/4	cup cider vinegar	2	tablespoons olive oil
1/4	cup reduced-sodium soy sauce	3	tablespoons chopped pecans, toasted

1. In a large skillet, bring 3 cups water to a boil. Add asparagus; cover and boil for 3 minutes. Drain and immediately place asparagus in ice water. Drain and pat dry.

2. In a large resealable plastic bag, combine the vinegar, soy sauce, sugar and oil. Add the asparagus; seal bag and turn to coat. Refrigerate for up to 3 hours.

3. Drain and discard marinade. Sprinkle asparagus with pecans.

Nutrition Facts: 1 serving equals 77 calories, 6 g fat (1 g saturated fat), 0 cholesterol, 164 mg sodium, 5 g carbohydrate, 1 g fiber, 2 g protein. **Diabetic Exchanges:** 1 vegetable, 1 fat.

FRESH ASPARAGUS WITH PECANS NOTES:

_____
_____
_____
_____

Asparagus Scones

Prep: 25 min. • **Bake:** 20 min. + cooling • **Yield:** 8 scones.
These moist scones have a mild, peppery bite and go great with soup for a light lunch. Feel free to substitute Parmesan or smoked mozzarella cheese for the cheddar.
—*Mary Ann Dell, Phoenixville, Pennsylvania*

1-3/4	cups cut fresh asparagus (1/4-inch pieces)	1/4	teaspoon pepper
2	cups all-purpose flour	1/4	teaspoon cayenne pepper
1	tablespoon sugar	1/4	cup cold butter, cubed
2	teaspoons baking powder	3/4	cup plus 2 tablespoons buttermilk, *divided*
1/2	teaspoon salt	1/2	cup shredded reduced-fat cheddar cheese
1/4	teaspoon baking soda		

1. In a large saucepan, bring 1/2 in. of water to a boil. Add asparagus; cover and boil for 3 minutes. Drain and immediately place asparagus in ice water. Drain and pat dry; set aside.

2. In a large bowl, combine flour, sugar, baking powder, salt, baking soda, pepper and cayenne. Cut in butter until mixture resembles coarse crumbs. Stir in 3/4 cup buttermilk just until moistened. Stir in cheese and asparagus.

3. Turn onto a floured surface; knead 10 times. Transfer dough to a baking sheet coated with cooking spray. Pat into a 9-in. circle. Cut into eight wedges, but do not separate.

4. Brush with remaining buttermilk. Bake at 425° for 18-20 minutes or until golden brown. Cool on a wire rack.

Nutrition Facts: 1 scone equals 211 calories, 8 g fat (5 g saturated fat), 21 mg cholesterol, 419 mg sodium, 29 g carbohydrate, 2 g fiber, 7 g protein. **Diabetic Exchanges:** 2 starch, 1-1/2 fat.

ASPARAGUS SCONES NOTES: _____
_____
_____
_____
_____

Tangy Asparagus Potato Salad

Prep/Total Time: 25 min. • **Yield:** 4 servings.
I look forward to making this whenever asparagus season rolls around. It's been a family favorite for years.
—*Debbie Konietzki, Neenah, Wisconsin*

4 small red potatoes, cut into 1/4-inch wedges	1 tablespoon lemon juice
1 pound fresh asparagus, trimmed	1/4 cup olive oil
1 tablespoon Dijon mustard	2 tablespoons minced chives
	1/8 teaspoon salt
	Dash pepper

1. Place potatoes in a large saucepan; cover with water. Bring to a boil; cook for 15-20 minutes or until tender.

2. Meanwhile, in a large skillet, bring 1/2 in. of water to a boil. Add asparagus; cover and boil for 3 minutes. Drain and immediately place asparagus in ice water. Drain and pat dry. Cut into 1-in. pieces.

3. Drain potatoes and place in a large bowl; add asparagus. In a small bowl, combine the mustard and lemon juice; whisk in oil until combined. Add the chives, salt and pepper. Pour over vegetables and toss to coat. Serve warm or at room temperature.

Nutrition Facts: 3/4 cup equals 172 calories, 14 g fat (2 g saturated fat), 0 cholesterol, 177 mg sodium, 11 g carbohydrate, 2 g fiber, 3 g protein.

```
TANGY ASPARAGUS POTATO SALAD
NOTES:_____
_____
_____
_____
_____
```

```
BOW TIES WITH ASPARAGUS AND
PROSCIUTTO NOTES: _____
_____
_____
_____
_____
```

Bow Ties with Asparagus and Prosciutto

Prep: 15 min. • **Cook:** 15 min. • **Yield:** 6 servings.
For a main course, I like this dish that lets the flavors of prosciutto and asparagus shine. With only five ingredients and a couple tablespoons of water, dinner is as easy as it is elegant. Sometimes I'll add a dash of nutmeg for a change of pace.
—*Jodi Trigg, Toledo, Illinois*

1 package (16 ounces) bow tie pasta	3 tablespoons water
1-1/2 cups heavy whipping cream	1/2 cup shredded Parmesan cheese
1 pound fresh asparagus, trimmed and cut into 1-inch pieces	6 ounces thinly sliced prosciutto *or* deli ham, cut into strips

1. Cook pasta according to package directions. Meanwhile, in a small saucepan, bring cream to a boil. Reduce heat; simmer, uncovered, for 6-7 minutes or until slightly thickened.

2. Place asparagus and water in a microwave-safe dish. Cover; microwave on high for 3-4 minutes or until crisp-tender. Drain.

3. Drain pasta and place in a large serving bowl. Add the cream, asparagus, cheese and prosciutto; toss to coat.

Nutrition Facts: 1-1/3 cup equals 573 calories, 29 g fat (17 g saturated fat), 112 mg cholesterol, 689 mg sodium, 58 g carbohydrate, 3 g fiber, 22 g protein.

EDITOR'S NOTE: This recipe was tested in a 1,100-watt microwave.

Fettuccine with Asparagus and Peas

Prep/Total Time: 30 min. • **Yield:** 6 servings.
I found this years ago, and it has consistently been a crowd pleaser.
I often use whole wheat pasta instead; it's a great substitution!
—*Vicki Kamstra, Spokane, Washington*

- 8 ounces uncooked fettuccine
- 2 medium leeks (white portion only), sliced
- 1 tablespoon olive oil
- 1 pound fresh asparagus, trimmed and cut into 1-inch pieces
- 2 garlic cloves, minced
- 1 cup frozen peas, thawed
- 1/2 teaspoon salt
- 1/4 teaspoon pepper
- 1/2 cup part-skim ricotta cheese
- 1/4 cup plus 6 teaspoons grated Parmesan cheese, *divided*
- 2 tablespoons lemon juice
- 1 tablespoon grated lemon peel

1. Cook fettuccine according to package directions. Meanwhile, in a large nonstick skillet coated with cooking spray, saute leeks in oil for 1 minute. Add asparagus and garlic; saute until asparagus is crisp-tender. Stir in peas, salt and pepper.

2. Drain fettuccine, reserving 1/2 cup cooking liquid. Place ricotta cheese in a small bowl; whisk in reserved cooking liquid. Whisk in 1/4 cup Parmesan cheese, lemon juice and peel. Add to the skillet; heat through.

3. Add fettuccine; toss to coat. Sprinkle with remaining Parmesan cheese.

Nutrition Facts: 1-1/3 cups equals 250 calories, 7 g fat (2 g saturated fat), 10 mg cholesterol, 363 mg sodium, 38 g carbohydrate, 4 g fiber, 12 g protein. **Diabetic Exchanges:** 2 starch, 1 vegetable, 1 fat.

FETTUCCINE WITH ASPARAGUS AND PEAS
NOTES: _____
_____
_____
_____

BAKED ASPARAGUS DIP NOTES:
_____
_____
_____
_____

Baked Asparagus Dip

Prep/Total Time: 30 min. • **Yield:** 8 servings
Since I'm from Wisconsin, it was only logical to put together a vegetable and a cheese—two things this state produces in abundance.
—*Sandra Baratka, Phillips, Wisconsin*

- 1 pound diced cooked fresh asparagus, drained
- 1 cup grated Parmesan cheese
- 1 cup mayonnaise
- Snack rye bread

1. In a large bowl, combine the asparagus, cheese and mayonnaise. Place in a 2-cup ovenproof bowl. Bake at 375° for 20 minutes or until heated through. Serve warm with bread.

Nutrition Facts: 1 serving (2 tablespoons) equals 259 calories, 25 g fat (5 g saturated fat), 18 mg cholesterol, 340 mg sodium, 3 g carbohydrate, 1 g fiber, 6 g protein.

Bacon-Wrapped Asparagus

Prep: 20 min. • **Grill:** 10 min. • **Yield:** 2-3 servings.
My husband and I grill dinner almost every night. In the spring, this makes a tasty flame-kissed side dish.
—*Patricia Kitts, Dickinson, Texas*

10 fresh asparagus spears, trimmed
1/8 teaspoon pepper
5 bacon strips, halved lengthwise

1. Place the asparagus on a sheet of waxed paper; coat with cooking spray. Sprinkle with pepper; turn to coat. Wrap a bacon piece around each spear; secure the ends with toothpicks.

2. Grill, uncovered, over medium heat for 4-6 minutes on each side or until bacon is crisp. Discard toothpicks.

Nutrition Facts: 5 pieces equals 222 calories, 22 g fat (8 g saturated fat), 25 mg cholesterol, 281 mg sodium, 2 g carbohydrate, 1 g fiber, 5 g protein.

BACON-WRAPPED ASPARAGUS NOTES:
_____
_____
_____
_____
_____

Asparagus Snack Squares

Prep: 25 min. • **Bake:** 15 min. • **Yield:** 3 dozen.
We try to enjoy crisp, nutrition-packed asparagus as often as we can during its short growing season in the Midwest. Here is a simple pizza-like dish that's great for an appetizer or main course.
—*Judy Wagner, Chicago, Illinois*

1 cup chopped sweet onion
3 tablespoons butter
2 garlic cloves, minced
1 pound fresh asparagus, trimmed
1/4 teaspoon pepper
2 tubes (8 ounces *each*) refrigerated crescent rolls
1 cup (4 ounces) shredded part-skim mozzarella cheese
1 cup (4 ounces) shredded Swiss cheese

1. In a large skillet, saute onion in butter until tender. Add garlic; cook 1 minute longer.

2. Cut asparagus into 1-in. pieces; set the tips aside. Add remaining asparagus to skillet; saute until crisp-tender. Add asparagus tips and pepper; saute 1-2 minutes longer or until asparagus is tender.

3. Press dough into an ungreased 15-in. x 10-in. x 1-in. baking pan; seal seams and perforations. Bake at 375° for 6-8 minutes or until lightly browned. Top with asparagus mixture; sprinkle with cheeses. Bake 6-8 minutes longer or until cheese is melted. Cut into squares.

Nutrition Facts: 1 serving equals 56 calories, 4 g fat (2 g saturated fat), 7 mg cholesterol, 82 mg sodium, 3 g carbohydrate, trace fiber, 2 g protein.

ASPARAGUS SNACK SQUARES NOTES:
_____
_____
_____
_____

Asparagus with Lemon Sauce

Prep: 5 min. • **Cook:** 10 min. • **Yield:** 4 servings.

We didn't have an oven or stove in our first years of marriage, so we relied heavily on our microwave. This side of asparagus in a creamy lemon sauce was always a favorite. Garnished with fresh lemon wedges, it's a pretty addition to any menu.
—*Janice Gerbitz, Woodland, California*

- 3 cups cut fresh asparagus (2-inch pieces)
- 1 can (8 ounces) sliced water chestnuts, drained
- 1/4 cup cream cheese, softened
- 2 tablespoons water
- 2 tablespoons milk
- 1/2 teaspoon grated lemon peel
- 1 tablespoon sliced almonds, toasted

1. Place the asparagus and water chestnuts in a shallow microwave-safe dish; add 1/2 in. of water. Cover and microwave on high for 6-8 minutes or until asparagus is crisp-tender; drain and keep warm.

2. In a small microwave-safe bowl, combine the cream cheese, water, milk and lemon peel. Cover and microwave on high for 1 to 1-1/2 minutes or until heated through, stirring occasionally. Pour over asparagus mixture; sprinkle with almonds.

Nutrition Facts: 3/4 cup equals 115 calories, 6 g fat (3 g saturated fat), 17 mg cholesterol, 53 mg sodium, 13 g carbohydrate, 4 g fiber, 4 g protein.

EDITOR'S NOTE: This recipe was tested in a 1,100-watt microwave.

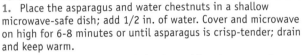

ASPARAGUS WITH LEMON SAUCE TIP:
When fresh asparagus is plentiful and inexpensive, stock up. Blanch, cool and store it covered with water in containers in the freezer. When thawed, it tastes just like fresh-picked. —Estelle M., Gobles, Michigan

EGGS WITH FETA AND ASPARAGUS NOTES:

Eggs with Feta and Asparagus

Prep: 10 min. • **Cook:** 10 min. • **Yield:** 2 servings.

Perfect for entertaining, this yummy brunch recipe can be easily doubled or tripled for your family. The flavor is irresistible.
—*Carol Heine, New Prague, Minnesota*

- 1 cup cut fresh asparagus (2-inch pieces)
- 1 tablespoon butter
- 4 eggs
- 1/8 to 1/4 teaspoon seasoned salt
- 4 strips ready-to-serve fully cooked bacon, crumbled
- 1/4 cup crumbled feta cheese

1. Place 1 in. of water in a saucepan; add asparagus. Bring to a boil. Reduce heat; cover and simmer for 3-5 minutes or until crisp-tender.

2. Meanwhile, in a large skillet, heat butter until hot. Add eggs; reduce heat to low. Cook until whites are completely set and yolks begin to thicken but are not hard. Sprinkle with seasoned salt.

3. Transfer eggs to serving plates; top with asparagus, bacon and cheese.

Nutrition Facts: 1 serving equals 296 calories, 21 g fat (9 g saturated fat), 448 mg cholesterol, 467 mg sodium, 5 g carbohydrate, 2 g fiber, 20 g protein.

FENNEL

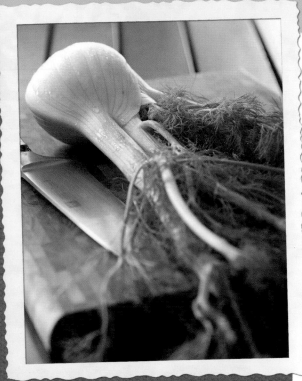

A cool-weather crop, fennel is often overwintered and therefore one of the first veggies on the farmers market scene. It adds a delicate anise flavor and satisfying crunch to salads and spring dishes.

SEASON: Spring to fall.

AT THE MARKET: Choose large, firm, crisp fennel with creamy white bulbs and bright green fronds.

STORAGE: Before storing, cut stalks off. Wrap stalks separately from the bulb in plastic bags. Store in the crisper section of the refrigerator for 3 to 4 days.

Aromatic Fennel Chicken

Prep: 35 min. • **Cook:** 50 min. • **Yield:** 6 servings.
Fennel adds something special to this wonderful chicken dish, along with lemon, capers, wine, spices and a bit of bacon.
—*Rebecca Hunt, Santa Paula, California*

- 4 bacon strips, chopped
- 1 broiler/fryer chicken (3-1/2 to 4 pounds), cut up, skin removed
- 1/2 teaspoon salt
- 1/2 teaspoon pepper
- 2 fennel bulbs, sliced
- 2 medium onions, chopped
- 6 garlic cloves, minced
- 3/4 cup white wine *or* reduced-sodium chicken broth
- 1/4 cup lemon juice
- 1 tablespoon grated lemon peel
- 2 bay leaves
- 2 teaspoons dried thyme
- Pinch cayenne pepper
- 3 tablespoons capers, drained

1. In a large nonstick skillet, cook bacon over medium heat until crisp. Using a slotted spoon, remove to paper towels; drain, reserving 1 tablespoon drippings.

2. Sprinkle chicken with salt and pepper. Brown chicken on all sides in reserved drippings; remove and keep warm. Add fennel and onions to the pan; cook and stir for 3-4 minutes or until onions are tender. Add garlic; cook 1 minute longer.

3. Stir in the wine, lemon juice and peel, bay leaves, thyme and cayenne. Return chicken to the pan. Bring to a boil. Reduce heat; cover and simmer for 20-25 minutes or until chicken juices run clear. Remove chicken and keep warm.

4. Cook the fennel mixture, uncovered, for 8-10 minutes or until slightly thickened, stirring occasionally. Stir in capers and reserved bacon. Discard bay leaves. Serve with chicken.

Nutrition Facts: about 4 ounces cooked chicken with 1/2 cup fennel mixture equals 290 calories, 12 g fat (4 g saturated fat), 92 mg cholesterol, 520 mg sodium, 13 g carbohydrate, 4 g fiber, 31 g protein. **Diabetic Exchanges:** 4 lean meat, 2 vegetable, 1 fat.

AROMATIC FENNEL CHICKEN NOTES:

Fennel Waldorf Salad

Prep/Total Time: 25 min. • **Yield:** 4 servings.
The old standby Waldorf salad is simply too good to let slip away!
Here's a new slant featuring fresh fennel. I like to use local
apples for a fresh, crisp flavor.
—Donna Noel, Gray, Maine

1-1/2 cups sliced fennel bulb	1-1/2 teaspoons grated onion
1-1/2 cups sliced apples	1/8 teaspoon salt
3 tablespoons fat-free mayonnaise	1/3 cup chopped pecans, toasted
1-1/2 teaspoons fat-free milk	

1. In a large bowl, combine fennel and apples. In a small
bowl, whisk mayonnaise, milk, onion and salt. Pour over fennel
mixture; toss to coat. Before serving, stir in pecans.

Nutrition Facts: 3/4 cup equals 112 calories, 8 g fat (1 g saturated fat),
1 mg cholesterol, 172 mg sodium, 12 g carbohydrate, 3 g fiber, 1 g protein.
Diabetic Exchanges: 1-1/2 fat, 1 vegetable, 1/2 fruit.

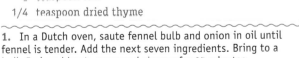

FENNEL WALDORF SALAD NOTES: _____
_____
_____
_____
_____

Italian Chicken Soup

Prep: 10 min. • **Cook:** 45 min. • **Yield:** 4 servings.
This satisfying soup gets its Italian flair from fennel, thyme, basil
and orzo pasta. If you don't start with a low-sodium or
sodium-free stock, decrease the amount of salt.
—Taste of Home Test Kitchen

1 fennel bulb, chopped	1/4 teaspoon dried basil
1/2 cup chopped onion	1/4 teaspoon pepper
2 teaspoons olive oil	2 cups cubed cooked chicken breast
2 cups hot water	
4 cups reduced-sodium chicken broth	1/2 cup uncooked orzo pasta
1-1/2 cups chopped carrots	2 tablespoons finely chopped fennel fronds
1 teaspoon salt	
1/4 teaspoon dried thyme	

1. In a Dutch oven, saute fennel bulb and onion in oil until
fennel is tender. Add the next seven ingredients. Bring to a
boil. Reduced heat; cover and simmer for 15 minutes.

2. Stir in chicken and orzo. Cover and cook for 20 minutes or
until orzo is tender. Stir in fennel fronds.

Nutrition Facts: 1 1/2 cup equals 282 calories, 5 g fat (1 g saturated fat),
55 mg cholesterol, 769 mg sodium, 33 g carbohydrate, 5 g fiber, 26 g protein.
Diabetic Exchanges: 3 lean meat, 1-1/2 starch, 1 vegetable.

ITALIAN CHICKEN SOUP NOTES: _____
_____
_____
_____
_____
_____

FISH WITH FENNEL NOTES: _____
_____
_____
_____

HOW TO PREPARE FENNEL

1. Cut stalks and fronds off the bulb. The fibrous stalks can be used to flavor fish stock. The fronds are delicious and can be used to garnish any dish that contains fennel. If the bulb is discolored or tough, discard the outer layer.

2. Set bulb on the flat end, then cut it in half and slice as desired.

Fish with Fennel

Prep: 30 min. • **Cook:** 10 min. • **Yield:** 4 servings.
This brightly flavored fish is a great showcase for fennel.
You'll use the seeds, bulb and fronds.
—*Barbara Stelluto, Devon, Pennsylvania*

1 medium lime	2 garlic cloves, minced
1 teaspoon fennel seeds	4 striped bass *or* barramundi fillets (8 ounces *each*)
1 large fennel bulb, sliced	
1/4 teaspoon salt	1 tablespoon chopped fennel fronds
4 teaspoons olive oil, *divided*	

1. Cut lime in half; cut four slices from one half for garnish. Finely grate enough peel from remaining half to measure 3/4 teaspoon; squeeze juice from lime half. Set aside.

2. In a small dry skillet over medium heat, toast fennel seeds until aromatic, about 1-2 minutes. Cool. Crush seeds in a spice grinder or with a mortar and pestle.

3. In a large saucepan, bring 1 in. of water to a boil. Add sliced fennel and salt; cover and boil for 6-10 minutes or until crisp-tender. Drain and pat dry.

4. In a large nonstick skillet, saute fennel in 2 teaspoons oil for 3 minutes or until fennel is lightly browned. Add garlic; cook 1 minute longer. Remove from the pan and set aside.

5. In the same skillet over medium-high heat, cook fillets in remaining oil for 3-4 minutes on each side or until fish flakes easily with a fork.

6. Drizzle with lime juice; sprinkle with lime peel and crushed fennel seeds. Serve with sauteed fennel. Garnish with fennel fronds and lime slices.

Nutrition Facts: 1 fillet with 1/4 cup fennel equals 285 calories, 8 g fat (1 g saturated fat), 80 mg cholesterol, 276 mg sodium, 7 g carbohydrate, 3 g fiber, 46 g protein. **Diabetic Exchanges:** 6 lean meat, 1 vegetable, 1 fat.

Roasted Fennel and Peppers

Prep: 10 min. • **Cook:** 45 min. • **Yield:** 6 servings.
Fennel makes for a tasty change of pace in this versatile side that goes great with grilled meats. Best of all, it's full of flavor, easy to do and doesn't taste "light" at all!
—*Taste of Home Test Kitchen*

2 fennel bulbs, halved and sliced
2 medium sweet red peppers, cut into 1-inch pieces
1 medium onion, cut into 1-inch pieces
3 garlic cloves, minced
1 tablespoon olive oil
1/2 teaspoon salt
1/2 teaspoon pepper
1/2 teaspoon rubbed sage
Fresh sage leaves, thinly sliced, optional

1. Place fennel, peppers, onion and garlic in a 15-in. x 10-in. x 1-in. baking pan coated with cooking spray. Drizzle with oil; sprinkle with salt, pepper and rubbed sage. Toss to coat.

2. Bake, uncovered, at 425° for 20-25 minutes or until tender, stirring twice. Garnish dish with fresh sage if desired.

Nutrition Facts: 2/3 cup equals 90 calories, 3 g fat (trace saturated fat), 0 cholesterol, 277 mg sodium, 17 g carbohydrate, 6 g fiber, 3 g protein.
Diabetic Exchanges: 1 starch, 1/2 fat.

ROASTED FENNEL AND PEPPERS
NOTES:_____
_____
_____
_____

Asparagus-Fennel Pasta Salad

Prep: 25 min. • **Cook:** 20 min. • **Yield:** 14 servings.
Asparagus delivers delightful spring flavor in this hearty side salad. Served warm, it includes a wonderful mix of fresh-tasting ingredients.
—*Linda Lacek, Winter Park, Florida*

1 pound fresh asparagus, trimmed and cut into 3/4-inch pieces
2 medium onions, halved and thinly sliced
1 small fennel bulb, sliced
2 tablespoons olive oil
8 ounces uncooked penne pasta
4 medium tomatoes, seeded and diced
12 pitted Greek olives, sliced
1 cup minced fresh parsley
VINAIGRETTE:
1/4 cup olive oil
1/4 cup lemon juice
2 garlic cloves, minced
1/2 teaspoon Dijon mustard
1/2 teaspoon salt
1/4 teaspoon pepper
1 cup (4 ounces) crumbled feta cheese

1. Place asparagus, onions and fennel in a 15-in. x 10-in. x 1-in. baking pan. Drizzle with oil; toss to coat. Bake at 400° for 20-25 minutes or until lightly browned and crisp-tender, stirring occasionally.

2. Meanwhile, cook pasta according to package directions. Drain; place in a large serving bowl. Add tomatoes, olives, parsley and roasted vegetables.

3. In a small bowl, whisk the oil, lemon juice, garlic, mustard, salt and pepper. Drizzle over salad and toss to coat. Sprinkle with feta cheese.

Nutrition Facts: 3/4 cup equals 167 calories, 8 g fat (2 g saturated fat), 4 mg cholesterol, 278 mg sodium, 19 g carbohydrate, 3 g fiber, 5 g protein.

ASPARAGUS-FENNEL PASTA SALAD NOTES:
_____
_____
_____
_____

Garlic Fennel Bisque

Prep: 10 min. • **Cook:** 45 min. • **Yield:** 14 servings.
I usually serve this in the spring as a wonderful side. The
fennel creamy bisque is so refreshing.
—*Janet Ondrich, Thamesville, Ontario*

4 cups water	2 tablespoons chopped fennel fronds
2-1/2 cups half-and-half cream	
24 garlic cloves, peeled and halved	1/2 teaspoon salt
3 medium fennel bulbs, cut into 1/2-inch pieces	1/8 teaspoon pepper
	1/2 cup pine nuts, toasted

1. In a Dutch oven, bring water, cream and garlic to a
boil. Reduce heat; cover and simmer for 15 minutes or until
garlic is very soft. Add fennel and fennel fronds; cover and
simmer 15 minutes longer or until fennel is very soft.

2. Cool slightly. In a blender, process soup in batches until
blended. Return all to the pan. Season with salt and pepper;
heat through. Sprinkle each serving with pine nuts.

Nutrition Facts: 1/2 cup equals 108 calories, 7 g fat (3 g saturated
fat), 21 mg cholesterol, 133 mg sodium, 8 g carbohydrate, 2 g fiber,
4 g protein. **Diabetic Exchanges:** 1-1/2 fat, 1 vegetable.

GARLIC FENNEL BISQUE NOTES:
_____
_____
_____
_____
_____

Herbed Fennel and Onion

Prep: 15 min. • **Cook:** 15 min. • **Yield:** 3 servings.
Wondering what to do with those fennel bulbs you brought home from
the market? Try them in this aromatic and savory side dish that's so
rich no one will guess it's healthy. Vinegar adds a slight tang.
—*Meghann Minton, Portland, Oregon*

1 large sweet onion, halved and sliced	2 teaspoons minced fresh rosemary *or* 1/2 teaspoon dried rosemary, crushed
1 medium fennel bulb, halved and cut into 1/2-inch slices	
1 tablespoon olive oil	2 teaspoons balsamic vinegar
1 cup reduced-sodium chicken broth	1/4 teaspoon salt
1 tablespoon minced fresh sage *or* 1 teaspoon dried sage leaves	1/4 teaspoon pepper

1. In a large skillet, saute onion and fennel in oil until crisp-
tender. Add the broth, sage and rosemary. Bring to a boil; cook
until broth is evaporated.

2. Remove from the heat; stir in the vinegar, salt and pepper.

Nutrition Facts: 1/2 cup equals 109 calories, 5 g fat (1 g saturated fat),
0 cholesterol, 437 mg sodium, 15 g carbohydrate, 3 g fiber, 3 g protein.
Diabetic Exchanges: 2 vegetable, 1 fat.

HERBED FENNEL AND ONION NOTES:
_____
_____
_____
_____
_____

Chicken with Fennel Stuffing

Prep: 10 min. • **Cook:** 20 min. • **Yield:** 6 servings.
We stuff a beautiful golden bird with fantastic fennel stuffing
for an easy yet impressive entree for guests.
—*Taste of Home Test Kitchen*

1 fennel bulb, chopped	1 tablespoon minced fresh thyme
1 large onion, chopped	1 teaspoon rubbed sage
4 tablespoons butter, *divided*	1 teaspoon salt, *divided*
5 cups unseasoned stuffing cubes	3/4 teaspoon pepper, *divided*
1-1/2 cups chicken broth	1 roasting chicken (7 to 8 pounds)

1. In a large skillet, saute fennel and onion in 2 tablespoons butter until tender. Place in a large bowl. Stir in the stuffing cubes, broth, thyme, sage, 3/4 teaspoon salt and 1/2 teaspoon pepper. Just before baking, loosely stuff chicken with 3 cups stuffing. Place remaining stuffing in a greased 1-qt. baking dish; refrigerate until ready to bake.

2. Place chicken breast side up on a rack in a roasting pan. Melt remaining butter; brush over chicken. Sprinkle with remaining salt and pepper. Bake, uncovered, at 350° for 2-3/4 to 3-1/4 hours or until a meat thermometer reads 180° for chicken and 165° for stuffing.

3. Bake additional stuffing, covered, for 20 minutes. Uncover; bake 15-20 minutes longer or until lightly browned. Cover chicken and let stand for 10 minutes before removing stuffing and carving.

Nutrition Facts: 1 serving equals 774 calories, 41 g fat (14 g saturated fat), 200 mg cholesterol, 1,230 mg sodium, 38 g carbohydrate, 4 g fiber, 63 g protein.

CHICKEN WITH FENNEL STUFFING TIP:
Fennel's feathery leaves have a
delicate, mild flavor and look simply
elegant when used as a garnish. If
the fennel you're using doesn't have
fronds, garnish with flat leaf parsley
instead. —Taste of Home

FENNEL-POTATO AU GRATIN NOTES:

Fennel-Potato au Gratin

Prep: 40 min. • **Cook:** 1 hour 15 min. • **Yield:** 12 servings.
The tender potato slices in this casserole have a mild fennel flavor
with a hint of nutmeg. Add a creamy sauce and a sprinkling of
Parmesan, and you have a side dish your family will request often.
—*Karen Haen, Sturgeon Bay, Wisconsin*

9 cups sliced peeled potatoes	1 cup heavy whipping cream
2 medium fennel bulbs, sliced	1 teaspoon salt
1 tablespoon butter	1/2 teaspoon pepper
2 tablespoons all-purpose flour	1/4 teaspoon ground nutmeg
1-1/4 cups chicken broth	3/4 cup shredded Parmesan cheese

1. In a greased shallow 3-qt. baking dish, combine the potatoes and fennel; set aside.

2. In a small saucepan, melt butter. Stir in flour until smooth; gradually add the broth, cream, salt, pepper and nutmeg. Bring to a boil; cook and stir for 2 minutes or until thickened. Pour over potato mixture; gently toss to coat.

3. Cover and bake at 350° for 1 hour or until potatoes are tender. Uncover; sprinkle with cheese. Bake 15 minutes longer or until cheese is melted.

Nutrition Facts: 3/4 cup equals 218 calories, 10 g fat (6 g saturated fat), 34 mg cholesterol, 423 mg sodium, 28 g carbohydrate, 3 g fiber, 5 g protein.

fresh HERBS

Eating local doesn't get any closer than shopping in your own backyard. And one of the easiest ways to begin living a locavore lifestyle is by growing a kitchen herb garden.

A nice feature of an herb garden is that it can occupy as much or as little space as you'd like. You can easily grow enough plants in small pots—even in reusable containers gathered from around the house—to make it feasible and affordable to enjoy fresh herbs all year long.

Many varieties even double as beautiful ornamentals that add a punch of color, fragrance and texture to your existing garden or landscape.

But which herbs are the best ones to cultivate?

To get you started, here's a list of our favorite herbs and the best ways to grow—and eat—them.

TOP 10 HERBS

Can't tell parsley from oregano? That's ok. This top 10 list will have you knowing—and growing—your own herbs in no time.

1. **BASIL:** Want to add zest to pasta sauces? Just leaf it to basil. This herb has more than 30 varieties, but sweet basil is the most common. Space plants 1 foot apart; they'll grow 1 to 2 feet high. To promote bushiness, pinch off growing tips and blooms as they appear. Consider colorful varieties, such as Purple Ruffles.

2. **BAY LEAVES:** Bay leaves come from a shrub that's a perennial in warmer climates. In colder regions, buy a small plant and grow it indoors for the winter and even year-round. It will reach 5 to 6 feet in height if kept pruned. Warning: Be sure you buy a culinary bay tree, as other relatives produce toxic leaves.

3. **CHIVE:** Versatility, thy name is chive. Stir this recipe-friendly herb into soups and sauces; whip it with butter, cream cheese, sour cream and dips; or sprinkle it on omelets and potatoes. Chives are kissing cousins of onions but taste slightly sweeter and milder (and won't make you cry). They grow 10 to 15 inches tall with bright blossoms and leaves.

4. **CILANTRO:** Strongly associated with Mexican food, cilantro also is a popular ingredient in Middle Eastern, Indian, South American and Asian cuisines. And talk about getting bang for your buck—its seeds produce the spice coriander. Cilantro grows 1 to 3 feet tall. For a continuous harvest, plant successive crops every two to four weeks.

5. **DILL:** A member of the carrot family, dill is well-known as a pickling ingredient. But its seeds and leaves also taste great in breads, dips and soups. It grows best when sown directly in soil; it reseeds itself regularly. Common dill grows to about 3 feet tall but is leggy enough to warrant planting in a location protected from wind.

6. **OREGANO:** This drought-tolerant Mediterranean herb typically grows about a foot tall. It's the ultimate low-maintenance herb, as it requires little watering. In fact, you don't even have to cover the seeds with dirt; just mist them and watch 'em grow. To maximize flavor and to keep plants compact, pinch off blooms as they appear.

7. **PARSLEY:** Popular as a garnish, this member of the carrot family also enhances the flavor of meats, salads and soups. The plants are slowpokes when it comes to germination, so it helps to soak the seeds overnight before planting. Mature parsley will reach 10 to 18 inches in height and spread 6 to 9 inches.

8. **ROSEMARY:** This aromatic herb is packed with medicinal powers. The scent of its oil enhances memory, and the herb is a powerful antioxidant that reduces the risk of blood clots, cancer, heart attacks and strokes. It's also a crowd-pleaser when roasted with chicken, fish, lamb, pork and potatoes. It grows up to 3 feet tall.

9. **SAGE:** Savory sage is a true multitasker. It adds color, texture and fragrance to gardens, not to mention distinctive flavor to pasta, meats and breads. Most types of culinary sage feature purplish-blue flowers and fuzzy leaves that range from gray-green to variegated colors. Plants grow up to 2-1/2 feet tall and wide. Pinched for space? One plant is probably plenty. Bon appétit!

10. **THYME:** Make time to grow thyme. This aromatic herb complements everything from tomato sauces and marinades to vegetables and jellies. It also doubles as an eye-pleasing, 6- to 10-inch-high ground cover. Best of all, this woody perennial doesn't demand much attention at all, especially when it comes to watering. In fact, too much water tends to reduce its flavor.

Caroline's Basil Boats

Prep/Total Time: 15 min. • **Yield:** 8 appetizers.
Inspired by my grandfather's garden, I created these fresh, simple boats that are always gobbled up in a snap.
—*Judy Blackburn, Myrtle Beach, South Carolina*

- 8 large fresh basil leaves
- 1/2 cup finely chopped tomato
- 1/2 cup finely chopped carrot
- 3 tablespoons shredded part-skim mozzarella cheese
- 4 teaspoons shredded Parmesan cheese
- 3 tablespoons Italian salad dressing

1. Place basil leaves on a serving plate. In a large bowl, combine the tomato, carrot and mozzarella cheese; spoon into basil leaves. Sprinkle with Parmesan cheese; drizzle with dressing.

Nutrition Facts: 1 filled basil leaf equals 36 calories, 3 g fat (1 g saturated fat), 2 mg cholesterol, 127 mg sodium, 2 g carbohydrate, trace fiber, 1 g protein. **Diabetic Exchanges:** 1/2 fat.

CAROLINE'S BASIL BOATS NOTES:

_____
_____
_____
_____

Dilled Salmon Omelets with Creme Fraiche

Prep: 15 min. • **Cook:** 5 min./batch • **Yield:** 6 servings.
Here is one of our biggest hits on our weekend menu. It has so much flavor with the dill and rich salmon that it will impress everyone.
—*Susan Goodman, Wilmington, Vermont*

- 12 eggs
- 2 tablespoons milk
- Salt and pepper to taste
- 2 tablespoons butter
- 1 pound salmon fillets, cooked and flaked
- 3 cups (12 ounces) shredded Swiss cheese
- 2 tablespoons snipped fresh dill
- 3/4 cup creme fraiche *or* sour cream
- 6 fresh dill sprigs

1. In a large bowl, whisk the eggs, milk, salt and pepper together until blended.

2. For each omelet, in an 8-in. ovenproof skillet, melt 1 teaspoon butter over medium heat. Pour 1/2 cup egg mixture into the pan. Sprinkle with 1/3 cup salmon, 1/2 cup cheese and 1 teaspoon snipped dill. As eggs set, lift edges, letting uncooked portion flow underneath. Cook until eggs are nearly set.

3. Broil 6 in. from the heat for 1-2 minutes or until eggs are completely set. Fold omelet in half; transfer to a plate. Top with 2 tablespoons creme fraiche and a dill sprig. Repeat for remaining omelets.

Nutrition Facts: 1 omelet equals 632 calories, 48 g fat (24 g saturated fat), 553 mg cholesterol, 374 mg sodium, 4 g carbohydrate, trace fiber, 44 g protein.

DILLED SALMON OMELETS WITH CREME FRAICHE NOTES: _____

_____
_____
_____
_____

Basil Marmalade Scones

Prep: 20 min. • **Bake:** 15 min. • **Yield:** 8 scones.

Orange marmalade and fragrant basil give these delightful scones a slightly sweet and unique garden-fresh flavor. They're tender and moist and perfect with morning or afternoon tea.

—*Hannah Wallace, Wenatchee, Washington*

2 cups all-purpose flour	3 tablespoons minced fresh basil *or* 1 tablespoon dried basil
3 tablespoons sugar	
2 teaspoons baking powder	2 eggs
1/2 teaspoon salt	1/3 cup fat-free milk
3 tablespoons cold butter	1/3 cup orange marmalade

1. In a small bowl, combine the flour, sugar, baking powder and salt. Cut in butter until mixture resembles coarse crumbs. Stir in basil. Whisk eggs and milk; stir into crumb mixture just until moistened. Turn onto a floured surface; knead 5 times.

2. Divide dough in half. Transfer one portion to a baking sheet coated with cooking spray. Pat into a 7-in. circle. Spread marmalade to within 1/2 in. of edge. Pat remaining dough into a 7-in. circle. Place over marmalade; seal edges. Cut into eight wedges, but do not separate.

3. Bake at 400° for 15-20 minutes or until golden brown. Serve scones warm.

Nutrition Facts: 1 scone equals 224 calories, 6 g fat (3 g saturated fat), 64 mg cholesterol, 308 mg sodium, 38 g carbohydrate, 1 g fiber, 5 g protein.

BASIL MARMALADE SCONES TIP:
To mince fresh herbs quickly, easily and with very little cleanup, hold a small bunch over a small bowl or glass and make 1/8-in to 1/4-in. cuts with kitchen shears. —Taste of Home

BASIL CORN ON THE COB NOTES:
_____
_____
_____
_____
_____

Basil Corn on the Cob

Prep: 25 min. + soaking • **Grill:** 25 min. • **Yield:** 6 servings.

Steaming the basil under the husks adds lots of flavor to these fantastic ears. Lime makes their sweet taste pop even more.

—*Diane Eaton, Campbell, California*

6 large ears sweet corn in husks	1/4 teaspoon sugar
	Dash salt
6 tablespoons butter, softened	Dash garlic salt
	1 cup fresh basil leaves
1/2 teaspoon dried basil	Lime wedges

1. Carefully peel back corn husks to within 1 in. of bottoms; remove silk. In a small bowl, combine the butter, dried basil, sugar, salt and garlic salt; spread over corn. Place basil leaves over butter mixture. Rewrap corn in husks and secure with kitchen string. Place in a stockpot; cover with cold water. Soak for 20 minutes; drain.

2. Grill corn, covered, over medium heat for 25-30 minutes or until tender, turning often. Serve with lime wedges.

Nutrition Facts: 1 ear of corn equals 225 calories, 13 g fat (7 g saturated fat), 30 mg cholesterol, 145 mg sodium, 28 g carbohydrate, 4 g fiber, 5 g protein.

HOMEMADE HERB VINEGAR
Not only does herb-infused vinegar taste great on salads and veggies, it's easy to make, too.

STEP ONE: After sterilizing the container, gather your fresh herbs. Wash and pat herbs dry, then place into the container. (It's better to use too many than too few.)

STEP TWO: Add enough vinegar at room temperature to cover herbs. Seal with a non-metallic lid and let stand for 24 hours. Strain and remove old herbs. Place fresh herbs in bottle, pour in strained herb vinegar and seal. Store vinegar in a cool dark place.

Herb Vinegar

Prep: 20 min. + cooling • **Yield:** 1-1/4 cups.
This is a creative way to use up herbs from an herb garden. The vinegar can be used to marinate meat or add dimension to salad dressings.
—*Taste of Home Test Kitchen*

1 garlic clove, optional
12 to 18 inches fresh oregano, basil *or* tarragon sprigs
1-1/4 cups white vinegar *or* white wine vinegar

1. If desired, cut garlic in half and skewer with a toothpick. Place in a glass jar or bottle. Add oregano; set aside. In a small saucepan, bring vinegar to a simmer (do not boil). Carefully pour into containers. Let cool to room temperature.
2. Remove the garlic after 24 hours. Cover and store in a cool dry place.

Basil Vinegar

Prep: 10 min. + standing • **Yield:** 2 cups.
This fresh tasting herb-infused vinegar is a must when cooking up an Italian feast. It looks stunning and tastes amazing.
—*Taste of Home Test Kitchen*

1 cup fresh basil leaves, crushed
2 cups white wine vinegar
Basil sprigs, optional

1. Place crushed basil leaves in a sterilized pint jar. Heat vinegar just until simmering; pour over basil. Cool to room temperature. Cover; let stand in a cool dark place for 24 hours.
2. Strain and discard basil. Pour into a sterilized jar or decorative bottle. Add a basil sprig if desired. Store in a cool dark place.

Tarragon Vinegar

Prep: 10 min. + standing • **Yield:** 2 cups.
Add fresh tarragon sprigs to basic white wine vinegar in a decorative jar, and you'll have a lovely, contemporary gift for that special cook on your gift list.
—*Sue Gronholz, Beaver Dam, Wisconsin*

1 cup tarragon sprigs
2 cups white wine vinegar
Additional fresh tarragon sprig, optional

1. Wash tarragon and pat dry. Place in a sterilized jar. Using a wooden spoon, gently bruise the tarragon. Add the vinegar. Cover and store mixture in a cool dark place for 2-3 weeks to let flavors develop.
2. Strain and discard tarragon. Pour vinegar into a sterilized decorative bottle. Add additional tarragon if desired. Store in a cool dark place.

ALL DRESSED UP.
Don't limit your use of herb
vinegars to salads! Use them in
any recipe that calls for vinegar,
add a dash in sauces and spreads
or drizzle some over sauteed
veggies. (Pictured from left to
right: Herb Vinegar, Tarragon
Vinegar and Basil Vinegar.)

Pesto Muffins

Prep/Total Time: 30 min. • **Yield:** 1 dozen.
Who would think to put fresh herbs in muffins? These tender bites prove it's a tasty idea. I often freeze extra basil so I can enjoy them during the fall and winter months, too.
—*Cheryl Hindrichs, Columbus, Ohio*

1-1/2 cups all-purpose flour
1/2 cup whole wheat flour
1/2 teaspoon baking powder
1/2 teaspoon baking soda
1/4 teaspoon salt
1 egg
1 cup buttermilk
3/4 cup vegetable broth
3 tablespoons canola oil
1/2 cup grated Parmesan cheese, *divided*
1/2 cup loosely packed basil leaves, chopped
1/4 cup chopped walnuts
2 garlic cloves, minced

1. In a large bowl, combine the first five ingredients. In another bowl, whisk the egg, buttermilk, broth and oil. Stir into dry ingredients just until moistened.

2. Set aside 1 tablespoon cheese. Fold the basil, walnuts, garlic and remaining cheese into batter. Fill paper-lined muffin cups two-thirds full; sprinkle with reserved cheese.

3. Bake at 400° for 15-20 minutes or until a toothpick inserted near the center comes out clean. Cool for 5 minutes before removing from pan to a wire rack. Serve warm.

Nutrition Facts: 1 muffin equals 153 calories, 7 g fat (1 g saturated fat), 21 mg cholesterol, 270 mg sodium, 17 g carbohydrate, 1 g fiber, 6 g protein. **Diabetic Exchanges:** 1-1/2 fat, 1 starch.

PESTO MUFFINS NOTES: _____
_____
_____
_____

Parsley Butter

Prep/Total Time: 5 min. • **Yield:** 1/2 cup.
Making herb butter is very simple and will add lots of flavor to your food. It will impress your guests, too—they'll be asking for the recipe!
—*Taste of Home Test Kitchen*

1/2 cup butter, softened
1 tablespoon minced fresh parsley *or* 1 teaspoon dried parsley flakes
1 tablespoon minced fresh tarragon *or* 1 teaspoon dried tarragon
1/2 teaspoon minced chives
1/4 teaspoon minced garlic
Dash pepper

1. In a small bowl, combine all the ingredients. Refrigerate leftovers.

Nutrition Facts: 1 serving (1 tablespoon) equals 101 calories, 11 g fat (7 g saturated fat), 31 mg cholesterol, 116 mg sodium, trace carbohydrate, trace fiber, trace protein.

PARSLEY BUTTER NOTES: _____
_____
_____
_____

Pesto Swirled Cheesecake

Prep: 30 min. • **Bake:** 35 min. + chilling • **Yield:** 24 servings.

My husband never got a bite of this savory cheesecake—it was that popular at our last family party. It will be at your gathering, too.
—*Elizabeth Jackson, Portland, Oregon*

2/3 cup dry bread crumbs
5 tablespoons finely chopped pine nuts, toasted
2 tablespoons butter, melted

FILLING:
1 carton (15 ounces) ricotta cheese
1/2 cup half-and-half cream
2 tablespoons grated Parmesan cheese
2 tablespoons all-purpose flour
1/2 teaspoon salt
1/4 teaspoon garlic salt
2 eggs, lightly beaten

PESTO TOPPING:
1/2 cup loosely packed basil leaves
2 tablespoons grated Parmesan cheese
1 tablespoon pine nuts, toasted
2 garlic cloves, peeled
2 tablespoons olive oil

Assorted crackers

1. In a small bowl, combine the bread crumbs, pine nuts and butter. Press onto the bottom of a greased 9-in. springform pan; set aside.

2. In a small bowl, beat the ricotta cheese, cream, Parmesan cheese, flour, salt and garlic salt until smooth. Add eggs; beat on low speed just until combined. Pour into the crust.

3. For topping, combine the basil, Parmesan cheese, pine nuts and garlic in a food processor; cover and process until finely chopped. While processing, gradually add oil in a steady stream. Drop by teaspoonfuls over filling; cut through with a knife to swirl.

4. Place pan on a baking sheet. Bake at 350° for 35-40 minutes or until center is almost set. Cool on a wire rack for 10 minutes. Carefully run a knife around edge of pan to loosen; cool 1 hour longer. Refrigerate overnight.

5. Serve with crackers. Refrigerate leftovers.

Nutrition Facts: 1 slice (calculated without crackers) equals 87 calories, 6 g fat (2 g saturated fat), 28 mg cholesterol, 144 mg sodium, 4 g carbohydrate, trace fiber, 4 g protein.

Herb Butter

Prep/Total Time: 5 min. • **Yield:** 2/3 cup.

We love to use this savory butter on fresh corn on the cob, but it's also yummy on many fresh vegetables. This is a super way to use your summer herbs.

—*Donna Smith, Victor, New York*

1/2 cup butter, softened	1/2 teaspoon dried thyme
1 tablespoon minced chives	1/4 teaspoon salt
1 tablespoon minced fresh dill	Dash garlic powder
1 tablespoon minced fresh parsley	Dash cayenne pepper
	Hot cooked corn on the cob

1. In a small bowl, combine the first eight ingredients. Serve with corn. Refrigerate leftovers.

Nutrition Facts: 1 tablespoon equals 203 calories, 10 g fat (6 g saturated fat), 24 mg cholesterol, 130 mg sodium, 29 g carbohydrate, 4 g fiber, 4 g protein.

HERB BUTTER NOTES: _____
_____
_____
_____

Tuna Salad with Basil Dressing

Prep/Total Time: 30 min. • **Yield:** 2 servings.

I came up with this no-fuss salad one night when my husband and I wanted a light meal. We now enjoy it a few times each month.

—*Laura McAllister, Morganton, North Carolina*

	DRESSING:
1/2 pound fresh asparagus, trimmed and cut into 2-inch pieces	1/4 cup minced fresh basil
1 tuna steak (8 ounces)	1/4 cup olive oil
1/8 teaspoon salt	1 tablespoon orange juice
1/8 teaspoon pepper	1 tablespoon balsamic vinegar
2 tablespoons olive oil	1 teaspoon grated orange peel
4 cups torn romaine	1 garlic clove, minced
2 medium navel oranges, peeled and sectioned	1/2 teaspoon Dijon mustard
1 cup cherry tomatoes, halved	1/4 teaspoon sugar
	1/8 teaspoon pepper
	Dash salt

1. In a large saucepan bring 4 cups water to a boil. Add asparagus; cover and boil for 3 minutes. Drain and immediately place asparagus in ice water. Drain and pat dry; set aside.

2. Sprinkle tuna with salt and pepper. In a small skillet, cook tuna in oil over medium heat for 3-4 minutes on each side for medium-rare or until slightly pink in the center.

3. Meanwhile, in a large bowl, combine the romaine, oranges, tomatoes and asparagus. In a small bowl, whisk the dressing ingredients. Divide romaine mixture between two serving plates. Slice tuna; arrange over salads. Serve with dressing.

Nutrition Facts: 1 serving equals 603 calories, 42 g fat (6 g saturated fat), 51 mg cholesterol, 315 mg sodium, 29 g carbohydrate, 6 g fiber, 31 g protein.

TUNA SALAD WITH BASIL DRESSING NOTES: _____
_____
_____
_____
_____

Cilantro Corn Saute

Prep/Total Time: 15 min. • **Yield:** 4 servings.
This is an easy side dish that goes with most anything. With cilantro and cumin, it's strong on Southwest flavor.
—*Lisa Langston, Conroe, Texas*

3-1/3 cups fresh *or* frozen corn, thawed	2 tablespoons butter
1 medium green pepper, chopped	1/2 cup minced fresh cilantro
1 tablespoon finely chopped onion	1-1/2 teaspoons ground cumin

1. In a large skillet, saute the corn, green pepper and onion in butter until tender. Stir in cilantro and cumin; saute 1-2 minutes longer or until heated through.

Nutrition Facts: 3/4 cup equals 173 calories, 7 g fat (4 g saturated fat), 15 mg cholesterol, 80 mg sodium, 27 g carbohydrate, 4 g fiber, 5 g protein.
Diabetic Exchanges: 1-1/2 starch, 1 fat.

CILANTRO CORN SAUTE TIP:
To easily trim cilantro, hold the bunch, then angle the blade of a chef's knife almost parallel with the stems. With short, downward strokes, shave off the leaves where they meet the stems. —Taste of Home

Tomato-Basil Bruschetta

Prep/Total Time: 25 min. • **Yield:** about 2 dozen.
It's easy to double this great recipe for a crowd. You can make the tomato topping ahead, or keep it simple and serve it as a dip for the French bread slices.
—*Marie Cosenza, Cortlandt Manor, New York*

3 plum tomatoes, chopped	1/2 teaspoon dried oregano
1/3 cup thinly sliced green onions	1/4 teaspoon salt
4 tablespoons olive oil, *divided*	1/8 teaspoon pepper
1 tablespoon minced fresh basil *or* 1 teaspoon dried basil	1 loaf (1 pound) French bread, cut into 1/2-inch slices
1 tablespoon red wine vinegar	2 garlic cloves, peeled and halved

1. In a small bowl, combine tomatoes, onions, 2 tablespoons oil, basil, vinegar, oregano, salt and pepper; set aside.

2. Lightly brush both sides of bread slices with remaining oil. Arrange on ungreased baking sheets. Broil 3-4 in. from the heat for 2-3 minutes on each side or until golden brown.

3. Rub garlic over bread slices. With a slotted spoon, top each slice with tomato mixture.

Nutrition Facts: 1 appetizer equals 84 calories, 3 g fat (trace saturated fat), 0 cholesterol, 162 mg sodium, 12 g carbohydrate, 1 g fiber, 3 g protein.
Diabetic Exchange: 1 starch.

TOMATO-BASIL BRUSCHETTA NOTES:
_____
_____
_____
_____

GARLIC

Back in the day, Greek athletes gobbled up garlic before competition for stamina. Modern-day studies prove they were on to something. Thankfully for you—and those next to you—you won't need to eat garlic all by itself. Instead, enjoy one of these yummy garlic-infused dishes.

SEASON: First harvest in early spring, but available year-round in most markets.

AT THE MARKET: Look for heads that are firm with plenty of dry, papery covering. Heads that are showing signs of sprouting are past their prime.

STORAGE: Keep whole bulbs in a cool, dark place away from direct sunlight. Do not store in the refrigerator.

Roasted Goat Cheese with Garlic

Prep: 45 min. • **Bake:** 15 min. • **Yield:** About 1-1/4 cups

When we entertain, this savory spread is a must. The combination of goat cheese, garlic and onions always earns recipe requests.
—*Carol Barlow, Berwyn, Illinois*

- 6 to 8 garlic cloves, peeled
- 1 tablespoon canola oil
- 1 medium red onion, thinly sliced
- 2 tablespoons butter
- 1 tablespoon brown sugar
- 8 ounces crumbled goat *or* feta cheese
- 1 tablespoon white balsamic vinegar

Salt and pepper to taste

- 1/4 cup thinly sliced fresh basil

Thinly sliced French bread *or* assorted crackers

1. Place garlic and oil in a pie plate. Cover and bake at 350° for 30 minutes.

2. Meanwhile, in a small skillet, saute onion in butter until tender and lightly browned. Add brown sugar; cook and stir until sugar is dissolved. Remove from the heat.

3. Remove garlic from pie plate. Spread onion mixture in pie plate; top with cheese. Place garlic over cheese. Bake, uncovered, for 15-20 minutes or until cheese is melted.

4. Mash garlic mixture with a fork. Stir in vinegar, salt and pepper. Transfer to a serving bowl; sprinkle with basil. Serve warm with French bread or crackers.

Nutrition Facts: 4 tablespoon equals 213 calories, 17 g fat (10 g saturated fat), 40 mg cholesterol, 236 mg sodium, 6 g carbohydrate, trace fiber, 9 g protein.

ROASTED GOAT CHEESE WITH GARLIC
NOTES:_____
_____
_____
_____
_____

Onion-Garlic Bubble Bread

Prep: 10 min. • **Bake:** 20 min. • **Yield:** 1 loaf (24 pieces).
This lovely golden loaf has great onion-garlic flavor in every bite. Try dipping bite-size pieces in herb-seasoned olive oil or warm pasta sauce for a unique appetizer.
—*Taste of Home Test Kitchen*

2 loaves (1 pound *each*) frozen bread dough *or* 24 frozen unbaked white dinner rolls, thawed	1/2 cup butter, melted
	2 garlic cloves, minced
	1 teaspoon dried parsley flakes
1/2 cup finely chopped sweet onion	1/4 teaspoon salt
	Herb-seasoned olive oil, optional

1. Divide dough into 24 pieces. In a small bowl, combine the onion, butter, garlic, parsley and salt. Dip each piece of dough into butter mixture; place in a 10-in. fluted tube pan coated with cooking spray. Cover and let rise in a warm place until doubled, about 1 hour.

2. Bake at 375° for 20-25 minutes or until golden brown. Serve warm with olive oil if desired.

Nutrition Facts: 1 piece equals 141 calories, 5 g fat (2 g saturated fat), 10 mg cholesterol, 263 mg sodium, 19 g carbohydrate, 2 g fiber, 4 g protein.

ONION-GARLIC BUBBLE BREAD NOTES:

_____
_____
_____
_____

Garlic-Kissed Tomatoes

Prep/Total Time: 15 min. • **Yield:** 12 servings.
Everyone I know loves this recipe—even my husband who normally doesn't like garlic! These tomatoes are a hit at potlucks...folks always ask for the recipe.
—*Margaret Zickert, Deerfield, Wisconsin*

6 medium tomatoes	1/2 teaspoon salt
1/4 cup canola oil	1/2 teaspoon dried oregano
3 tablespoons lemon juice	1/8 teaspoon pepper
2 garlic cloves, thinly sliced	

1. Peel and cut tomatoes in half horizontally. Squeeze tomatoes lightly to release seeds. Discard seeds and juices. Place tomato halves in a container with a tight-fitting lid.

2. In a small bowl, combine the canola oil, lemon juice, garlic, salt, oregano and pepper. Pour over tomatoes. Seal lid and turn to coat. Refrigerate tomatoes for at least 4 hours or up to 2 days, turning occasionally.

Nutrition Facts: 1 each equals 58 calories, 5 g fat (1 g saturated fat), 0 cholesterol, 105 mg sodium, 4 g carbohydrate, 1 g fiber, 1 g protein.

GARLIC-KISSED TOMATOES NOTES:

_____
_____
_____
_____

Garlic-Onion Pizza Wedges

Prep: 10 min. • **Bake:** 10 min. • **Yield:** 8 servings.
Using a prebaked crust, you can have this delicious appetizer hot and ready to serve in just 20 minutes. The wedges can even make a light main dish.
—*Clyda Conrad, Yuma, Arizona*

1/2 cup grated Parmesan cheese
1/2 cup chopped red onion
1/2 cup mayonnaise
1/4 cup minced fresh basil
4 garlic cloves, minced
Pepper to taste
1 prebaked 12-inch thin pizza crust

1. In a small bowl, combine the cheese, onion, mayonnaise, basil, garlic and pepper; spread over crust.

2. Place on an ungreased baking sheet or pizza pan. Bake at 450° for 8-10 minutes or until crust is lightly browned. Cut into wedges.

Nutrition Facts: 1 slice equals 234 calories, 15 g fat (3 g saturated fat), 9 mg cholesterol, 357 mg sodium, 19 g carbohydrate, 1 g fiber, 6 g protein.

GARLIC-ONION PIZZA WEDGES NOTES:
_____
_____
_____
_____
_____

Garlic-Rosemary Cornish Hen

Prep: 20 min. • **Bake:** 30 min. • **Yield:** 2 servings.
I have served these hens for backyard cookouts as well as formal dinners. The garlic is mild and pleasant and, combined with rosemary and lemon, results in meat that's tender and moist.
—*Jane Ashworth, Beavercreek, Ohio*

1 Cornish game hen (20 to 24 ounces), split lengthwise
1/2 medium lemon, cut into wedges
2 fresh rosemary sprigs
1 tablespoon olive oil
1/4 teaspoon salt
1/8 teaspoon pepper
10 garlic cloves
2 tablespoons chicken broth
1/4 cup white wine *or* additional chicken broth

1. Place hens, breast side up, over lemon and rosemary in an ungreased 11-in. x 7-in. baking dish. Brush with oil and sprinkle with salt and pepper. Add garlic to pan. Bake, uncovered, at 450° for 20 minutes. Reduce heat to 350°.

2. Pour broth and wine over hen and bake 10-15 minutes longer or until juices run clear, basting twice with pan juices. Remove hen to serving plates and keep warm.

3. Transfer pan juices to a saucepan. Bring to a boil. Reduce heat; simmer, uncovered, for 5-7 minutes or until pan juices reach desired consistency. Strain juices and serve with hen.

Nutrition Facts: 1/2 game hen with 1 tablespoon of sauce equals 846 calories, 59 g fat (15 g saturated fat), 371 mg cholesterol, 540 mg sodium, 7 g carbohydrate, 1 g fiber, 64 g protein.

GARLIC-ROSEMARY CORNISH HEN NOTES:
_____
_____
_____
_____

SAVE IT FOR LATER.
You can store whole or partial garlic bulbs in a cool-dry-dark place in a well-ventilated container, like a mesh bag, for up to 2 months. Leaving the cloves on the bulb with the papery skin attached will help prevent them from drying out.

Penne Gorgonzola with Chicken

Prep/Total Time: 30 min. • **Yield:** 8 servings.
You'll never believe how quickly you can throw together this rich and comforting pasta dish. You can substitute another cheese for the Gorgonzola if you like.
—*Taste of Home Test Kitchen*

- 1 package (16 ounces) penne pasta
- 1 pound boneless skinless chicken breasts, cut into 1/2-inch pieces
- 1 tablespoon olive oil
- 1 large garlic clove, minced
- 1/4 cup white wine
- 1 cup heavy whipping cream
- 1/4 cup chicken broth
- 2 cups (8 ounces) crumbled Gorgonzola cheese
- 6 to 8 fresh sage leaves, thinly sliced

Salt and pepper to taste

Grated Parmigiano-Reggiano cheese and minced fresh parsley

1. Cook pasta according to package directions. Meanwhile, in a large skillet over medium heat, brown chicken in oil on all sides. Add garlic; cook 1 minute longer. Add wine, stirring to loosen browned bits from pan.

2. Add cream and broth; cook until sauce is slightly thickened and chicken is no longer pink. Stir in the Gorgonzola cheese, sage, salt and pepper; cook just until cheese is melted.

3. Drain pasta; toss with sauce. Sprinkle with Parmigiano-Reggiano cheese and parsley.

Nutrition Facts: 1-1/4 cups equals 489 calories, 23 g fat (14 g saturated fat), 97 mg cholesterol, 453 mg sodium, 43 g carbohydrate, 3 g fiber, 26 g protein.

Warm Garlicky Grape Tomatoes

Prep: 10 min. • **Bake:** 20 min. • **Yield:** 4 servings.
This is one of our favorite quick ways to use up a large crop of grape tomatoes and garlic.
—*Rose Gulledge, Crofton, Maryland*

2 cups grape tomatoes	1/8 teaspoon pepper
3 garlic cloves, minced	1 teaspoon olive oil, *divided*
1-1/2 teaspoons minced fresh basil	1/4 cup soft whole wheat bread crumbs
1/2 teaspoon salt-free garlic seasoning blend	1/4 cup crumbled feta cheese
1/4 teaspoon salt	

1. In a small bowl, combine the tomatoes, garlic, basil, seasoning blend, salt and pepper. Add 1/2 teaspoon oil; toss to coat. Transfer to a 3-cup baking dish coated with cooking spray.

2. Bake at 425° for 15 minutes. Combine bread crumbs and remaining oil; sprinkle over the top. Sprinkle with cheese. Bake 5-10 minutes longer or until cheese is softened and tomatoes are tender.

Nutrition Facts: 1/2 cup equals 64 calories, 3 g fat (1 g saturated fat), 4 mg cholesterol, 259 mg sodium, 8 g carbohydrate, 2 g fiber, 3 g protein.
Diabetic Exchanges: 1 vegetable, 1/2 fat.

WARM GARLICKY GRAPE TOMATOES NOTES:
_____
_____
_____
_____

Broccoli Rabe & Garlic Pasta

Prep: 15 min. • **Bake:** 15 min. • **Yield:** 4 servings.
I created this because I needed a quick entree with few ingredients. The garlic-flavored oil makes the broccoli rabe less bitter, and with toasted garlic, it's a great dish.
—*Mary Ann Lee, Clifton Park, New York*

12 ounces uncooked linguine	1/4 teaspoon crushed red pepper flakes
1 pound broccoli rabe	1 cup chicken broth, *divided*
3 garlic cloves, minced	1/4 cup minced fresh parsley
2 tablespoons olive oil	1/4 cup shredded Parmesan cheese
1/4 teaspoon salt	
1/4 teaspoon pepper	

1. Cook linguine according to package directions. Meanwhile, trim 1/2 in. from broccoli rabe stems; discard any coarse or damaged leaves. Rinse broccoli rabe in cold water and cut into 2-in. pieces; set aside.

2. In a large skillet, saute garlic in oil for 1 minute. Add the broccoli rabe, salt, pepper, pepper flakes and 1/2 cup broth. Bring to a boil.

3. Reduce heat; cover and cook for 3-5 minutes or until broccoli rabe is tender. Drain linguine; add to the pan. Stir in parsley and enough remaining broth to moisten the linguine. Sprinkle with cheese.

Nutrition Facts: 1-1/2 cup equals 428 calories, 10 g fat (2 g saturated fat), 5 mg cholesterol, 518 mg sodium, 69 g carbohydrate, 3 g fiber, 18 g protein.

BROCCOLI RABE & GARLIC PASTA NOTES:
_____
_____
_____

greens & LETTUCE

Parmesan, Walnut & Arugula Baskets

Prep: 20 min. • **Cook:** 10 min. • **Yield:** 6 servings.
Want to impress your guests? Serve up salad in crispy Parmesan baskets and just watch the reaction!
—*Anna Maria Wharton, Staten Island, New York*

- 1 cup plus 2 tablespoons shredded Parmesan cheese
- 2 tablespoons finely chopped walnuts

SALAD:

- 4 cups fresh arugula or spring mix salad greens
- 1/2 cup green grapes, halved
- 2 tablespoons chopped walnuts
- 2 tablespoons olive oil
- 1 tablespoon raspberry vinegar
- 1/4 teaspoon salt
- 1/8 teaspoon pepper

1. Heat a small nonstick skillet over medium-high heat. Sprinkle 3 tablespoons cheese and 1 teaspoon walnuts over the bottom of the skillet. Cook for 1-2 minutes or until edges are golden brown and cheese is bubbly. Remove from the heat and let stand for 30 seconds.

2. Using a spatula, carefully remove cheese mixture and immediately drape over an inverted glass with a 2-in.-diameter bottom; cool completely. Repeat with remaining cheese and walnuts, forming five more baskets.

3. For salad, in a large bowl, combine the arugula, grapes and walnuts. Whisk the oil, vinegar, salt and pepper. Pour over arugula mixture; toss to coat. Place 1/2 cup salad in each basket.

Nutrition Facts: 1 serving equals 147 calories, 12 g fat (3 g saturated fat), 11 mg cholesterol, 357 mg sodium, 4 g carbohydrate, 1 g fiber, 7 g protein.

Nothing says spring like the crunch of a fresh salad. Lucky for you, lettuce and greens are some of the first stars to appear on the farmers market scene. Cousins of lettuce, kale and spinach are considered superfoods for the nutritional punch they pack.

SEASON: Peaks late spring through early summer; available year-round.

AT THE MARKET: Select crisp, dark green, tender leaves; avoid yellowed or wilted leaves.

STORAGE: Refrigerate unwashed in sealed plastic bag for up to 5 days.

PARMESAN, WALNUT & ARUGULA
BASKETS NOTES: _____
_____
_____
_____
_____

Penne with Kale and Onion

Prep: 15 min. • **Cook:** 20 min. • **Yield:** 6 servings.
I love kale; my husband hates it. But when I swapped it into a favorite penne-with-spinach recipe, it was so delicious, he asked for seconds!
—*Kimberly Hammond, Kingwood, Texas*

- 1 medium onion, sliced
- 2 tablespoons olive oil, *divided*
- 8 garlic cloves, thinly sliced
- 3 cups uncooked penne pasta
- 6 cups chopped fresh kale
- 1/2 teaspoon salt

1. In a large skillet, cook the onion in 1 tablespoon oil over medium heat for 15-20 minutes or until the onion is golden brown, stirring frequently and adding the garlic during the last 2 minutes of cooking time.

2. Meanwhile, in a large saucepan, cook the penne according to package directions. In a Dutch oven, bring 1 in. of water to a boil. Add the kale; cover and cook for 10-15 minutes or until tender; drain.

3. Drain penne; drizzle with remaining oil. Stir the salt, penne and kale into the onion mixture; heat through.

Nutrition Facts: 1 cup equals 191 calories, 5 g fat (1 g saturated fat), 0 cholesterol, 206 mg sodium, 31 g carbohydrate, 2 g fiber, 6 g protein.
Diabetic Exchanges: 1-1/2 starch, 1 vegetable, 1 fat.

PENNE WITH KALE AND ONION NOTES:
_____
_____
_____
_____

Arugula Salad with Sugared Pecans

Prep: 15 min. • **Cook:** 10 min. • **Yield:** 6 servings.
Sugared pecans make a sweet addition to this picture-perfect salad with tangy dressing. Keep a close eye on the pecans, because they toast quickly.
—*Taste of Home Test Kitchen*

- 3/4 teaspoon butter
- 1/3 cup chopped pecans
- 1 teaspoon sugar
- 4 cups torn leaf lettuce
- 2 cups fresh arugula *or* baby spinach
- 1 small fennel bulb, thinly sliced
- 1/2 cup grape tomatoes
- 2 tablespoons lemon juice
- 2 tablespoons olive oil
- 1 tablespoon water
- 1 tablespoon honey
- 1/8 teaspoon salt

1. In a small heavy skillet, melt butter. Add pecans; cook over medium heat until toasted, about 4 minutes. Sprinkle with sugar; cook and stir for 2-4 minutes or until sugar is melted. Spread on foil to cool.

2. In a large salad bowl, combine the lettuce, arugula, fennel and tomatoes. In a jar with a tight-fitting lid, combine the remaining ingredients; shake well. Drizzle over salad and toss to coat. Top with sugared pecans. Serve immediately.

Nutrition Facts: 1 cup equals 127 calories, 10 g fat (1 g saturated fat), 1 mg cholesterol, 81 mg sodium, 10 g carbohydrate, 3 g fiber, 2 g protein.
Diabetic Exchanges: 2 fat, 1 vegetable.

ARUGULA SALAD WITH SUGARED PECANS NOTES: _____
_____
_____
_____
_____

Arugula Summer Salad

Prep/Total Time: 15 min. • **Yield:** 6 servings.
This simple summer-fresh salad stars arugula and tomatoes.
We love them both. Olive oil—the only oil I use in my
kitchen—flavors the light vinaigrette dressing.
—*Marie Forte, Raritan, New Jersey*

4 cups fresh arugula
  or baby spinach

1 large sweet onion,
  thinly sliced

2 medium tomatoes,
  cut into wedges

DRESSING:

2 tablespoons olive
  oil

1 tablespoon lemon
  juice

1 tablespoon red
  wine vinegar

Salt and pepper to taste

1. In a salad bowl, combine the arugula, onion and tomatoes. In a small bowl, whisk the dressing ingredients; drizzle over salad and gently toss to coat.

Nutrition Facts: 3/4 cup equals 63 calories, 5 g fat (1 g saturated fat), 0 cholesterol, 7 mg sodium, 5 g carbohydrate, 1 g fiber, 1 g protein. **Diabetic Exchanges:** 1 vegetable, 1 fat.

ARUGULA SUMMER SALAD NOTES:

_____
_____
_____
_____

Spinach Pesto

Prep/Total Time: 15 min. • **Yield:** 2 cups.
Serve this vibrant pesto on pasta, pizza, sandwiches and more. If you
don't have fresh oregano on hand, you can omit it.
—*Susan Westerfield, Albuquerque, New Mexico*

2 cups fresh baby
  spinach

2 cups loosely packed
  basil leaves

1 cup grated Romano
  cheese

2 tablespoons fresh
  oregano

2 teaspoons minced
  garlic

1/2 teaspoon salt

1/2 cup chopped walnuts,
  toasted

1 tablespoon lemon
  juice

2 teaspoons grated
  lemon peel

1 cup olive oil

Hot cooked pasta

1. Place the first six ingredients in a food processor; cover and pulse until chopped. Add the walnuts, lemon juice and peel; cover and process until blended. While processing, gradually add oil in a steady stream.

2. Serve desired amount of pesto with pasta. Transfer remaining sauce to ice cube trays. Cover and freeze for up to 1 month.

3. **To use frozen pesto:** Thaw in the refrigerator for 3 hours. Serve with pasta.

Nutrition Facts: 2 tablespoons (calculated without pasta) equals 177 calories, 18 g fat (4 g saturated fat), 8 mg cholesterol, 205 mg sodium, 1 g carbohydrate, 1 g fiber, 4 g protein.

SPINACH PESTO NOTES: _____

_____
_____
_____
_____

Chicken Thighs with Shallots & Spinach

Prep: 10 min. • **Cook:** 20 min. • **Yield:** 6 servings.

This moist and tender chicken comes complete with its own creamy and flavorful vegetable side! It makes a pretty presentation and goes together in no time flat for a nutritious weeknight meal.

—Genna Johannes, Wrightstown, Wisconsin

- 6 boneless skinless chicken thighs (about 1-1/2 pounds)
- 1/2 teaspoon seasoned salt
- 1/2 teaspoon pepper
- 1-1/2 teaspoons olive oil
- 4 shallots, thinly sliced
- 1/3 cup white wine *or* reduced-sodium chicken broth
- 1/4 cup fat-free sour cream
- 1/4 teaspoon salt
- 1 package (10 ounces) fresh spinach

1. Sprinkle chicken with seasoned salt and pepper. In a large nonstick skillet coated with cooking spray, cook chicken in oil over medium heat for 6 minutes on each side or until chicken juices run clear. Remove and keep warm.

2. In the same skillet, saute shallots until tender. Add the wine, sour cream and salt. Bring to a boil; cook and stir for 2-3 minutes or until slightly thickened. Add spinach; cook and stir until spinach is wilted. Serve with chicken.

Nutrition Facts: 1 each equals 225 calories, 10 g fat (2 g saturated fat), 77 mg cholesterol, 338 mg sodium, 8 g carbohydrate, 1 g fiber, 24 g protein.
Diabetic Exchanges: 3 lean meat, 1-1/2 fat, 1 vegetable.

CHICKEN THIGHS WITH SHALLOTS & SPINACH NOTES: _____

_____

_____

_____

_____

Spinach Pizza

Prep: 15 min. • **Bake:** 10 min. • **Yield:** 4-6 servings.

Layered with Alfredo sauce, fresh spinach, tomatoes and, of course, cheese, this pizza makes a family-pleasing, veggie-filled meal.

—Dawn Bartholomew, Raleigh, North Carolina

- 1/2 cup Alfredo sauce
- 1 prebaked 12-inch pizza crust
- 4 cups chopped fresh spinach
- 2 medium tomatoes, chopped
- 2 cups (8 ounces) shredded Italian cheese blend

1. Spread Alfredo sauce over pizza crust to within 1 in. of edges. Top with spinach, tomatoes and cheese.

2. Bake at 450° for 10-15 minutes or until cheese is melted and crust is golden brown.

Nutrition Facts: 1 slice equals 270 calories, 11 g fat (7 g saturated fat), 33 mg cholesterol, 549 mg sodium, 27 g carbohydrate, 2 g fiber, 13 g protein.

SPINACH PIZZA NOTES:_____

_____

_____

_____

_____

STUFFING A TENDERLOIN

STEP ONE: Cut a lengthwise slit down the center of the tenderloin to within 1/2 in. of bottom.

STEP TWO: Open tenderloin so it lies flat. On each half, make another lengthwise slit down the center to within 1/2 in. of bottom.

STEP THREE: Cover with plastic wrap. Flatten to 1/4-in. thickness.

STEP FOUR: Remove plastic wrap. Layer or stuff as recipe directs.

STEP FIVE: Roll up jelly-roll style, starting with a long side. Tie roast at 1-1/2-in. to 2-in. intervals with kitchen string.

Spinach-Stuffed Pork Tenderloin

Prep: 15 min. • **Bake:** 25 min. • **Yield:** 4 servings.
For a truly elegant and hearty meal, turn to this impressive roast. Just follow the directions (and helpful how-to photos) on the left.
—*Taste of Home Test Kitchen*

1	pork tenderloin (about 1 pound)	1/2	teaspoon pepper, *divided*
1/2	teaspoon celery salt, *divided*	4	slices provolone cheese
1/2	teaspoon garlic powder, *divided*	2	cups fresh spinach
		2	thin slices deli ham (1/2 ounce *each*)

1. Cut a lengthwise slit down the center of the tenderloin to within 1/2 in. of bottom. Open tenderloin so it lies flat.

2. On each half, make another lengthwise slit down the center to within 1/2 in. of bottom.

3. Cover with plastic wrap. Flatten to 1/4-in. thickness.

4. Remove plastic wrap; sprinkle pork with 1/4 teaspoon celery salt, 1/4 teaspoon garlic powder and 1/4 teaspoon pepper. Layer with the cheese, spinach and ham. Press down gently. Roll up jelly-roll style, starting with a long side.

5. Tie the roast at 1-1/2-inch to 2-inch intervals with kitchen string. Sprinkle with remaining celery salt, garlic powder and pepper. Place on a rack in a shallow baking pan.

6. Bake, uncovered, at 425° for 25-30 minutes or until a meat thermometer reads 160°. Transfer to a serving platter. Let stand for 10 minutes before slicing.

Nutrition Facts: 1 each equals 248 calories, 12 g fat (6 g saturated fat), 87 mg cholesterol, 588 mg sodium, 2 g carbohydrate, 1 g fiber, 32 g protein.

SPINACH-STUFFED PORK TENDERLOIN
NOTES:_____
_____
_____
_____

Fruited Mixed Greens Salad

Prep/Total Time: 15 min. • **Yield:** 6 servings.

Thanks to all the fruits and veggies in this attention-getting side salad, you'll enjoy a good dose of antioxidants.

—Ann Baker, Texarkana, Texas

- 1 package (5 ounces) spring mix salad greens
- 2 cups fresh baby spinach
- 1 cup fresh arugula *or* additional fresh baby spinach
- 1 can (11 ounces) mandarin oranges, drained
- 2/3 cup chopped walnuts
- 1/2 cup fresh raspberries
- 1/2 cup canned diced beets
- 1/2 cup fresh blueberries
- 1/4 cup sliced radishes

DRESSING:
- 2/3 cup fat-free poppy seed salad dressing
- 3 tablespoons red raspberry preserves
- 1 teaspoon white wine vinegar

1. In a large bowl, combine the first nine ingredients. In a small bowl, whisk the dressing ingredients. Drizzle over salad; toss to coat.

Nutrition Facts: 1-2/3 cups equals 197 calories, 8 g fat (1 g saturated fat), 4 mg cholesterol, 116 mg sodium, 28 g carbohydrate, 3 g fiber, 6 g protein.
Diabetic Exchanges: 1 starch, 1 vegetable, 1 fat, 1/2 fruit.

FRUITED MIXED GREENS SALAD TIP:
After washing salad greens, use a salad spinner to remove excess water. Then put the greens in a serving bowl, place a wet paper towel over the top and chill. The greens get extra-crisp.
—Sandy R., Cocoa Beach, Florida

Spinach Vermicelli

Prep: 15 min. • **Cook:** 15 min. • **Yield:** 6 servings.

Not only is this simple, meatless dish tasty, it also offers the bright color and nutrition of spinach.

—Charleen Berker, Palgrave, Ontario.

- 8 ounces uncooked vermicelli
- 1 large red onion, sliced and separated into rings
- 1 tablespoon olive oil
- 2 garlic cloves, minced
- 1 package (10 ounces) fresh spinach, torn
- 2 tablespoons lemon juice
- 1 tablespoon minced fresh tarragon *or* 1 teaspoon dried tarragon
- 1/4 teaspoon salt
- 1/8 teaspoon pepper
- 1/3 cup crumbled Gorgonzola cheese

1. Cook vermicelli according to package directions. Meanwhile, in a large nonstick skillet, saute onion in oil until crisp-tender. Add garlic; saute 1 minute longer. Add the spinach, lemon juice, tarragon, salt and pepper; saute for 2 minutes or until spinach is wilted.

2. Drain vermicelli; toss with spinach mixture. Sprinkle with the cheese.

Nutrition Facts: 1 cup pasta with about 1 tablespoon cheese equals 220 calories, 6 g fat (3 g saturated fat), 8 mg cholesterol, 296 mg sodium, 33 g carbohydrate, 3 g fiber, 9 g protein. **Diabetic Exchanges:** 2 starch, 1 vegetable, 1 fat.

SPINACH VERMICELLI NOTES: _____
_____
_____
_____
_____

Grilled Steak Bruschetta Salad

Prep: 15 min. • **Grill:** 15 min. • **Yield:** 6 servings.
You'll want to fire up the grill just to make this impressive entree. The steaks cook quickly, and the salad prep takes almost no time at all.
—*Devon Delaney, Princeton, New Jersey*

1-1/2	pounds beef tenderloin steaks (1 inch thick)
1/2	teaspoon salt
1/4	teaspoon pepper
6	slices Italian bread (1/2 inch thick)
3	cups fresh arugula *or* baby spinach
3/4	cup prepared bruschetta topping *or* vegetable salad of your choice

Crumbled blue cheese, optional

3/4	cup blue cheese salad dressing

1. Sprinkle steaks with salt and pepper. Grill, covered, over medium heat for 6-8 minutes on each side or until meat reaches desired doneness (for medium-rare, a meat thermometer should read 145°; medium, 160°; well-done, 170°). Let stand for 5 minutes.

2. Grill bread, covered, for 1-2 minutes on each side or until toasted; place on salad plates.

3. Thinly slice steak; arrange over toast. Top with arugula and bruschetta topping; sprinkle with cheese if desired. Drizzle with dressing.

Nutrition Facts: 1 each equals 412 calories, 26 g fat (7 g saturated fat), 76 mg cholesterol, 950 mg sodium, 16 g carbohydrate, 1 g fiber, 28 g protein.

EDITOR'S NOTE: Look for bruschetta topping in the pasta aisle or your grocer's deli case.

GRILLED STEAK BRUSCHETTA SALAD NOTES:_____
_____
_____
_____
_____

Salmon Mousse Endive Leaves

Prep/Total Time: 20 min. • **Yield:** 2 dozen.
I recently made this deliciously different appetizer and received rave reviews. This thick mousse has a lovely presentation that is well suited for special occasions.
—*Doreen Matthew, San Marcos, California*

2	packages (3 ounces each) smoked salmon *or* lox	1/2	teaspoon onion powder
2	packages (3 ounces each) cream cheese, softened	1/2	teaspoon prepared horseradish
1	tablespoon dill weed	24	endive leaves
1	tablespoon lemon juice		Watercress and diced pimientos, optional

1. Place the first six ingredients in a food processor; cover and process until smooth. Pipe or spoon about 1 tablespoon filling onto each endive leaf. Garnish with watercress and pimientos if desired.

Nutrition Facts: 1 each equals 45 calories, 3 g fat (2 g saturated fat), 9 mg cholesterol, 177 mg sodium, 3 g carbohydrate, 2 g fiber, 3 g protein.

SALMON MOUSSE ENDIVE LEAVES NOTES:
_____
_____
_____
_____
_____

leeks & ONIONS

Relatives to the onion, leeks produce white stalks instead of a bulbous roots. Their mild, onion-like taste makes them perfect for soups, stews and casseroles. They're even tasty when steamed or sauteed.

Sweet or sharp, onions are a farmers market and recipe staple. Whether sliced, chopped or caramelized, they add flavor and richness to your favorite recipes.

SEASON: Year-round

AT THE MARKET: Look for leeks with roots and dark green leaves intact.

Select firm onions that have dry, papery skins; avoid those with soft spots, blemishes or freen sprouts.

STORAGE: Do not trim or wash before storing. Store in the vegetable drawer of your refrigerator. Leeks will keep 5-10 days.

Keep onions in a dark, cool, dry, well-ventialed area for up to 3 weeks.

Sage Onion Quiche

Prep: 15 min. • **Bake:** 35 min. + standing • **Yield:** 6-8 servings.
I reach for this recipe often because it's so versatile—you can serve it for brunch, as a side dish or as a meatless entree. The fresh sage adds great flavor to the onions.
—*Shelley Johnson, Indianapolis, Indiana*

- 2   large onions, thinly sliced
- 2   tablespoons butter
- 2   tablespoons minced fresh sage
- 1   teaspoon minced fresh thyme *or* 1/4 teaspoon dried thyme
- 1   unbaked pastry shell (9 inches)
- 1   cup (4 ounces) shredded cheddar cheese
- 4   eggs
- 1   can (12 ounces) evaporated milk
- 1/2 teaspoon salt
- 1/8 teaspoon pepper
- 1/8 teaspoon ground nutmeg

1. In a large skillet, saute onions in butter until tender; drain. Stir in sage and thyme. Spoon into pastry shell. Sprinkle with cheese. In a bowl, whisk the eggs, milk, salt, pepper and nutmeg. Pour over cheese.

2. Bake at 425° for 15 minutes. Reduce heat to 375°; bake 20-25 minutes longer or until a knife inserted near center comes out clean. Let stand for 10 minutes before cutting.

Nutrition Facts: 1 piece sage quiche equals 302 calories, 19 g fat (11 g saturated fat), 147 mg cholesterol, 435 mg sodium, 21 g carbohydrate, 1 g fiber, 10 g protein.

SAGE ONION QUICHE NOTES: _____

Brie-Leek Tartlets

Prep/Total Time: 30 min. • **Yield:** 15 appetizers.
I have a family of picky eaters, but everyone loves these cheesy bites. I make dozens of them at a time because they disappear from the tray the second I turn my back.
—*Colleen MacDonald, Port Moody, British Columbia*

1 medium leek (white portion only), finely chopped	Dash salt and white pepper
3 tablespoons butter	Dash ground nutmeg
1 garlic clove, minced	1 package (1.9 ounces) frozen miniature phyllo tart shells
1/2 cup heavy whipping cream	2 ounces Brie cheese, rind removed

1. In a small skillet, saute leek in butter until tender. Add the garlic; cook 1 minute longer. Stir in the cream, salt, pepper and nutmeg; cook and stir for 1-2 minutes or until thickened.

2. Place tart shells on a baking sheet. Slice cheese into 15 pieces; place one piece in each tart shell. Top each with 1-1/2 teaspoons leek mixture.

3. Bake at 350° for 6-8 minutes or until heated through. Refrigerate leftovers.

Nutrition Facts: 1 tartlet equals 86 calories, 7 g fat (4 g saturated fat), 21 mg cholesterol, 64 mg sodium, 4 g carbohydrate, trace fiber, 2 g protein.

BRIE-LEEK TARTLETS NOTES: _____

_____
_____
_____
_____

Leek Potato Pancakes

Prep: 30 min. + chilling • **Cook:** 5 min./batch • **Yield:** 12 pancakes.
I received this recipe from my great-grandmother who brought this over from England, where they enjoyed leeks in many dishes.
—*Suzanne Kesel, Cohocton, New York*

1/2 pound russet potatoes, peeled and quartered	1/3 cup grated Parmesan cheese
2 pounds medium leeks (white portion only), thinly sliced	1 teaspoon salt
	1/4 teaspoon pepper
4 eggs, lightly beaten	1/4 cup canola oil, *divided*
1/2 cup dry bread crumbs	6 tablespoons sour cream

1. Place potatoes in a large saucepan and cover with water. Bring to a boil. Reduce heat; cover and cook for 15-20 minutes or until tender, adding leeks during the last 3 minutes. Drain.

2. Transfer potatoes to a large bowl; mash with eggs, bread crumbs, cheese, salt and pepper. Stir in leeks. Cover and refrigerate for 1 hour.

3. Heat 1 tablespoon oil in a large nonstick skillet over medium heat. Drop batter by 1/4 cupfuls into oil. Fry in batches until golden brown on both sides, using remaining oil as needed. Drain on paper towels. Serve with sour cream.

Nutrition Facts: 2 pancakes with 1 tablespoon sour cream equals 338 calories, 17 g fat (5 g saturated fat), 155 mg cholesterol, 611 mg sodium, 36 g carbohydrate, 4 g fiber, 11 g protein.

LEEK POTATO PANCAKES NOTES:

_____
_____
_____
_____

French Onion Soup

Prep: 15 min. • **Cook:** 8 hours • **Yield:** 4 servings.
It's hard to believe something this delightful came from a slow cooker! Topped with a slice of French bread and provolone cheese, individual servings are sure to be enjoyed by everyone at your dinner table.
—*Kris Ritter, Pittsburgh, Pennsylvania*

1 large sweet onion, thinly sliced (about 4 cups)

1/4 cup butter, cubed

2 cans (14-1/2 ounces *each*) beef broth

2 tablespoons sherry *or* additional beef broth

1/2 teaspoon pepper

4 slices French bread (1/2 inch thick), toasted

4 slices provolone cheese

1. Place onion and butter in a 1-1/2-qt. slow cooker coated with cooking spray. Cover and cook on low for 6 hours or until onion is tender. Stir in the broth, sherry and pepper. Cover and cook 2-3 hours longer or until heated through.

2. Ladle soup into ovenproof bowls. Top each with a slice of toast and cheese. Broil 4-6 in. from the heat for 2-3 minutes or until cheese is melted. Serve immediately.

Nutrition Facts: 1 cup equals 267 calories, 20 g fat (12 g saturated fat), 50 mg cholesterol, 1,324 mg sodium, 10 g carbohydrate, 1 g fiber, 11 g protein.

FRENCH ONION SOUP NOTES: _____
_____
_____
_____
_____
_____

TOMATO LEEK TARTS NOTES: _____
_____
_____
_____

Tomato Leek Tarts

Prep/Total Time: 30 min. • **Yield:** 2 tarts.
These attractive tarts are ideal for a special lunch or as a light supper. The crisp pastry crust cuts easily into wedges.
—*Kathleen Tribble, Santa Ynez, California*

1 package (15 ounces) refrigerated pie pastry

4 ounces provolone cheese, shredded

1 pound leeks (white portion only), sliced

6 medium plum tomatoes, thinly sliced

1/4 cup grated Parmesan cheese

1-1/2 teaspoons garlic powder

1/8 teaspoon pepper

1 cup (8 ounces) shredded part-skim mozzarella cheese

1. Place both pastry sheets on greased baking sheets. Sprinkle each with provolone cheese, leaving 1 in. around edges. Arrange leeks and tomato slices over provolone cheese. Sprinkle with Parmesan cheese, garlic powder and pepper. Top with mozzarella cheese. Fold edges over filling.

2. Bake at 425° for 18-22 minutes or until crusts are lightly browned. Cut into wedges. Serve warm.

Nutrition Facts: 1 serving (1 slice) equals 280 calories, 16 g fat (8 g saturated fat), 25 mg cholesterol, 346 mg sodium, 25 g carbohydrate, 1 g fiber, 10 g protein.

Orange-Scented Leeks & Mushrooms

Prep: 20 min. • **Cook:** 40 min. • **Yield:** 7 servings.
This simple side is great for seasonal celebrations. The sherry and orange juice add a unique flavor twist that makes this dish special.
—*Carole Bess White, Portland, Oregon*

4 pounds medium leeks (white and light green portions only), thinly sliced (about 8 cups)

1 pound sliced fresh mushrooms

2 tablespoons olive oil

1/4 cup sherry *or* reduced-sodium chicken broth

1/2 cup reduced-sodium chicken broth

1 tablespoon balsamic vinegar

1 teaspoon orange juice

1/2 teaspoon grated orange peel

1/4 teaspoon salt

1/4 teaspoon minced fresh thyme *or* dash dried thyme

1/8 teaspoon pepper

1. In a Dutch oven, cook leeks and mushrooms in oil in batches over medium heat for 15-20 minutes or until tender, stirring occasionally. Return all to the pan. Add sherry, stirring to loosen browned bits from pan.

2. Stir in the remaining ingredients; cook and stir for 10-15 minutes or until liquid is almost evaporated.

Nutrition Facts: 2/3 cup equals 215 calories, 5 g fat (1 g saturated fat), 0 cholesterol, 180 mg sodium, 40 g carbohydrate, 5 g fiber, 6 g protein.

ORANGE-SCENTED LEEKS & MUSHROOMS TIP: Leeks often contain sand between their layers. Before using in your recipe, cut them lengthwise in half and rinse under cold water, gently separating the leaves to flush out any trapped sand. —Taste of Home

Baked Sweet Onions

Prep: 25 min. • **Cook:** 40 min. • **Yield:** 8 servings.
Baking enhances the natural sweetness of my family's favorite Vidalia onions. Perfect alongside beef entrees, this side dish has a similar taste to French onion soup.
—*Ann Yarber, Goldsby, Oklahoma*

8 large sweet onions, peeled

1/2 cup butter, melted

1/2 cup Burgundy wine *or* beef broth

8 teaspoons beef bouillon granules

1 teaspoon dried thyme

1 teaspoon pepper

1-1/2 cups shredded Swiss cheese

1. Cut each onion into six wedges to within 1/2 in. of the bottom. Place each onion on a piece of heavy-duty foil (about 12 in. square).

2. In a small bowl, combine the butter, wine, bouillon, thyme and pepper. Spoon over onions; sprinkle with cheese. Fold foil around each onion and seal tightly. Place on a baking sheet. Bake at 425° for 40-45 minutes or until onions are tender. Open foil carefully to allow steam to escape.

Nutrition Facts: 1 onion equals 294 calories, 17 g fat (11 g saturated fat), 49 mg cholesterol, 948 mg sodium, 27 g carbohydrate, 3 g fiber, 9 g protein.

BAKED SWEET ONIONS NOTES: _____
_____
_____
_____

Rustic Fig, Onion & Pear Tart

Prep: 50 min. • **Cook:** 15 min. • **Yield:** 12 servings.
The rich, sweet flavors of fig, onion and pear work so well
together and are perfectly suited for the rustic crust.
—*Tina MacKissock, Manchester, New Hampshire*

- 3 large sweet onions, halved and thinly sliced
- 3 medium pears, peeled and sliced
- 4-1/2 teaspoons olive oil
- 4-1/2 teaspoons butter
- 1 cup fig preserves
- 1 tablespoon plus 1 teaspoon cider vinegar
- 1/8 teaspoon salt
- 1 sheet refrigerated pie pastry
- 1/8 teaspoon pepper
- 1 egg, beaten

1. In a large skillet, saute onions and pears in oil and butter until softened. Reduce heat to medium-low; cook, stirring occasionally, for 30 minutes or until deep golden brown.

2. Add the preserves, vinegar and salt. Bring to a boil; cook for 5 minutes or until thickened. Cool slightly.

3. Place half of the onion mixture in a food processor; cover and process until pureed. Set the remaining onion mixture aside.

4. Place pie pastry on a greased 12-in. pizza pan. Spoon pureed onion mixture over the pastry to within 2 in. of edges; sprinkle with pepper. Top with reserved onion mixture. Fold up edges of pastry over filling, leaving center uncovered. Brush edges of tart with egg.

5. Bake at 450° for 15-20 minutes or until crust is golden and filling is bubbly.

Nutrition Facts: 1 slice equals 228 calories, 8 g fat (3 g saturated fat), 16 mg cholesterol, 111 mg sodium, 39 g carbohydrate, 2 g fiber, 2 g protein.

RUSTIC FIG, ONION & PEAR TART
NOTES:_____
_____
_____
_____
_____
_____
_____

Caramelized Onion Focaccia

Prep: 30 min. • **Cook:** 15 min. • **Yield:** 15 servings.

For a melt-in-your-mouth experience, top premade or refrigerated pizza crust with sweet cooked onions and your favorite cheese. The result is a focaccia-style snack that's fantastic!

—Deirdre Dee Cox, Milwaukee, Wisconsin

3 large sweet onions, thinly sliced	2 tablespoons butter
2 tablespoons brown sugar	1 tube (13.8 ounces) refrigerated pizza crust
1 tablespoon marsala wine *or* apple juice	1 tablespoon olive oil
1/4 teaspoon salt	1/4 cup shredded Parmesan cheese
1/4 teaspoon pepper	

1. In a large skillet, cook the onions, brown sugar, wine, salt and pepper in butter over medium heat for 15-20 minutes or until onions are golden brown, stirring frequently.

2. On a greased baking sheet, roll out pizza crust into a 13-in. x 10-in. rectangle. Brush with oil. Top with onions and cheese.

3. Bake at 400° for 15-18 minutes or until lightly browned. Serve warm.

Nutrition Facts: 1 piece equals 116 calories, 4 g fat (1 g saturated fat), 5 mg cholesterol, 246 mg sodium, 17 g carbohydrate, 1 g fiber, 3 g protein.
Diabetic Exchanges: 1 starch, 1/2 fat.

CARAMELIZED ONION FOCACCIA TIP:
When it comes to caramelizing onions, patience is key. Sweet onions (such as Vidalias), low heat and a cast-iron skillet don't hurt either. As they cook, stir often to prevent burning.
—Taste of Home

Potato & Red Onion Frittata

Prep: 30 min. • **Cook:** 15 min. • **Yield:** 4 servings.

Frittata is an Italian classic perfect for any meal of the day, especially a special-occasion brunch. In this recipe, market-fresh red onions and potatoes take center stage.

—Maria Regakis, Somerville, Massachusetts

1 large red onion, chopped	1/2 pound red potatoes (about 5 small), thinly sliced
1/2 teaspoon minced fresh rosemary *or* 1/8 teaspoon dried rosemary, crushed	6 eggs, lightly beaten
	1/3 cup 2% milk
4 tablespoons butter, *divided*	1/2 teaspoon salt
	1/4 teaspoon pepper
1 garlic clove, minced	1/2 cup shredded Gruyere *or* Swiss cheese

1. In a 10-in. ovenproof skillet, saute onion and rosemary in 1 tablespoon butter until tender. Add garlic; cook 1 minute longer. Remove from the pan and set aside. In the same skillet, cook potatoes in 2 tablespoons butter until tender and golden brown. Remove and keep warm.

2. In a large bowl, whisk the eggs, milk, salt and pepper. Stir in cheese and onion mixture. Melt remaining butter in the skillet; tilt pan to evenly coat. Add egg mixture. Bake at 350° for 8-10 minutes or until nearly set.

3. Top with potatoes; bake for 3-5 minutes or until eggs are completely set. Let stand for 5 minutes. Cut into wedges.

Nutrition Facts: 1 each equals 326 calories, 23 g fat (12 g saturated fat), 361 mg cholesterol, 531 mg sodium, 15 g carbohydrate, 2 g fiber, 16 g protein.

POTATO & RED ONION FRITTATA NOTES:
_____
_____
_____
_____

MUSHROOMS

Spinach and Mushrooms

Prep/Total Time: 30 min • **Yield:** 4 servings.
Fresh, garlicky mushrooms and warm sauteed spinach make for a combination that tastes incredible and looks impressive, too.
—*Joyce Frey, Macksville, Kansas*

- 1/2 pound sliced fresh mushrooms
- 1 tablespoon butter
- 1 tablespoon olive oil
- 2 garlic cloves, minced
- 1/4 cup dry white wine *or* reduced-sodium chicken broth
- 3 tablespoons Worcestershire sauce
- 1 teaspoon minced fresh oregano *or* 1/2 teaspoon dried oregano
- 3/4 teaspoon minced fresh thyme *or* 1/4 teaspoon dried thyme
- 1/4 teaspoon salt
- 1/4 teaspoon pepper
- 1 package (6 ounces) fresh baby spinach
- 1 can (8 ounces) sliced water chestnuts, drained

1. In a large nonstick skillet, saute mushrooms in butter and oil until tender. Add garlic; cook 1 minute longer. Stir in the wine, Worcestershire sauce and seasonings. Bring to a boil. Reduce heat; simmer, uncovered, for 7-8 minutes or until liquid has evaporated.

2. Add spinach; cook and stir until wilted. Stir in water chestnuts; heat through.

Nutrition Facts: 3/4 cup equals 124 calories, 7 g fat (2 g saturated fat), 8 mg cholesterol, 334 mg sodium, 14 g carbohydrate, 3 g fiber, 4 g protein. **Diabetic Exchanges:** 2 vegetable, 1 fat.

Love 'em or hate 'em, mushrooms are packed with vitamins and nutrients. They're also a tasty meat substitute in casseroles, sandwiches and more.

SEASON: Foraging is typically in the early spring; available year-round.

BUYING: Select mushrooms with fresh, firm, smooth caps and closed gills; avoid cracks, brown spots or blemishes or ones that are shriveled.

STORAGE: Refrigerate unwashed, loose mushrooms in a brown paper bag for up to 5-10 days depending on variety. Store away from veggies with strong aromas.

SPINACH AND MUSHROOMS NOTES:
_____
_____
_____
_____
_____

Creamed Spinach and Mushrooms

Prep: 5 min. • **Cook:** 5 min. • **Yield:** 2 servings.
When my family was snowed in one time, we had to make do with what we had on hand. I was able to pull this recipe together. We found it was very versatile and quick—10 minutes to make from start to finish.
—*Michelle Ferrario, Ijamsville, Maryland*

1-1/2	cups sliced fresh mushrooms	3	ounces reduced-fat cream cheese, cubed
2	tablespoons olive oil	1/4	teaspoon salt
1/2	teaspoon butter	1/8	teaspoon pepper
1	package (6 ounces) fresh baby spinach		

1. In a small skillet, saute the mushrooms in oil and butter until tender. Add the spinach; cover and cook for 1 minute or until wilted.

2. Stir in cream cheese, salt and pepper. Serve immediately.

Nutrition Facts: 1/2 cup equals 266 calories, 24 g fat (9 g saturated fat), 33 mg cholesterol, 551 mg sodium, 7 g carbohydrate, 3 g fiber, 8 g protein.

CREAMED SPINACH AND MUSHROOMS
NOTES:_____
_____
_____
_____

Havarti Shrimp Quesadillas

Prep/Total Time: 25 min. • **Yield:** 2 dozen.
Apricot preserves add a subtle touch of sweetness to the sauteed mushrooms, tender shrimp and Havarti cheese tucked inside these crispy, grilled quesadillas.
—*Susan Manning, Burlington, North Carolina*

1/2	pound fresh mushrooms, chopped	6	ounces Havarti cheese, thinly sliced
1	tablespoon canola oil	1/2	pound cooked medium shrimp, peeled and deveined and chopped
1	tablespoon butter		
6	tablespoons apricot preserves	2	tablespoons butter, melted
6	flour tortillas (10 inches)		

1. In a large skillet, saute mushrooms in oil and butter until tender. Spread 1 tablespoon preserves over half of each tortilla; top with cheese, shrimp and mushrooms. Fold tortillas over. Brush both sides with melted butter.

2. Grill quesadillas, uncovered, over medium heat for 1-2 minutes on each side or until golden brown and cheese is melted. Cut each quesadilla into four wedges. Serve warm.

Nutrition Facts: 1 wedge equals 123 calories, 5 g fat (3 g saturated fat), 26 mg cholesterol, 166 mg sodium, 12 g carbohydrate, 2 g fiber, 6 g protein.
Diabetic Exchanges: 1 starch, 1 fat.

HAVARTI SHRIMP QUESADILLAS
NOTES:_____
_____
_____
_____
_____

Spinach, Mushroom & Three-Cheese Pizza

Prep: 30 min. • **Bake:** 15 min. • **Yield:** 6 pieces.
The magic of mushrooms caps off this yummy pie. A knife-and-fork pizza, it's loaded with spinach, onion, garlic and a trio of cheeses.
—*Lily Julow, Gainesville, Florida*

1 loaf (1 pound) frozen pizza dough, thawed	2 garlic cloves, minced
3 tablespoons olive oil, *divided*	1 package (10 ounces) frozen chopped spinach, thawed and squeezed dry
2 thin slices prosciutto *or* deli ham, julienned	1 log (4 ounces) fresh goat cheese, crumbled
1 pound sliced baby portobello mushrooms	2 cups (8 ounces) shredded fontina cheese
1/2 small red onion, sliced	1/2 cup grated Romano cheese
1 tablespoon minced fresh rosemary	

1. Roll dough into a 12-in. x 9-in. rectangle; transfer to a greased baking sheet and build up edges slightly. Brush with 1 tablespoon oil.

2. In a large skillet, saute prosciutto in remaining oil until crispy. Add mushrooms and onion; saute until tender. Stir in rosemary and garlic; cook 1 minute longer.

3. Place spinach over dough; top with mushroom mixture and goat cheese. Sprinkle with fontina. Bake at 450° for 15-20 minutes or until edges are golden brown and cheese is bubbly. Sprinkle with Romano cheese.

Nutrition Facts: 1 piece equals 492 calories, 25 g fat (11 g saturated fat), 66 mg cholesterol, 964 mg sodium, 42 g carbohydrate, 2 g fiber, 24 g protein.

SPINACH, MUSHROOM & THREE-CHEESE
PIZZA NOTES: _____
_____
_____
_____
_____

Stuffed Asiago-Basil Mushrooms

Prep: 25 min. • **Bake:** 10 min. • **Yield:** 2 dozen.
Don't like mushrooms? Guess again...you will now! These pretty appetizers taste divine. For a main dish, double the filling and use large portobellos.
—*Lorraine Caland, Thunder Bay, Ontario*

24 baby portobello mushrooms, stems removed
1/2 cup reduced-fat mayonnaise
3/4 cup shredded Asiago cheese
1/2 cup loosely packed basil leaves, stems removed
1/4 teaspoon white pepper
12 cherry tomatoes, halved
2 tablespoons grated Parmesan cheese, optional

1. Place mushrooms on a greased 15-in. x 10-in. x 1-in. baking pan. Bake at 375° for 10 minutes. Drain liquid from the mushrooms.

2. Meanwhile, in a food processor, place the mayonnaise, Asiago cheese, basil and pepper; cover and process until mixture is blended.

3. Fill mushrooms with a heaping teaspoonful mayonnaise mixture; top with tomato. Bake 8-10 minutes longer or until lightly browned. Sprinkle with Parmesan cheese if desired.

Nutrition Facts: 1 each equals 35 calories, 3 g fat (1 g saturated fat), 5 mg cholesterol, 50 mg sodium, 2 g carbohydrate, trace fiber, 2 g protein.

STUFFED ASIAGO-BASIL MUSHROOMS NOTES:
_____
_____
_____
_____
_____

NO-FUSS STUFFED 'SHROOMS.
A rubber-tipped baby spoon makes quick work of stuffing smaller foods, like baby portobello caps. The spoon fits nicely inside the mushroom, and the filling mixture doesn't stick to the rubber coating.

Couscous with Mushrooms

Prep: 10 min. • **Cook:** 5 min. • **Yield:** 4 servings.
Fluffy and flavorful, couscous takes only moments to prepare and can be used with a variety of ingredients. I think it's delicious dressed up with fresh mushrooms, butter and chicken bouillon.
—*Claudia Ruiss, Massapequa, New York*

1-1/4	cups water	1/4	teaspoon pepper
2	tablespoons butter	1	cup uncooked couscous
2	teaspoons chicken bouillon granules	1	can (7 ounces) mushroom stems and pieces, drained
1/4	teaspoon salt		

1. In a large saucepan, bring the water, butter, bouillon, salt and pepper to a boil. Stir in couscous and mushrooms. Cover and remove from the heat; let stand for 5 minutes. Fluff with a fork.

Nutrition Facts: 3/4 cup equals 230 calories, 6 g fat (4 g saturated fat), 15 mg cholesterol, 794 mg sodium, 37 g carbohydrate, 3 g fiber, 8 g protein.

COUSCOUS WITH MUSHROOMS NOTES:

Mushroom Barley Soup

Prep: 25 min. + soaking • **Cook:** 5 hours • **Yield:** 12 servings.
Here's a hearty soup that is delicious and chock-full of vegetables. I think it's best served with a chunk of crusty bread smothered in real butter.
—*Constance Sullivan, Oceanside, California*

1/2	cup dried great northern beans	3	celery ribs, thinly sliced
1	pound sliced fresh mushrooms	3	large carrots, chopped
2	cups chopped onions	1/2	cup medium pearl barley
1	medium leek (white portion only), sliced	2	teaspoons dried parsley flakes
2	tablespoons butter	1-1/2	teaspoons salt
1	to 2 garlic cloves, minced	1	bay leaf
2	cartons (32 ounces *each*) chicken broth	1/4	teaspoon white pepper

1. Soak the beans according to package directions. In a large skillet, cook the mushrooms, onions and leek in butter over medium heat until tender. Add garlic; cook 1 minute longer.

2. Transfer to a 6-quart slow cooker. Drain and rinse beans, discarding liquid. Add the beans, broth, celery, carrots, barley, parsley, salt, bay leaf and pepper. Cover and cook on low for 5-6 hours or until beans and vegetables are tender. Discard bay leaf.

Nutrition Facts: 1 cup equals 116 calories, 3 g fat (1 g saturated fat), 8 mg cholesterol, 988 mg sodium, 19 g carbohydrate, 5 g fiber, 5 g protein.

MUSHROOM BARLEY SOUP NOTES:

Risotto-Stuffed Portobello Mushrooms

Prep: 45 min. • **Bake:** 15 min. • **Yield:** 8 servings.
These elegant, stuffed mushroom caps make a lovely special-occasion side dish perfect for the holidays. Green and red sweet peppers add festive color to the creamy and tender risotto.
—*Christie Szabo, Helotes, Texas*

1   cup balsamic vinaigrette
8   large portobello mushrooms (4 to 4-1/2 inches), stems removed
4   cups chicken broth, *divided*
2   large sweet onions, chopped
1   medium green pepper, diced
1   medium sweet red pepper, diced
1   tablespoon pine nuts
2   garlic cloves, minced
3   tablespoons butter
2   cups uncooked arborio rice
1/2 cup plus 2 tablespoons grated Parmesan cheese, *divided*
1/4 cup minced fresh parsley
1/4 teaspoon pepper

1. Place vinaigrette in a large resealable plastic bag; add the mushrooms. Seal bag and turn to coat; refrigerate for at least 30 minutes.

2. Drain and discard marinade. Place mushroom caps in a 15-in. x 10-in. x 1-in. baking pan. Bake, uncovered, at 425° for 15-20 minutes or until tender.

3. Meanwhile, in a small saucepan, heat broth and keep warm. In a Dutch oven, saute the onions, peppers, pine nuts and garlic in butter until tender, about 3 minutes. Add rice; cook and stir for 2-3 minutes. Carefully stir in 1 cup warm broth. Cook and stir until all of the broth is absorbed.

4. Add remaining broth, 1/2 cup at a time, stirring constantly. Allow the liquid to absorb between additions. Cook until risotto is creamy and rice is almost tender. (Cooking time is about 20 minutes.)

5. Stir in 1/2 cup cheese, parsley and pepper. Place 3/4 cup risotto in each mushroom cap. Sprinkle with remaining cheese; serve immediately.

Nutrition Facts: 1 stuffed mushroom equals 353 calories, 11 g fat (4 g saturated fat), 19 mg cholesterol, 813 mg sodium, 53 g carbohydrate, 3 g fiber, 9 g protein.

PEAS

There are two kinds of peas: garden peas, which require shelling, and snow or sugar peas, which yield edible pods. Whichever you prefer, we have you stocked with plenty of yummy spring recipes for both.

SEASON: Garden peas peak May-June; Snow peas available year-round; sugar snap peas available in spring and fall.

AT THE MARKET: For garden peas, select peas that are in their pods, crisp, firm and have a bright green color. Avoid large pods or those with thick skin.

For snow peas, select peas that are flat, are about 3 in. long and have a light green color with a shiny appearance.

For sugar snap peas, select peas that have crisp, plump-looking, dark green pods. Avoid dry or moldy pods.

STORAGE: Refrigerate unwashed, unshelled garden peas in an open plastic bag for up to 2 days.

Refrigerate unwashed snow or sugar snap peas in an open plastic bag for up to 2 days.

Snow Pea & Carrot Saute

Prep: 15 min. • **Cook:** 5 min. • **Yield:** 5 servings.
With bright carrot strips and green snow peas, this makes a colorful dish with any entree. Short on time? You can also buy matchstick carrots at the grocery store.
—*Taste of Home Test Kitchen*

- 1 pound fresh snow peas
- 1 tablespoon butter
- 2 medium carrots, julienned
- 1 garlic clove, minced
- 3 tablespoons honey
- 1/4 teaspoon salt
- 1/8 teaspoon pepper

1. In a large skillet, saute the snow peas in butter for 3 minutes. Add the carrots and garlic; saute 1-2 minutes longer or until vegetables are crisp-tender. Add remaining ingredients; heat through.

Nutrition Facts: 3/4 cup equals 108 calories, 3 g fat (1 g saturated fat), 6 mg cholesterol, 155 mg sodium, 20 g carbohydrate, 3 g fiber, 3 g protein. **Diabetic Exchanges:** 2 vegetable, 1/2 starch.

SNOW PEA & CARROT SAUTE NOTES:
_____
_____
_____
_____

Spring Pea Soup

Prep: 10 min. • **Cook:** 35 min. • **Yield:** 16 servings.
I've had this tried-and-true recipe for years. The pleasing pea soup is easy to prepare and has wonderful texture and flavor.
—Denise Patterson, Bainbridge, Ohio

4 cups cubed peeled potatoes	4 cups fresh *or* frozen peas
1/4 cup butter, cubed	1/4 cup minced chives
12 cups chicken broth	

1. In a Dutch oven, saute potatoes in butter until lightly browned. Stir in broth. Bring to a boil. Reduce heat; cover and simmer for 12 minutes. Stir in peas; cook 5-8 minutes longer or until potatoes and peas are tender. Cool slightly. In a blender, process soup in batches until smooth. Return all to pan and heat through. Sprinkle with chives.

Nutrition Facts: 1 cup equals 99 calories, 3 g fat (2 g saturated fat), 11 mg cholesterol, 759 mg sodium, 14 g carbohydrate, 3 g fiber, 3 g protein.

SPRING PEA SOUP NOTES: _____
_____
_____
_____
_____

Sesame Chicken Salad

Prep/Total Time: 15 min. • **Yield:** 2 servings.
You can toss together this fresh, flavorful Asian salad in no time. Brimming with color and crunch, it's perfectly portioned for two.
—Taste of Home Test Kitchen

1/3 cup fat-free mayonnaise	1/2 cup chopped fresh snow peas
1 tablespoon reduced-sodium soy sauce	1 small sweet red pepper, chopped
1/8 teaspoon ground ginger	1 tablespoon sesame seeds, toasted
1-1/3 cups cubed cooked chicken breast	4 lettuce leaves
	1 tablespoon chopped cashews

1. In a small bowl, combine the mayonnaise, soy sauce and ginger. Stir in the chicken, peas, pepper and sesame seeds. Serve over lettuce leaves; sprinkle with cashews.

Nutrition Facts: 1 cup salad with 1-1/2 teaspoons cashews equals 254 calories, 8 g fat (2 g saturated fat), 76 mg cholesterol, 736 mg sodium, 14 g carbohydrate, 4 g fiber, 31 g protein. **Diabetic Exchanges:** 4 very lean meat, 1 vegetable, 1 fat, 1/2 starch.

SESAME CHICKEN SALAD NOTES:
_____
_____
_____
_____

Pea Soup with Mushroom Cream Sauce

Prep: 25 min. • **Cook:** 15 min. • **Yield:** 6 servings.
Fresh garden peas combine with a hint of basil for a
delightfully light spring soup. A unique mushroom drizzle
adds extra depth to this beautiful creation.
—*Sally Sibthorpe, Shelby Township, Michigan*

1/2   pound sliced baby portobello mushrooms, *divided*
   1   tablespoon butter
1/4   cup chopped onion
   1   garlic clove, minced
1/2   cup half-and-half cream
   3   tablespoons sherry *or* reduced-sodium chicken broth
   1   tablespoon minced fresh thyme *or* 1 teaspoon dried thyme
3/4   teaspoon salt, *divided*
   5   cups fresh *or* frozen peas, *divided*
   3   cups reduced-sodium chicken broth
   2   tablespoons lemon juice
4-1/2   teaspoons minced fresh basil *or* 1-1/2 teaspoons dried basil

PEA SOUP WITH MUSHROOM CREAM
SAUCE NOTES:_____
_____
_____
_____
_____
_____

1. Set aside 3 tablespoons mushrooms for garnish. In a large skillet, saute the remaining mushrooms in butter until tender.

2. Add the onion to skillet; saute until tender. Add garlic; cook 1 minute longer. Stir in the cream, sherry, thyme and 1/4 teaspoon salt. Bring to a boil. Reduce heat; simmer, uncovered, for 2 minutes. Cool slightly. Transfer to a blender; process until smooth. Set aside.

3. In a Dutch oven, combine 4-1/2 cups peas, chicken broth and remaining salt. Bring to a boil. Reduce heat; simmer, uncovered, for 4 minutes or until peas are tender. Stir in lemon juice and basil; heat through. Transfer to a blender; process in batches until blended.

4. Ladle soup into serving bowls; top with mushroom cream sauce. Garnish with reserved mushrooms and remaining peas.

Nutrition Facts: 3/4 cup soup with 2 tablespoons sauce equals 169 calories, 5 g fat (3 g saturated fat), 15 mg cholesterol, 612 mg sodium, 22 g carbohydrate, 7 g fiber, 10 g protein. **Diabetic Exchanges:** 1-1/2 starch, 1 fat.

Pretty Stuffed Spring Peas

Prep: 30 min. + chilling • **Yield:** 3 dozen.

These stuffed peas are the perfect way to welcome spring and sail right through summer. I serve the yummy bites on a platter surrounded by juicy strawberries.

—*Phyllis Cooper, Yarmouth Port, Massachusetts*

1 package (8 ounces) cream cheese, softened

2 teaspoons minced chives

1 teaspoon dried basil

1 garlic clove, minced

1/2 teaspoon caraway seeds

1/2 teaspoon dill weed

1/4 teaspoon lemon-pepper seasoning

36 fresh snow peas (about 1/4 pound), trimmed

1. In a large bowl, combine the first seven ingredients. Cover and refrigerate overnight.

2. Let filling stand at room temperature for 30 minutes. Meanwhile, in a large saucepan, bring 6 cups water to a boil. Add snow peas; cover and boil for 1-2 minutes. Drain and immediately place peas in ice water. Drain and pat dry.

3. Gently split peas open; pipe about 1 teaspoonful of filling into each pod.

Nutrition Facts: 1 appetizer equals 23 calories, 2 g fat (1 g saturated fat), 7 mg cholesterol, 22 mg sodium, trace carbohydrate, trace fiber, 1 g protein. **Diabetic Exchange:** 1/2 fat.

PRETTY STUFFED SPRING PEAS NOTES:

_____

_____

_____

_____

_____

Vegetable Barley

Prep: 10 min. • **Cook:** 50 min. • **Yield:** 4 servings.

Here is a hearty side dish of colorful green snow peas, red pepper and just a hint of lemon (for a fresh springtime taste). Serve it warmed or chilled.

—*Ellen Govertsen, Wheaton, Illinois*

2-2/3 cups water

1/2 cup medium pearl barley

1/2 teaspoon salt

1 cup fresh snow peas

1 small sweet red pepper, chopped

1 tablespoon canola oil

4 green onions, thinly sliced

2 tablespoons lemon juice

1 teaspoon grated lemon peel

1. In a large saucepan, bring water to a boil. Stir in the barley and salt. Reduce heat; cover and simmer for 45-50 minutes or until tender.

2. In a small skillet, saute snow peas and red pepper in oil for 2 minutes. Add the onions; saute 2 minutes longer or until vegetables are tender.

3. Remove barley from the heat; stir in the lemon juice, lemon peel and vegetable mixture.

Nutrition Facts: 3/4 cup equals 148 calories, 4 g fat (trace saturated fat), 0 cholesterol, 302 mg sodium, 25 g carbohydrate, 6 g fiber, 4 g protein. **Diabetic Exchanges:** 1-1/2 starch, 1 vegetable, 1/2 fat.

VEGETABLE BARLEY NOTES: _____

_____

_____

_____

_____

Dilled Peas with Walnuts

Prep/Total Time: 20 min. • **Yield:** 2 servings.
This simple yet delicious side dish is a family favorite. The addition of fresh dill, onion and walnut dresses up the bright green peas without overpowering them.
—*Kristen Johnson, Aloha, Oregon*

- 1 cup fresh *or* frozen peas, thawed
- 2 tablespoons chopped onion
- 1-1/2 teaspoons butter
- 3/4 teaspoon snipped fresh dill *or* 1/4 teaspoon dill weed
- 1/8 teaspoon salt
- 1/8 teaspoon pepper
- 1 tablespoon chopped walnuts

1. In a small saucepan, combine peas and onion. Cover with water. Bring to a boil. Reduce heat; cover and simmer for 4-5 minutes or until peas are tender. Drain.

2. Stir in the butter, dill, salt and pepper; heat through. Sprinkle with walnuts.

Nutrition Facts: 1/2 cup equals 109 calories, 5 g fat (2 g saturated fat), 8 mg cholesterol, 249 mg sodium, 11 g carbohydrate, 4 g fiber, 5 g protein. **Diabetic Exchanges:** 1 starch, 1 fat.

DILLED PEAS WITH WALNUTS NOTES:
_____
_____
_____
_____
_____

Asian Quinoa

Prep: 20 min. • **Cook:** 20 min. • **Yield:** 4 servings
I love to cook and come up with new recipes. I serve this dish at least once a month and sometimes more. For a different twist, I'll occasionally add a scrambled egg or use soy sauce instead of the rice vinegar.
—*Sonya Labbe, Los Angeles, California*

- 1 cup water
- 2 tablespoons rice vinegar
- 2 tablespoons plum sauce
- 2 garlic cloves, minced
- 1 teaspoon minced fresh gingerroot
- 1 teaspoon sesame oil
- 1/4 teaspoon salt
- 1/4 teaspoon crushed red pepper flakes
- 1/2 cup quinoa, rinsed
- 1 medium sweet red pepper, chopped
- 1/2 cup sliced water chestnuts, chopped
- 1/2 cup fresh sugar snap peas, trimmed and halved
- 2 green onions, thinly sliced

1. In a large saucepan, combine the first eight ingredients; bring to a boil. Add quinoa. Reduce heat; cover and simmer for 12-15 minutes or until water is absorbed.

2. Remove from heat. Add the red pepper, water chestnuts, peas and onions; fluff with a fork. Cover; let stand 10 minutes.

Nutrition Facts: 2/3 cup equals 138 calories, 3 g fat (trace saturated fat), 0 cholesterol, 205 mg sodium, 25 g carbohydrate, 3 g fiber, 4 g protein.

EDITOR'S NOTE: Look for quinoa in the cereal, rice or organic food aisle.

ASIAN QUINOA NOTES: _____
_____
_____
_____
_____

Chicken & Vegetable Alfredo

Prep/Total Time: 25 min. • **Yield:** 2 servings.

This hearty pasta dish offers great garlic-basil flavor in a fraction of the time. Just think of how pretty this colorful dish will look on your table tonight! If you can't find basil and garlic goat cheese, buy plain goat cheese and add 1 teaspoon dried basil leaves to chicken and toss before cooking in butter.
—*Linda Morten, Somerville, Texas*

- 3 ounces uncooked fettuccine
- 1 boneless skinless chicken breast (6 ounces), cubed
- 3/4 cup fresh sugar snap peas
- 2 teaspoons butter
- 1/2 cup grape tomatoes
- 1 garlic clove, minced
- 1/2 teaspoon all-purpose flour
- 1/8 teaspoon salt
- 1/8 teaspoon pepper
- 1/3 cup half-and-half cream
- 1/4 cup basil and roasted garlic goat cheese
- 2 tablespoons minced fresh parsley

1. Cook fettuccine according package directions. Meanwhile, in a large skillet, saute chicken and peas in butter until chicken is no longer pink. Add tomatoes and garlic; cook 2 minutes longer.

2. Combine the flour, salt, pepper and cream; stir into the chicken mixture. Bring to a boil. Cook and stir for 1-2 minutes or until thickened.

3. Stir in goat cheese and parsley; cook and stir until cheese is melted. Drain fettuccine; toss with chicken mixture.

Nutrition Facts: 1-3/4 cup equals 438 calories, 16 g fat (10 g saturated fat), 97 mg cholesterol, 403 mg sodium, 39 g carbohydrate, 4 g fiber, 35 g protein.

CHICKEN & VEGETABLE ALFREDO NOTES:
_____
_____
_____
_____

HERBED PEAS NOTES: _____
_____
_____
_____

Herbed Peas

Prep: 10 min. • **Cook:** 15 min. • **Yield:** 8 servings.

Fresh herbs produce peas that please! Here's a great dish I love serving with my favorite meat dishes.
—*Mary Ann Dell, Phoenixville, Pennsylvania*

- 3/4 cup thinly sliced green onions
- 1/3 cup butter
- 6 cups fresh *or* frozen peas, thawed
- 3 tablespoons minced fresh parsley
- 3 tablespoons minced fresh basil
- 1 teaspoon sugar
- 3/4 teaspoon salt
- 1/2 teaspoon pepper

1. In a large skillet, saute the onions in butter until tender. Stir in the peas, parsley, basil, sugar, salt and pepper; saute for 3 minutes.

2. Reduce heat; cover and cook 3-5 minutes longer or until peas are tender. Serve with a slotted spoon.

Nutrition Facts: 3/4 cup equals 161 calories, 8 g fat (5 g saturated fat), 20 mg cholesterol, 283 mg sodium, 17 g carbohydrate, 6 g fiber, 6 g protein.
Diabetic Exchanges: 1 starch, 1 lean meat, 1 fat.

rhubarb & SWISS CHARD

A vegetable that functions as an easy-to-grow fruit—now there's a concept. Can it, freeze it, bake it or turn it into a sauce—rhubarb's slightly tart flavor is a match made in heaven when combined with apples, cherries and most berries.

SEASON: April to June.

AT THE MARKET: Select rhubarb that is firm and crisp. Avoid limp stalks.

STORAGE: Refrigerate unwashed for up to 1 week.

A NOTE ABOUT RHUBARB: If using frozen rhubarb, measure rhubarb while still frozen, then thaw completely. Drain in a colander, but do not press liquid out.

The Swiss army knife of garden vegetables, chard (also called Swiss chard) is packed with nutrition, tastes great in a variety of dishes and, when home-grown, even makes a nice ornamental addition to your landscaping.

SEASON: Spring to mid-summer.

AT THE MARKET: Look for leaves that are bright green; avoid vegetables with leaves that are browning, yellowing or wilted.

STORAGE: Refrigerate unwashed for 2-3 days.

MISHMASH APPLESAUCE

Prep: 30 min. • **Bake:** 30 min. • **Yield:** 8 cups.
This fun, colorful recipe is easy because you don't need to peel the apples. Berries and rhubarb give the flavor a boost.
—*Beverly Rice, Elm Grove, Wisconsin*

3 pounds tart apples, chopped	1 cup fresh *or* frozen cranberries
2 cups chopped fresh *or* frozen rhubarb	1 cup orange juice
1 cup chopped fresh *or* frozen strawberries	2 packages (.3 ounce *each*) sugar-free strawberry gelatin
1 cup fresh *or* frozen blueberries	

1. In a Dutch oven, combine the fruit and orange juice. Bring to a boil over medium heat, stirring frequently. Sprinkle gelatin over fruit mixture; stir until combined. Reduce heat; cover and simmer for 15-20 minutes or until apples are tender.

2. Remove from the heat; mash fruit. Let stand for 15 minutes. Serve warm or chilled.

Nutrition Facts: 1/2 cup equals 75 calories, trace fat (trace saturated fat), 0 cholesterol, 24 mg sodium, 18 g carbohydrate, 3 g fiber, 1 g protein. **Diabetic Exchanges:** 1 fruit.

MISHMASH APPLESAUCE NOTES: _____
_____
_____
_____
_____

Swiss Chard Bean Soup

Prep: 25 min. • **Cook:** 30 min. • **Yield:** 10 servings.
This hearty soup combines nutritious Swiss chard with other garden favorites. Its light broth is surprisingly rich in flavor and the grated Parmesan packs an additional punch.
—*Taste of Home Test Kitchen*

1 medium carrot, coarsely chopped	4 cups chopped Swiss chard
1 small zucchini, coarsely chopped	1 can (15-1/2 ounces) great northern beans, rinsed and drained
1 small yellow summer squash, coarsely chopped	1 can (14-1/2 ounces) diced tomatoes, undrained
1 small red onion, chopped	1 teaspoon dried thyme
2 tablespoons olive oil	1/2 teaspoon salt
2 garlic cloves, minced	1/2 teaspoon dried oregano
3 cans (14-1/2 ounces *each*) reduced-sodium chicken broth	1/4 teaspoon pepper
	1/4 cup grated Parmesan cheese

1. In a Dutch oven, saute the carrot, zucchini, yellow squash and onion in oil until tender. Add garlic; saute 1 minute longer. Add the broth, Swiss chard, beans, tomatoes, thyme, salt, oregano and pepper.

2. Bring to a boil. Reduce heat; simmer, uncovered, for 15 minutes or until chard is tender. Just before serving, sprinkle with cheese.

Nutrition Facts: 1 cup equals 94 calories, 4 g fat (1 g saturated fat), 2 mg cholesterol, 452 mg sodium, 12 g carbohydrate, 4 g fiber, 5 g protein.

SWISS CHARD BEAN SOUP NOTES:
_____
_____
_____
_____

Swiss Chard Bundles

Prep: 50 min. • **Bake:** 35 min. • **Yield:** 8 servings.
Tired of sauteed greens, I created this unique "stuffed" side dish that makes use of Swiss chard. A robust blend of seasonings and two types of cheese pack the tender bundles with loads of flavor.
—*Laurie Bock, Lynden, Washington*

- 1 bunch Swiss chard
- 3 medium potatoes (about 1 pound), peeled and cubed
- 1 medium onion, chopped
- 1 tablespoon olive oil
- 6 garlic cloves, minced
- 1/4 cup white wine *or* chicken broth
- 1/4 cup minced fresh oregano
- 1/2 teaspoon crushed red pepper flakes
- 1/3 cup sour cream
- 1/4 cup grated Parmesan cheese
- 3 tablespoons shredded cheddar cheese
- 1/4 teaspoon salt
- 1/4 teaspoon pepper
- 2 medium tomatoes, chopped
- 1/4 cup shredded Parmesan cheese

1. Cook Swiss chard in boiling water for 2-3 minutes or until tender. Drain and pat dry. Cut out the thick vein from the bottom of eight leaves, making a V-shaped cut; set aside. (Refrigerate remaining Swiss chard for another use.)

2. Place potatoes in a large saucepan and cover with water. Bring to a boil. Reduce heat; cover and cook 15-20 minutes or until potatoes are tender.

3. Meanwhile, in a small skillet, cook onion in oil until tender. Add garlic; cook 1 minute longer. Stir in the wine, oregano and pepper flakes. Bring to a boil; set aside.

4. Drain potatoes and mash. Stir in the wine mixture, sour cream, grated Parmesan cheese, cheddar cheese, salt and pepper. Overlapping cut ends of leaves, place about 1/3 cup potato mixture on each leaf. Fold in sides. Roll up completely to enclose filling.

5. Place seam side down in a greased 8-in. square baking dish. Cover and bake at 350° for 25 minutes. Sprinkle with tomatoes and shredded Parmesan cheese. Bake, uncovered, 10-15 minutes longer or until Swiss chard is tender and cheese is melted.

Nutrition Facts: 1 bundle equals 143 calories, 6 g fat (3 g saturated fat), 13 mg cholesterol, 231 mg sodium, 17 g carbohydrate, 2 g fiber, 5 g protein. **Diabetic Exchanges:** 1 vegetable, 1 fat, 1 starch.

Cherry Rhubarb Pie

Prep: 25 min. • **Bake:** 40 min. • **Yield:** 4 servings.

I share this recipe as often as I can. The slightly sweet, slightly tart pie is a must in our house during rhubarb season.
—*Shirley Steel, San Jose, California*

1-2/3 cups sliced fresh *or* frozen rhubarb

2/3 cup sugar

2/3 cup drained pitted tart cherries

4 teaspoons quick-cooking tapioca

2 to 3 drops red food coloring, optional

1 sheet refrigerated pie pastry

1. In a large bowl, combine the rhubarb, sugar, cherries, tapioca and food coloring if desired; stir gently and let stand for 15 minutes.

2. Meanwhile, cut pastry sheet in half. On a lightly floured surface, roll out one half to fit a 7-in. pie plate. Transfer pastry to pie plate; add filling. Roll out remaining pastry to fit top of pie. Place over filling. Trim, seal and flute edges. Cut slits in pastry.

3. Bake at 400° for 40-45 minutes or until crust is golden and filling is bubbly. Cover edges with foil during the last 15 minutes to prevent overbrowning if necessary. Cool on a wire rack.

Nutrition Facts: 1 piece equals 432 calories, 14 g fat (6 g saturated fat), 10 mg cholesterol, 206 mg sodium, 75 g carbohydrate, 1 g fiber, 3 g protein.

CHERRY RHUBARB PIE NOTES: _____

_____

_____

_____

_____

Salmon with Gingered Rhubarb Compote

Prep: 30 min. • **Bake:** 20 min. • **Yield:** 4 servings.

Rhubarb plays the role of lemon in this recipe, brightening and accenting the rich taste of the fish. I like to double the amount of compote and save half for another fast and healthy meal.
—*Susan Asanovic, Wilton, Connecticut*

1 medium onion, thinly sliced

4 green onions, sliced

2 tablespoons butter

4 cups sliced fresh *or* frozen rhubarb

1/4 cup packed brown sugar

1/2 cup sweet white wine *or* white grape juice

1 tablespoon minced fresh gingerroot

1/2 teaspoon salt

1/4 teaspoon pepper

4 salmon fillets (6 ounces *each*)

Additional sliced green onions, optional

1. In a large ovenproof skillet, cook onions in butter over medium heat for 15-20 minutes or until onions are golden brown, stirring frequently.

2. Add rhubarb and brown sugar; cook 3 minutes longer. Stir in the wine, ginger, salt and pepper. Bring to a boil. Reduce heat; simmer, uncovered, for 5-10 minutes or until rhubarb is tender, stirring occasionally.

3. Place salmon over rhubarb mixture. Bake, uncovered, at 350° for 20-25 minutes or until fish flakes easily with a fork. Sprinkle with additional green onions if desired.

Nutrition Facts: 1 salmon fillet with about 1/3 cup compote equals 464 calories, 24 g fat (7 g saturated fat), 115 mg cholesterol, 450 mg sodium, 25 g carbohydrate, 3 g fiber, 36 g protein.

SALMON WITH GINGERED RHUBARB COMPOTE NOTES: _____

_____

_____

_____

Rhubarb Popover Pie

Prep: 25 min. • **Bake:** 20 min. • **Yield:** 6 servings.
This fabulous spring breakfast "pie" is also delicious
when fresh strawberries are mixed in with the tart and
tangy rhubarb filling. Yum!
—*Patricia Kile, Elizabethtown, Pennsylvania*

1/2 cup all-purpose flour
1/4 teaspoon salt
2 eggs
1/2 cup 2% milk
2 tablespoons butter

FILLING:
1-1/2 cups sliced fresh *or* frozen rhubarb, thawed
1/2 cup canned pineapple chunks
1/3 cup butter, cubed
1/2 cup packed brown sugar

Whipped cream *or* vanilla ice cream, optional

1. In a large bowl, combine flour and salt. In another bowl, whisk eggs and milk.

2. Place butter in an 9-in. pie plate; heat in a 425° oven for 3-5 minutes or until butter is melted. Meanwhile, stir egg mixture into dry ingredients just until moistened.

3. Carefully swirl the butter in the pan to coat the sides and bottom of pan; add batter. Bake at 425° for 16-20 minutes or until puffed and golden brown.

4. Meanwhile, in a large skillet, saute the rhubarb and pineapple in butter until rhubarb is tender. Stir in brown sugar; bring to a boil over medium heat, stirring constantly. Pour into the center of puffed pancake; cut into six wedges. Serve immediately with whipped cream if desired.

Nutrition Facts: 1 piece (calculated without whipped cream) equals 279 calories, 16 g fat (10 g saturated fat), 109 mg cholesterol, 239 mg sodium, 31 g carbohydrate, 1 g fiber, 4 g protein.

> RHUBARB POPOVER PIE TIP: If you don't have a 9-inch pie plate, you can use four 8-ounce custard cups instead. In each custard cup, use 1-1/2 teaspoons butter and 1/2 cup batter. Place the cups on a baking sheet and bake about 15 minutes. —Taste of Home

> RHUBARB LEMON MUFFINS NOTES: _____
> _____
> _____
> _____

Rhubarb Lemon Muffins

Prep: 15 min. • **Bake:** 20 min. • **Yield:** 1 dozen.
My father has a rhubarb plant and gives me some every spring. I
stew some of it for him, but I always save some for a new recipe.
This is one of the tastiest I've tried.
—*Kathleen Smith, Pittsburgh, Pennsylvania*

2 cups all-purpose flour
1 cup plus 1-1/2 teaspoons sugar, *divided*
3 teaspoons baking powder
1/2 teaspoon salt
1/2 teaspoon ground ginger
2 eggs
1/2 cup buttermilk
1/4 cup canola oil
1 tablespoon grated lemon peel
1-3/4 cups sliced fresh *or* frozen rhubarb

1. In a large bowl, combine the flour, 1 cup sugar, baking powder, salt and ginger. In a small bowl, combine the eggs, buttermilk, oil and lemon peel. Stir into dry ingredients just until moistened. Fold in rhubarb.

2. Fill paper-lined muffin cups two-thirds full. Sprinkle with remaining sugar. Bake at 375° for 20-25 minutes or until a toothpick inserted near the middle comes out clean. Cool for 5 minutes before removing from pan to a wire rack.

Nutrition Facts: 1 muffin equals 203 calories, 6 g fat (1 g saturated fat), 36 mg cholesterol, 221 mg sodium, 35 g carbohydrate, 1 g fiber, 4 g protein.

OH BABY! Although the modern-day Dutch Baby is thought to have derived from German Apfelpfannkuchen, it was the Seattle-based Manca Cafe that made the puffy, filled pancake famous. The family-owned restaurant even owned the trademark for the term Dutch Babies until the 1950s when the restaurant closed.

early to mid-
SUMMER

THE HEIGHT OF THE SEASON

By now the farmers markets are in full swing. It has never been easier to create colorful and flavorful dishes from local ingredients. Make the most of the season's offerings with these simple, tasty recipes starring garden-fresh beans, berries, cherries, corn, cucumbers, kohlrabi and peppers.

BEANS

Commonly known as string beans or snap beans, these veggies are one of the most popular around—and for good reason! They add crunch, color and health benefits to many dishes.

SEASON: Peaks early to mid-summer; some varieties produce into fall.

AT THE MARKET: Select brightly colored, straight, smooth and unblemished pods. They should be crisp and have a firm, velvety feel.

STORAGE: Store unwashed in a sealed plastic bag or covered container in the refrigerator crisper drawer for up to 3 days.

Festive Bean 'n' Pepper Bundles

Prep: 25 min. • **Cook:** 15 min. • **Yield:** 12 servings.
Here is a beautiful way to prepare vegetables. The flavor pairs well with a variety of entrees.
—*Judith Krucki, Lake Orion, Michigan*

- 1 pound fresh green beans, trimmed
- 1 pound fresh wax beans, trimmed
- 2 tablespoons chicken bouillon granules
- 1/2 teaspoon garlic powder
- 3 medium zucchini
- 2 medium sweet red peppers, julienned
- 1/4 cup butter, melted

1. In a large saucepan, combine the beans, bouillon and garlic powder; cover with water. Bring to a boil. Cook, uncovered, for 8-10 minutes or until crisp-tender; drain.

2. Cut zucchini into 1/2-in. slices. Hollow out centers, leaving 1/4-in. rings; discard the centers. Thread beans and peppers through squash rings.

3. Place in a greased 15-in. x 10-in. x 1-in. baking pan; drizzle with butter. Cover and bake at 350° for 15-20 minutes or until zucchini is crisp-tender.

Nutrition Facts: 1 serving equals 57 calories, 3 g fat (2 g saturated fat), 8 mg cholesterol, 372 mg sodium, 7 g carbohydrate, 3 g fiber, 2 g protein.

FESTIVE BEAN 'N' PEPPER BUNDLES
NOTES:_____
_____
_____
_____
_____

Stir-Fried Beans with Pecans

Prep: 10 min. • **Cook:** 10 min. • **Yield:** 5 servings.
Made with fresh-from-the-garden green beans and onions, this side dish gets gobbled up by our six kids. Pecans add a bit of crunch.
— *Kathy Klingensmith, Riesel, Texas*

1/2 pound fresh green beans, trimmed	2 tablespoons canola oil
	1 large onion, sliced
1/2 pound fresh wax beans, trimmed	1/2 cup pecan halves
	3/4 teaspoon salt

1. In a large skillet or wok, stir-fry beans in oil for 4-5 minutes. Add remaining ingredients; stir-fry for 2-3 minutes longer or until vegetables are crisp-tender.

Nutrition Facts: 3/4 cup equals 163 calories, 13 g fat (1 g saturated fat), 0 cholesterol, 361 mg sodium, 11 g carbohydrate, 5 g fiber, 3 g protein.

STIR-FRIED BEANS WITH PECANS
NOTES:_____
_____
_____
_____

Summer's Bounty Soup

Prep: 5 min. • **Cook:** 7 hours • **Yield:** 12-14 servings.
Lots of wonderfully fresh-tasting vegetables are showcased in this chunky soup. I like it because it's a great way to use up excess green beans, and it's a summer dish that uses the slow cooker.
—*Victoria Zmarzley-Hahn, Northampton, Pennsylvania*

4 medium tomatoes, chopped	2 celery ribs, thinly sliced
2 medium potatoes, peeled and cubed	1 cup cubed peeled eggplant
2 cups halved fresh green beans	1 cup sliced fresh mushrooms
2 small zucchini, cubed	1 small onion, chopped
1 medium yellow summer squash, cubed	1 tablespoon minced fresh parsley
4 small carrots, thinly sliced	1 tablespoon salt-free garlic and herb seasoning
	4 cups V8 juice

1. In a 5-qt. slow cooker, combine all the ingredients. Cover and cook on low for 7-8 hours or until vegetables are tender.

Nutrition Facts: 1 cup equals 60 calories, trace fat (0 saturated fat), 0 cholesterol, 59 mg sodium, 13 g carbohydrate, 0 fiber, 2 g protein.
Diabetic Exchanges: 2 vegetable.

SUMMER'S BOUNTY SOUP NOTES:
_____
_____
_____

Roasted Parmesan Green Beans

Prep: 15 min. • **Cook:** 15 min. • **Yield:** 4 servings.

I'm not a big fan of the traditional green bean casserole, so I came up with this easy, no-fuss version. It's so quick and versatile, you can make it anytime and for just about any main dish.

—*Christie Ladd, Mechanicsburg, Pennsylvania*

1 pound fresh green beans, trimmed	2 tablespoons shredded Parmesan cheese
2 teaspoons olive oil	
1-1/2 teaspoons Greek seasoning	

1. Place beans in a 15-in. x 10-in. x 1-in. baking pan coated with cooking spray. Drizzle with oil. Sprinkle with seasoning; stir to coat.

2. Bake, uncovered, at 425° for 12-15 minutes or until beans are tender, stirring once. Sprinkle with cheese.

Nutrition Facts: 2/3 cup equals 61 calories, 3 g fat (1 g saturated fat), 2 mg cholesterol, 410 mg sodium, 7 g carbohydrate, 3 g fiber, 3 g protein. **Diabetic Exchanges:** 1 vegetable, 1/2 fat.

ROASTED PARMESAN GREEN BEANS
NOTES: _____
_____
_____
_____

String Bean Salad

Prep: 10 min. • **Cook:** 15 min. • **Yield:** 2 servings.

I first tried this simple summer side dish at our condo potluck. The combination of crisp beans and tender potatoes coated with light vinaigrette is very refreshing.

—*Jean Grade, Sheboygan, Wisconsin*

1 small red potato, halved and cut into 1/4-inch slices	2 tablespoons olive oil
1/3 pound fresh green beans, trimmed	1 tablespoon chopped red onion
	1 garlic clove, minced
	Salt and pepper to taste

1. Place potato slices in a steamer basket; place in a small saucepan over 1 in. of water. Bring to a boil; cover and steam for 5 minutes. Add beans; steam 8-10 minutes longer or until vegetables are tender.

2. In a jar with a tight-fitting lid, combine the oil, onion and garlic; shake well. Transfer vegetables to a bowl; add dressing and toss to coat. Season with salt and pepper. Cover and refrigerate for at least 1 hour.

Nutrition Facts: 1 cup equals 161 calories, 14 g fat (2 g saturated fat), 0 cholesterol, 6 mg sodium, 9 g carbohydrate, 3 g fiber, 2 g protein.

STRING BEAN SALAD NOTES:
_____
_____
_____
_____
_____

Garlic Green and Wax Beans

Prep: 5 min. • **Cook:** 10 min. • **Yield:** 12 servings.
Even those who don't like to eat their veggies will enjoy
this fresh-tasting medley of fresh green and wax beans.
—*Marilou Robinson, Portland, Oregon*

1-1/2 pounds fresh green beans	1 teaspoon white wine vinegar
1-1/2 pounds fresh wax beans	1 teaspoon olive oil
7 garlic cloves, minced, *divided*	1/2 teaspoon salt
	1/8 teaspoon pepper
1/4 cup reduced-fat sour cream	1 cup (4 ounces) shredded part-skim mozzarella cheese
1/4 cup fat-free milk	Minced fresh parsley

1. Place beans and 6 garlic cloves in a steamer basket. Place in a large saucepan over 1 in. of water; bring to a boil. Cover and steam for 8-10 minutes or until beans are crisp-tender. Transfer to a large bowl; set aside.

2. In a small bowl, combine the sour cream, milk and vinegar; let stand for 1 minute. Whisk in the oil, salt, pepper and remaining garlic. Pour over beans and toss. Cover and refrigerate for at least 2 hours. Just before serving, sprinkle with cheese and parsley.

Nutrition Facts: 3/4 cup equals 76 calories, 2 g fat (1 g saturated fat), 7 mg cholesterol, 157 mg sodium, 9 g carbohydrate, 4 g fiber, 5 g protein.
Diabetic Exchanges: 2 vegetable, 1/2 fat.

GARLIC GREEN AND WAX BEANS TIP:
White wine vinegar is made from white
wine, and, although its flavor is
pungent, it is milder than distilled
white vinegar. For savory dishes,
most people prefer to use white wine
vinegar. —Taste of Home

Pretty Almond Green Beans

Prep: 15 min. • **Cook:** 10 min. • **Yield:** 6 servings.
Savor the traditional flavors of green beans, mushrooms and onions
without the calories packed into traditional green bean casserole!
You'll appreciate how easily this light and festive dish comes together.
—*Vikki Peck, Poland, Ohio*

1 pound fresh green beans, trimmed	1 small onion, chopped
1 medium sweet red pepper, julienned	1 tablespoon olive oil
1 cup sliced fresh mushrooms	1/4 cup sliced almonds, toasted

1. Place beans in a large saucepan and cover with water. Bring to a boil. Cover and cook for 4-7 minutes or until crisp-tender.

2. Meanwhile, in a large nonstick skillet, saute the pepper, mushrooms and onion in oil until tender. Drain beans; stir into vegetable mixture. Sprinkle with almonds.

Nutrition Facts: 3/4 cup equals 78 calories, 4 g fat (1 g saturated fat), 0 cholesterol, 6 mg sodium, 9 g carbohydrate, 4 g fiber, 3 g protein.
Diabetic Exchanges: 1 vegetable, 1 fat.

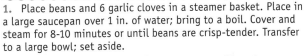

PRETTY ALMOND GREEN BEANS NOTES:
_____
_____
_____
_____

Green Beans with Pecans

Prep: 20 min. • **Cook:** 15 min. • **Yield:** 8 servings.
I collect cookbooks from all over the world and love to try new recipes. Pecans, a splash of orange juice and bit of maple syrup make this side dish something extra-special!
—*Sharon Delaney-Chronis, South Milwaukee, Wisconsin*

  1 tablespoon butter
  1 cup chopped pecans
  2 tablespoons maple syrup
1/8 teaspoon salt

BEANS:

1/4 cup finely chopped shallots
  2 tablespoons butter
  2 teaspoons all-purpose flour
1/2 teaspoon grated orange peel

Dash cayenne pepper

1-1/2 pounds fresh green beans, trimmed
2/3 cup reduced-sodium chicken broth
1/3 cup orange juice
  1 teaspoon fresh sage *or* 1/4 teaspoon dried sage leaves
1/4 teaspoon salt
1/8 teaspoon pepper

1. In a small heavy skillet, melt butter. Add pecans; cook over medium heat until toasted, about 4 minutes. Stir in syrup and salt. Cook and stir for 2-3 minutes or until pecans are glossy. Spread on foil to cool.

2. Meanwhile, in a large skillet, saute shallots in butter until tender; stir in the flour, orange peel and cayenne. Add the remaining ingredients; cover and cook for 5 minutes. Uncover; cook and stir 4-5 minutes longer or until the beans are crisp-tender. Transfer mixture to a serving bowl. Sprinkle with the pecans.

Nutrition Facts: 3/4 cup equals 192 calories, 15 g fat (4 g saturated fat), 11 mg cholesterol, 195 mg sodium, 14 g carbohydrate, 4 g fiber, 3 g protein.

Dilled Carrots & Green Beans

Prep/Total Time: 25 min. • **Yield:** 4 servings.
I never ate carrots before I found this recipe, but it's a family favorite for both weeknight dinners and special occasions.
—*Harriett Lee, Glasgow, Montana*

3/4 cup water	4 medium carrots, julienned
1 teaspoon sugar	1/2 pound fresh green beans
1/2 teaspoon salt	1/4 cup reduced-fat Italian salad dressing
1/2 teaspoon dill weed	

1. In small saucepan, bring the water, sugar, salt and dill to a boil. Add carrots and beans. Cook, uncovered, for 5-8 minutes or until vegetables are crisp-tender; drain.

2. Drizzle with dressing; toss to coat.

Nutrition Facts: 3/4 cup equals 69 calories, 2 g fat (trace saturated fat), trace cholesterol, 298 mg sodium, 11 g carbohydrate, 4 g fiber, 2 g protein. **Diabetic Exchanges:** 2 vegetable, 1/2 fat.

DILLED CARROTS & GREEN BEANS NOTES: _____

_____
_____
_____
_____

Fabulous Green Beans

Prep: 10 min. • **Cook:** 10 min. • **Yield:** 4 servings.
My family loves this butter sauce over green beans whether they are fresh or frozen. I've used this easy recipe over sugar snap peas as well with equally delicious results.
—*Lori Daniels, Beverly, West Virginia*

1 pound fresh green beans, trimmed	1/2 teaspoon Italian seasoning
1/4 cup butter, cubed	1/2 teaspoon lemon juice
1 tablespoon olive oil	1/4 teaspoon grated lemon peel
1/2 teaspoon salt	

1. Place beans in a steamer basket; place in a large saucepan over 1 in. of water. Bring to a boil; cover and steam for 8-10 minutes or until crisp-tender.

2. Meanwhile, in a small saucepan, heat the remaining ingredients until butter is melted. Transfer beans to a serving bowl; drizzle with butter mixture and toss to coat.

Nutrition Facts: 3/4 cup equals 165 calories, 15 g fat (8 g saturated fat), 30 mg cholesterol, 382 mg sodium, 8 g carbohydrate, 4 g fiber, 2 g protein.

FABULOUS GREEN BEANS NOTES: _____

_____
_____
_____
_____

BERRIES

Strawberries...blueberries... blackberries...raspberries...it just wouldn't be summer without these jewel-toned gems. Find plenty of uses for these sun-ripened beauties here.

SEASON: Blackberries peak May-September; blueberries peak May-October; raspberries peak June-July and September-October; strawberries peak April-June.

AT THE MARKET: Select plump berries free of bruises or mold.

STORAGE: Sort and discard any crushed, mushy or moldy fruit. Refrigerate in a paper towel-lined, moisture-proof container for 2 to 3 days.

Berry Cheese Torte

Prep: 40 min. + chilling • **Yield:** 12 servings.
Layers of gingersnap cookies, cream cheese and juicy berries make this recipe the ideal summer dessert. Its fancy presentation doesn't give away how easy it is to prepare.
—*Deborah Hitchcock, Granite Falls, Washington*

- 1 cup crushed gingersnap cookies (about 20 cookies)
- 3/4 cup crushed vanilla wafers (about 25 wafers)
- 1/4 cup finely chopped walnuts
- 1/3 cup butter, melted
- 1 envelope unflavored gelatin
- 1-3/4 cups white grape juice
- 1 package (8 ounces) cream cheese, softened
- 1/4 cup sugar
- 1 teaspoon vanilla extract
- 2-1/2 cups fresh blueberries
- 1-1/2 cups sliced fresh strawberries

1. In a small bowl, combine the cookie crumbs, wafer crumbs, walnuts and butter. Press onto the bottom and 1-1/2 in. up the sides of a greased 9-in. springform pan.

2. Bake at 350° for 8-10 minutes or until set. Cool on a wire rack.

3. In a small saucepan, sprinkle gelatin over grape juice; let stand for 1 minute. Heat over low heat, stirring until gelatin is completely dissolved. Cover and refrigerate until partially set, about 45 minutes.

4. Meanwhile, in a large bowl, beat the cream cheese, sugar and vanilla until smooth. Spread over crust.

5. Place berries in a large bowl; add gelatin mixture and gently stir to coat. Spoon over cream cheese layer. Refrigerate for at least 2 hours before serving. Carefully run a knife around edge of pan to loosen. Remove sides of pan.

Nutrition Facts: 1 slice equals 273 calories, 16 g fat (8 g saturated fat), 35 mg cholesterol, 196 mg sodium, 31 g carbohydrate, 2 g fiber, 4 g protein.

BERRY CHEESE TORTE NOTES:

Summer Strawberry Soup

Prep: 15 min. + chilling • **Yield:** 6 servings.
You'll be amazed that just five ingredients can create something so spectacular! This fruity chilled soup is certain to become a new summertime favorite.
—*Verna Bollin, Powell, Tennessee*

2 cups vanilla yogurt	1/2 cup sugar
1/2 cup orange juice	Additional vanilla yogurt and fresh mint leaves, optional
2 pounds fresh strawberries, halved (8 cups)	

1. In a blender, combine yogurt, orange juice, strawberries and sugar in batches; cover and process until blended. Refrigerate for at least 2 hours. Garnish with additional yogurt and mint leaves if desired.

Nutrition Facts: 1 cup (calculated without additional yogurt) equals 204 calories, 3 g fat (2 g saturated fat), 8 mg cholesterol, 54 mg sodium, 41 g carbohydrate, 3 g fiber, 5 g protein.

SUMMER STRAWBERRY SOUP NOTES:
_____
_____
_____
_____

Glazed Pork with Strawberry Couscous

Prep: 15 min. • **Bake:** 1 hour 20 min. + standing • **Yield:** 10 servings.
Combining strawberries and couscous may sound unusual, but one bite proves it's a delicious complement to a succulent pork roast.
—*Bernice Janowski, Stevens Point, Wisconsin*

2 teaspoons dried marjoram	1 can (14-1/2 ounces) chicken broth
1 teaspoon salt	1 package (10 ounces) plain couscous
1 teaspoon seasoned pepper	1 cup fresh strawberries, quartered
1 bone-in pork loin roast (5 pounds)	1/4 cup minced fresh mint
1/2 cup seedless strawberry jam	2 teaspoons grated orange peel
1/2 cup orange juice, *divided*	

1. Line the bottom of a large shallow roasting pan with foil; set aside. Combine the marjoram, salt and pepper; rub over roast. Place in pan. Bake, uncovered, at 350° for 1 hour.

2. Combine jam and 1/4 cup orange juice; brush half over pork. Bake 20-30 minutes longer or until a meat thermometer reads 160°, basting with remaining jam mixture every 10 minutes. Let stand for 10 minutes before slicing.

3. Meanwhile, in a small saucepan, bring broth to a boil. Stir in couscous. Cover and remove from the heat; let stand for 5 minutes or until liquid is absorbed. Fluff with a fork; stir in the strawberries, mint, orange peel and remaining orange juice. Serve with pork.

Nutrition Facts: 4 ounces cooked meat with 1/2 cup couscous mixture equals 383 calories, 11 g fat (4 g saturated fat), 92 mg cholesterol, 493 mg sodium, 35 g carbohydrate, 2 g fiber, 36 g protein. **Diabetic Exchanges:** 4 lean meat, 2 starch, 1 fat.

GLAZED PORK WITH STRAWBERRY
COUSCOUS NOTES: _____
_____
_____
_____
_____

Cocoa Meringues with Berries

Prep: 20 min. • **Bake:** 50 min. + standing
Yield: 2 servings.
Light...fruity...chocolaty...this dessert has it all!
Add the sweet homemade berry sauce, and you're all set!
—*Raymonde Bourgeois, Swastika, Ontario*

1 egg white
1/8 teaspoon cream of tartar
Dash salt
3 tablespoons sugar, *divided*
1 tablespoon baking cocoa
1/4 teaspoon vanilla extract
2 tablespoons finely chopped bittersweet chocolate

BERRY SAUCE:
2 tablespoons sugar
1 teaspoon cornstarch
2 tablespoons orange juice
1 tablespoon water
1/2 cup fresh *or* frozen blueberries, thawed
1/2 cup fresh *or* frozen raspberries, thawed

1. Place egg white in a small bowl; let stand at room temperature for 30 minutes. Add cream of tartar and salt; beat on medium speed until soft peaks form. Gradually beat in 2 tablespoons sugar.

2. Combine cocoa and remaining sugar; add to meringue with vanilla. Beat on high until stiff glossy peaks form and sugar is dissolved. Fold in chopped chocolate.

3. Drop two mounds onto a parchment paper-lined baking sheet. Shape into 3-in. cups with the back of a spoon. Bake at 275° for 50-60 minutes or until set and dry. Turn oven off; leave meringues in oven for 1 hour.

4. In a small saucepan, combine the sugar, cornstarch, orange juice and water. Bring to a boil; cook and stir for 1 minute or until thickened. Remove from the heat; stir in berries. Cool to room temperature. Spoon into meringues.

Nutrition Facts: 1 meringue with 1/2 cup sauce equals 215 calories, 4 g fat (2 g saturated fat), 0 cholesterol, 102 mg sodium, 46 g carbohydrate, 3 g fiber, 3 g protein.

Blackberry Whole Wheat Coffee Cake

Prep: 20 min. • **Bake:** 35 min. + cooling • **Yield:** 20 servings.
Here is a low-guilt coffee cake that is high in blackberry flavor.
Wonderfully moist and tender, it's also good made with
fresh blueberries or raspberries.
—*Carol Forcum, Marion, Illinois*

1-1/2	cups all-purpose flour	1 cup buttermilk
1-1/3	cups packed brown sugar	1/3 cup canola oil
1	cup whole wheat flour	1/3 cup unsweetened applesauce
2	teaspoons baking powder	2 teaspoons vanilla extract
1/2	teaspoon baking soda	2 cups fresh *or* frozen blackberries
Dash salt		
1	egg	

1. In a large bowl, combine the first six ingredients. In another large bowl, combine the egg, buttermilk, oil, applesauce and vanilla. Stir into dry ingredients just until moistened. Fold in blackberries.

2. Transfer to a 13-in. x 9-in. baking pan coated with cooking spray. Bake at 375° for 35-40 minutes or until a toothpick inserted near the center comes out clean. Cool on a wire rack.

Nutrition Facts: 1 piece equals 160 calories, 4 g fat (trace saturated fat), 11 mg cholesterol, 102 mg sodium, 28 g carbohydrate, 2 g fiber, 3 g protein. **Diabetic Exchanges:** 1-1/2 starch, 1 fat.

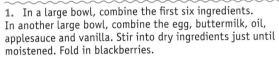

BLACKBERRY WHOLE WHEAT COFFEE CAKE
NOTES: _____

Broiled Halibut Steaks with Raspberry Sauce

Prep/Total Time: 15 min. • **Yield:** 4 servings.
This elegant and delicious entree is simply effortless. Salmon
can be used instead of halibut, and blackberry jam in place of
raspberry. Either way, it's outstanding!
—*Allene Bary-Cooper, Wichita Falls, Texas*

1/4	cup butter, cubed	3/4 cup seedless raspberry jam
1/4	teaspoon garlic powder	2 green onions, sliced
1/4	teaspoon salt	2 teaspoons Dijon mustard
1/4	teaspoon pepper	Fresh raspberries and lemon wedges, optional
4	halibut steaks (6 ounces *each*)	

1. In a microwave-safe bowl, melt butter; stir in the garlic powder, salt and pepper.

2. Broil halibut 4-6 in. from the heat for 5-6 minutes on each side or until fish flakes easily with a fork, basting occasionally with butter mixture.

3. Meanwhile, in a microwave-safe bowl, heat the jam, onions and mustard until jam is melted; stir until blended. Serve with fish. Garnish with raspberries and lemon wedges if desired.

Nutrition Facts: 1 halibut steak with 3 tablespoons sauce (calculated without raspberries and lemon) equals 443 calories, 15 g fat (8 g saturated fat), 85 mg cholesterol, 381 mg sodium, 40 g carbohydrate, trace fiber, 36 g protein.

BROILED HALIBUT STEAKS
WITH RASPBERRY SAUCE NOTES: _____

So Very Berry Brie

Prep: 15 min. + standing • **Bake:** 10 min. • **Yield:** 8 servings.

I needed a quick dish for a party and had some berries on hand. Combining them with warm Brie cheese made for an impressive and elegant starter.

—Kristin Larson, Newton, Kansas

- 1/2 cup sugar
- 2 tablespoons water
- 1/2 cup fresh *or* frozen raspberries, thawed
- 1/2 cup fresh *or* frozen blueberries, thawed
- 1/2 cup fresh *or* frozen blackberries, thawed
- 1 tablespoon cornstarch
- 2 tablespoons cold water
- 1 round (8 ounces) Brie cheese, halved horizontally

Bagel *and/or* baked pita chips

1. In a small saucepan, heat sugar and water until sugar is dissolved. Add berries. Bring to a boil. Reduce heat; simmer, uncovered, for 3 minutes. Combine cornstarch and cold water until smooth; gradually stir into the pan. Bring to a boil. Cook and stir for 2 minutes or until thickened. Remove from the heat; let stand for 10 minutes.

2. Place bottom half of cheese in an ungreased ovenproof serving dish; pour 1/2 cup berry mixture over cheese. Top with remaining cheese and berry mixture.

3. Bake, uncovered, at 400° for 8-10 minutes or until cheese is softened. Serve with chips.

Nutrition Facts: 1 serving (calculated without chips) equals 160 calories, 8 g fat (5 g saturated fat), 28 mg cholesterol, 179 mg sodium, 17 g carbohydrate, 1 g fiber, 6 g protein.

SO VERY BERRY BRIE NOTES:

_____
_____
_____
_____
_____

Strawberry Romaine Salad

Prep/Total Time: 30 min. • **Yield:** 10 servings.

Ruby red berries, crunchy almonds, crisp romaine and a homemade poppy seed dressing—what's not to love in this refreshing salad?

—Irene Keller, Kalamazoo, Michigan

- 1/4 cup sugar
- 1/3 cup slivered almonds
- 1 bunch romaine, torn
- 1 small onion, halved and thinly sliced
- 2 cups halved fresh strawberries

CREAMY POPPY SEED DRESSING:

- 1/4 cup mayonnaise
- 2 tablespoons sugar
- 1 tablespoon sour cream
- 1 tablespoon milk
- 2-1/4 teaspoons cider vinegar
- 1-1/2 teaspoons poppy seeds

1. In a small heavy skillet over medium-low heat, cook and stir the sugar until melted and caramel in color, about 10 minutes. Stir in almonds until coated. Spread on foil to cool; break into small pieces.

2. In a large bowl, combine the romaine, onion and strawberries. Combine the dressing ingredients; drizzle over salad and toss to coat. Sprinkle with coated almonds.

Nutrition Facts: 3/4 cup equals 112 calories, 7 g fat (1 g saturated fat), 2 mg cholesterol, 35 mg sodium, 12 g carbohydrate, 2 g fiber, 2 g protein.
Diabetic Exchanges: 1 vegetable, 1 fat, 1/2 starch.

STRAWBERRY ROMAINE SALAD NOTES:

_____
_____
_____
_____

Cedar Plank Salmon with Blackberry Sauce

Prep: 20 min. + soaking • **Grill:** 15 min. • **Yield:** 6 servings.
Here's my go-to entree for a warm-weather cookout. The salmon has a rich, grilled taste that's enhanced by the savory blackberry sauce. It's a nice balance of sweet, smoky and spicy.
—*Stephanie Matthews, Tempe, Arizona*

2 cedar grilling planks	1/4 teaspoon salt, *divided*
2 cups fresh blackberries	1/4 teaspoon pepper, *divided*
2 tablespoons white wine	
1 tablespoon brown sugar	1/4 cup finely chopped shallots
1-1/2 teaspoons honey	1 garlic clove, minced
1-1/2 teaspoons chipotle hot pepper sauce	6 salmon fillets (5 ounces *each*)

1. Soak grilling planks in water for at least 1 hour.

2. In a food processor, combine the blackberries, wine, brown sugar, honey, hot pepper sauce, 1/8 teaspoon salt and 1/8 teaspoon pepper; cover and process until blended. Strain and discard seeds. Stir the shallots and garlic into the sauce; set aside.

3. Place planks on grill over medium-high heat. Cover and heat until planks create a light to medium smoke and begin to crackle, about 3 minutes (this indicates planks are ready). Turn planks over.

4. Sprinkle salmon with remaining salt and pepper. Place on planks. Grill, covered, over medium heat for 12-15 minutes or until fish flakes easily with a fork. Serve with sauce.

Nutrition Facts: 1 salmon fillet with 2 tablespoons sauce equals 304 calories, 16 g fat (3 g saturated fat), 84 mg cholesterol, 186 mg sodium, 10 g carbohydrate, 3 g fiber, 29 g protein.

CEDAR PLANK SALMON WITH BLACKBERRY SAUCE TIP: For fillets, check for doneness by inserting a fork at an angle into the thickest portion of the fish and gently parting the meat. When it is opaque and flakes into sections, it's cooked completely. —Taste of Home

HEAVENLY FILLED STRAWBERRIES NOTES:

Heavenly Filled Strawberries

Prep/Total Time: 20 min. • **Yield:** about 3 dozen.
Stuffed with almond-flavored cream cheese and sprinkled with grated chocolate, these berries are a decadent way to usher in summer.
—*Stephen Munro, Beaverbank, Nova Scotia*

1 pound fresh strawberries	1/2 cup confectioners' sugar
2 packages (one 8 ounces, one 3 ounces) cream cheese, softened	1/4 teaspoon almond extract
	Grated chocolate

1. Remove stems from strawberries; cut a deep "X" in the tip of each berry. Gently spread berries open.

2. In a small bowl, beat the cream cheese, confectioners' sugar and almond extract until light and fluffy. Pipe or spoon about 2 teaspoons into each strawberry; sprinkle with grated chocolate. Chill until serving.

Nutrition Facts: 1 filled strawberry (calculated without chocolate) equals 41 calories, 3 g fat (2 g saturated fat), 10 mg cholesterol, 26 mg sodium, 3 g carbohydrate, trace fiber, 1 g protein. **Diabetic Exchange:** 1/2 fat.

Blackberry Cobbler

Prep: 25 min. • **Bake:** 30 min. • **Yield:** 9 servings.
We grow blackberries on our farm, and our family enjoys them in pies, jams, jellies and cobblers. I love to pull them out of the freezer in January and make this warm cobbler to enjoy summer's sweetness.
—*Lori Daniels, Beverly, West Virginia*

    3 cups fresh *or* frozen blackberries
    1 cup sugar
  1/4 teaspoon ground cinnamon
    3 tablespoons cornstarch
    1 cup cold water
    1 tablespoon butter
BISCUIT TOPPING:
1-1/2 cups all-purpose flour
    1 tablespoon sugar
1-1/2 teaspoons baking powder
  1/2 teaspoon salt
  1/2 cup cold butter, cubed
  1/2 cup 2% milk
Whipped topping *or* vanilla ice cream, optional

1. In a large saucepan, combine the blackberries, sugar and cinnamon. Cook and stir until mixture comes to a boil. Combine cornstarch and water until smooth; stir into fruit mixture. Bring to a boil; cook and stir for 2 minutes or until thickened. Pour into a greased 8-in. square baking dish. Dot with butter.

2. For topping, in a small bowl, combine the flour, sugar, baking powder and salt. Cut in butter until mixture resembles coarse crumbs. Stir in milk just until moistened. Drop by tablespoonfuls onto hot berry mixture.

3. Bake, uncovered, at 350° for 30-35 minutes or until filling is bubbly and topping is golden brown. Serve warm with whipped topping or ice cream.

Nutrition Facts: 1 serving (calculated without whipped topping or ice cream) equals 305 calories, 12 g fat (7 g saturated fat), 31 mg cholesterol, 286 mg sodium, 47 g carbohydrate, 3 g fiber, 3 g protein.

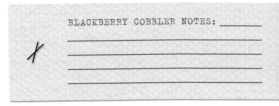

BLACKBERRY COBBLER NOTES: _____
_____
X _____
_____

Chicken 'n' Berry Salad

Prep: 15 min. + marinating • **Grill:** 10 min. • **Yield:** 9 servings.
We love this salad any time of year but especially in summer when blueberries and strawberries are in season.
—*Sheri Abernathy, Lemont, Illinois*

  1/2 cup sugar
  1/2 cup red wine vinegar
  1/2 cup olive oil
    1 garlic clove, minced
  1/2 teaspoon salt
  1/4 teaspoon pepper
    2 pounds boneless skinless chicken breasts
    6 cups torn romaine

    6 cups torn red leaf lettuce
    1 pint fresh blueberries
    1 pint fresh strawberries, sliced
    2 cups (8 ounces) shredded part-skim mozzarella cheese
    1 cup chopped walnuts

1. In a large bowl, whisk the first six ingredients. Pour 3/4 cup marinade into a large resealable plastic bag; add the chicken. Seal bag and turn to coat; refrigerate overnight. Cover and refrigerate remaining marinade.

2. Drain and discard marinade. Grill chicken, covered, over medium heat for 5-8 minutes on each side or until juices run clear. Cut into strips.

3. In a large bowl, combine the lettuces, blueberries, strawberries, cheese and walnuts. Add reserved marinade; toss to coat. Top with sliced chicken.

Nutrition Facts: 1-1/2 cups equals 426 calories, 25 g fat (5 g saturated fat), 70 mg cholesterol, 290 mg sodium, 22 g carbohydrate, 3 g fiber, 31 g protein.

CHICKEN 'N' BERRY SALAD NOTES:
_____
/ _____
_____
_____

CHANGE IT UP.
Add a dash of culinary creativity to your homemade cobbler recipe by varying the spices. Try substituting a teaspoon of aniseed or 1/4 teaspoon of ground nutmeg or ground cardamom for cinnamon.

Raspberry Mint Shakes

Prep/Total Time: 10 min. • **Yield:** 2 servings.
A creamy shake is the perfect way to cool down and relax at outdoor gatherings. Here's a fun option for dessert and also a great-tasting breakfast on the go.
—*Tiffanie Wright, Kempner, Texas*

1/3 cup honey	2 cups fresh *or* frozen raspberries
1/4 cup 2% milk	
1/4 cup heavy whipping cream	1 cup vanilla ice cream
1/4 teaspoon almond extract	2 tablespoons chopped fresh mint leaves

1. In a blender, combine all ingredients; cover and process for 30 seconds or until blended. Pour into chilled glasses; serve immediately.

Nutrition Facts: 1 cup equals 488 calories, 20 g fat (12 g saturated fat), 72 mg cholesterol, 83 mg sodium, 79 g carbohydrate, 9 g fiber, 5 g protein.

RASPBERRY MINT SHAKES NOTES:
_____
_____
_____
_____

Grilled Halibut with Blueberry Salsa

Prep/Total Time: 30 min. • **Yield:** 6 servings.
Give halibut a new, summery spin. The salsa may seem sophisticated, but it's really a cinch to prepare.
—*Donna Goutermont, Juneau, Alaska*

2 cups fresh blueberries, *divided*	1 tablespoon balsamic vinegar
1 small red onion, chopped	1 teaspoon plus 2 tablespoons olive oil, *divided*
1/4 cup minced fresh cilantro	
1 jalapeno pepper, seeded and chopped	1/8 teaspoon plus 1 teaspoon salt, *divided*
2 tablespoons orange juice	1/8 teaspoon pepper
	6 halibut fillets (5 ounces *each*)

1. In a small bowl, coarsely mash 1 cup blueberries. Stir in the onion, cilantro, jalapeno, orange juice, vinegar, 1 teaspoon oil, 1/8 teaspoon salt, pepper and remaining blueberries. Cover and chill until serving.

2. Meanwhile, drizzle fillets with remaining oil; sprinkle with remaining salt. Grill halibut, covered, over medium heat for 4-5 minutes on each side or until fish flakes easily with a fork. Serve with salsa.

Nutrition Facts: 1 fillet with 1/4 cup salsa equals 239 calories, 9 g fat (1 g saturated fat), 45 mg cholesterol, 521 mg sodium, 9 g carbohydrate, 1 g fiber, 30 g protein. **Diabetic Exchanges:** 4 lean meat, 1 fat, 1/2 starch.

EDITOR'S NOTE: We recommend wearing disposable gloves when cutting hot peppers. Avoid touching your face.

GRILLED HALIBUT WITH BLUEBERRY SALSA NOTES: _____
_____
_____
_____

Lemon-Mint Pound Cake with Strawberries

Prep: 45 min. • **Bake:** 1 hour + cooling • **Yield:** 12 servings.
Lemon and mint are two ingredients that shout summer to me. This twist on strawberry shortcake comes together like a charm and is great when you want to impress.
—*Nichole Jones, Pleasant Grove, Utah*

- 1/4 cup sugar
- 1/4 cup loosely packed fresh mint leaves
- 3/4 cup butter, softened
- 2-1/2 cups confectioners' sugar, *divided*
- 3 eggs
- 1-1/2 cups all-purpose flour
- 2-1/4 cups heavy whipping cream, *divided*
- 2 tablespoons lemon juice
- 2 teaspoons grated lemon peel
- 1 jar (10 ounces) lemon curd
- 1 quart fresh strawberries, sliced

1. Place sugar and mint in a small food processor; cover and process until blended. Set aside.

2. In a large bowl, cream butter and 1-3/4 cups confectioners' sugar until light and fluffy. Beat in 4-1/2 teaspoons reserved mint mixture. Add eggs, one at a time, beating well after each addition. Add flour alternately with 1/4 cup cream. Stir in lemon juice and peel.

3. Pour into a greased and floured 8-in. x 4-in. loaf pan. Bake at 325° for 60-70 minutes or until a toothpick inserted near the center comes out clean. Cool for 10 minutes before removing from pan to a wire rack to cool completely.

4. In a large bowl, beat remaining cream until it begins to thicken. Add 1/2 cup confectioners' sugar and 1 tablespoon mint mixture; beat until stiff peaks form. Fold in lemon curd; set aside.

5. In another bowl, combine strawberries with remaining mint mixture and confectioners' sugar. Slice cake; serve with strawberry mixture and lemon cream.

Nutrition Facts: 1 slice with 1/3 cup lemon cream and 3 tablespoons strawberries equals 542 calories, 31 g fat (18 g saturated fat), 162 mg cholesterol, 134 mg sodium, 63 g carbohydrate, 2 g fiber, 5 g protein.

LEMON-MINT POUND CAKE WITH
STRAWBERRIES NOTES:

_____

_____

_____

_____

CHERRIES

Stone Fruit Pie

Prep: 30 min. • Bake: 45 min. • Yield: 8 servings.
You can use any type of stone fruit in this pie. I love combining sour cherries with white peaches.
—*Crystal Bruns, Iliff, Colorado*

- 2 cups fresh *or* frozen pitted tart cherries, thawed
- 3 medium nectarines, chopped
- 3 apricots, sliced
- 2/3 cup sugar
- 1 tablespoon cornstarch
- 2 tablespoons plus 2 cups all-purpose flour, *divided*
- 1/8 teaspoon ground cinnamon
- 1 teaspoon salt
- 3/4 cup plus 2 tablespoons cold butter, *divided*
- 6 to 7 tablespoons ice water
- 1 egg yolk
- 1 teaspoon water

1. In a small bowl, combine the cherries, nectarines, apricots, sugar, cornstarch, 2 tablespoons flour and cinnamon; set aside.

2. In another bowl, combine salt and remaining flour; cut in 3/4 cup butter until crumbly. Gradually add ice water, tossing with a fork until dough forms a ball. Divide dough in half. Roll out one half to fit a 9-in. pie plate; transfer pastry to pie plate. Add filling; dot with remaining butter.

3. Roll out remaining pastry; make a lattice crust. Trim, seal and flute edges. In a small bowl, whisk egg yolk and water; brush over lattice top.

4. Bake at 400° for 45-50 minutes or until filling is bubbly and crust is golden brown. Cover edges with foil during the last 15 minutes to prevent overbrowning if necessary. Cool on a wire rack.

Nutrition Facts: 1 piece equals 360 calories, 21 g fat (13 g saturated fat), 78 mg cholesterol, 439 mg sodium, 42 g carbohydrate, 2 g fiber, 3 g protein.

Dubbed a "superfruit," cherries are packed with good-for-you antioxidants. Available in sweet and tart varieties, the ruby little darlings sure make one heck of a pie.

SEASON: May-July

AT THE MARKET: Select cherries that are plump and firm with a shiny skin.

STORAGE: Before refrigerating, sort through and discard any crushed, mushy or moldy fruit. Refrigerate unwashed cherries in a closed plastic bag for 1-2 days.

STONE FRUIT PIE NOTES: _____
_____
_____
_____
_____

Bing Cherry Sherbet

Prep: 30 min. • **Process:** 20 min./batch + freezing
Yield: about 3 quarts.

To whip up this pretty pink sherbet studded with dark, sweet cherries, you'll need an ice cream maker and a total of only four ingredients! It's delicious made with sliced peaches and peach soda, too.

—*Helen Humble, Longview, Texas*

4 cups fresh *or* frozen pitted dark sweet cherries, quartered

1 cup sugar

2 liters black cherry soda, chilled

1 can (14 ounces) sweetened condensed milk

1. In a large saucepan, bring cherries and sugar to a boil over medium heat, stirring constantly. **Reduce heat;** cover and simmer for 10 minutes, stirring occasionally. Cool slightly. Transfer to a large bowl; cover and refrigerate until chilled.

2. Stir in soda and milk. Fill ice cream freezer cylinder two-thirds full; freeze according to manufacturer's directions. Refrigerate remaining mixture until ready to freeze. Transfer to a freezer container; freeze for 2-4 hours or until firm. Remove from the freezer 10 minutes before serving.

Nutrition Facts: 3/4 cup equals 201 calories, 2 g fat (1 g saturated fat), 8 mg cholesterol, 45 mg sodium, 44 g carbohydrate, 1 g fiber, 2 g protein.

BING CHERRY SHERBET NOTES: _____
_____
_____
_____
_____
_____

Homemade Cherry Pie

Prep: 20 min. • **Bake:** 30 min. + cooling • **Yield:** 6-8 servings.

Fresh tart cherries give this pie filling a homemade flavor that's superior to canned.

—*Taste of Home Test Kitchen*

2/3 cup sugar

1/4 cup cornstarch

1/4 teaspoon salt

4 cups fresh tart cherries, pitted

1-1/2 cups water

2 tablespoons lemon juice

6 drops red food coloring, optional

ADDITIONAL INGREDIENT:

Pastry for double-crust pie (9 inches)

1. In a large saucepan, combine the sugar, cornstarch and salt. Add the cherries, water and lemon juice. Bring to a boil; cook and stir for 2 minutes or until thickened. Remove from the heat; stir in food coloring if desired. **Yield:** 4 cups.

2. **For a lattice-crust pie:** Line a 9-in. pie plate with bottom pastry; add filling. Make a lattice crust; trim, seal and flute edges. Cover edges loosely with foil.

3. Bake at 400° for 15 minutes. Remove foil; bake 15-20 minutes longer or until crust is golden and filling is bubbly. Cool on a wire rack.

Nutrition Facts: 1 serving (1 piece) equals 359 calories, 14 g fat (6 g saturated fat), 10 mg cholesterol, 277 mg sodium, 56 g carbohydrate, 1 g fiber, 3 g protein.

EDITOR'S NOTE: This recipe makes enough for a 9-in. pie. To use in other dessert recipes, a 21-oz. can of commercial pie filling is equal to 2 cups.

HOMEMADE CHERRY PIE NOTES: _____
_____
_____
_____
_____

Sour Cherry Sorbet

Prep: 10 min. + freezing • **Yield:** 6 servings.
My mother-in-law has a sour cherry tree in her yard that yields many quarts of cherries each June. We think this frosty, sweet-sour sorbet is a refreshing way to cool a hot summer day.
—*Carol Gaus, Elk Grove Village, Illinois*

3 cups frozen pitted tart cherries	1/2 teaspoon almond extract
1 cup sugar	1/2 teaspoon salt
1/3 cup white wine *or* grape juice	

1. Place cherries in a food processor; cover and process until smooth. Add remaining ingredients; cover and pulse until blended.

2. Pour into a freezer container. Cover; freeze until firm.

Nutrition Facts: 1/3 cup equals 175 calories, trace fat (trace saturated fat), 0 cholesterol, 198 mg sodium, 42 g carbohydrate, 1 g fiber, 1 g protein.

SOUR CHERRY SORBET NOTES:
_____
_____
_____
_____
_____

Pork Chops with Chipotle Cherry Glaze

Prep: 15 min. • **Cook:** 20 min. • **Yield:** 4 servings.
This delicious combination of pork and spicy cherry sauce is so quick and easy. Canned cherries work well, too.
—*Roxanne Chan, Albany, California*

1/4 teaspoon salt	2 tablespoons red wine vinegar
1/4 teaspoon sugar	1 tablespoon chopped chipotle pepper in adobo sauce
1/4 teaspoon ground cinnamon	1 tablespoon orange marmalade
4 boneless pork loin chops (5 ounces *each*)	1 garlic clove, minced
1 tablespoon olive oil	2 tablespoons sliced almonds, toasted
1 cup pitted dark sweet cherries, halved	1 tablespoon thinly sliced green onion
1/4 cup orange juice	
2 tablespoons dried cherries	

1. In a small bowl, combine the salt, sugar and cinnamon. Sprinkle over pork chops. In a large skillet, cook chops, uncovered, in oil over medium heat for 6-8 minutes on each side or until meat juices run clear. Remove to a serving platter and keep warm.

2. In the same skillet, combine the sweet cherries, orange juice, dried cherries, vinegar, chipotle peppers, marmalade and garlic. Cook and stir for 2-3 minutes or until heated through. Spoon over chops; sprinkle with almonds and green onion.

Nutrition Facts: 1 pork chop with 1/4 cup sauce equals 318 calories, 13 g fat (4 g saturated fat), 68 mg cholesterol, 217 mg sodium, 21 g carbohydrate, 2 g fiber, 28 g protein.

PORK CHOPS WITH CHIPOTLE CHERRY GLAZE NOTES: _____
_____
_____
_____
_____

Cherry-Berry Pie

Prep: 30 min. • **Bake:** 45 min. + cooling • **Yield:** 8 servings.
The red and blue fruit colors showing through the lattice crust make a
great patriotic presentation for any 4th of July celebration.
—*Cathi Henke, Wauwatosa, Wisconsin*

2 cups fresh tart cherries, pitted	1/2 teaspoon almond extract
2 cups fresh blueberries	Dash salt
1 cup chopped fresh strawberries	1 package (15 ounces) refrigerated pie pastry
3/4 cup sugar	2 tablespoons butter
3 tablespoons cornstarch	1 egg
2 teaspoons lemon juice	1 tablespoon water

1. In a large bowl, combine the first eight ingredients.

2. Line a 9-in. pie plate with bottom crust; trim pastry even
with edge. Fill with fruit mixture and dot with butter. Make a
lattice crust with remaining pastry. Trim, seal and flute edges.
Beat egg and water; brush over lattice top.

3. Bake at 400° for 45-55 minutes or until crust is golden
brown and filling is bubbly. Cover edges with foil during the last
20 minutes to prevent overbrowning if necessary. Let pie cool
on a wire rack.

Nutrition Facts: 1 piece equals 402 calories, 18 g fat (8 g saturated fat),
44 mg cholesterol, 246 mg sodium, 59 g carbohydrate, 2 g fiber, 4 g protein.

CHERRY-BERRY PIE TIP:
Did you know the same tool you use to
cut a pizza pie can come in handy when
making a traditional dessert pie? It's
true! Use your pizza cutter to cut
pastry dough into nice, even strips.
—Taste of Home

Summer Fruit Crisp

Prep: 30 min. • **Cook:** 20 min. • **Yield:** 10 servings.
What says summer more than this sweet dessert simply packed with
fresh cherries and juicy peaches? To beat the heat, dollop with
a scoop of low-fat frozen yogurt or ice cream.
—*Beth Garvin, Cisco, Texas*

4 cups fresh dark sweet cherries (about 1-1/4 pounds), pitted	TOPPING:
4 cups sliced peeled peaches	1/2 cup old-fashioned oats
1/3 cup sugar	1/2 cup packed brown sugar
2 tablespoons all-purpose flour	1/3 cup all-purpose flour
1/8 teaspoon salt	1/4 cup chopped pecans
	1/4 teaspoon salt
	1/4 teaspoon ground cinnamon
	3 tablespoons cold butter

1. In a large bowl, combine the cherries, peaches, sugar, flour
and salt. Transfer to a 13-in. x 9-in. baking dish coated with
cooking spray.

2. For topping, in a small bowl, combine the oats, brown sugar,
flour, pecans, salt and cinnamon. Cut in butter until crumbly.
Sprinkle over fruit mixture.

3. Bake at 400° for 20-25 minutes or until filling is bubbly and
topping is golden brown. Serve warm.

Nutrition Facts: 1 serving equals 234 calories, 6 g fat (2 g saturated fat),
9 mg cholesterol, 128 mg sodium, 45 g carbohydrate, 3 g fiber, 3 g protein.

SUMMER FRUIT CRISP NOTES:
_____
_____
_____
_____
_____

CORN

Cheese Tortellini with Tomatoes and Corn

Prep/Total Time: 25 min. • **Yield:** 4 servings.
Garden-fresh flavors make this cold pasta dish a culinary
delight! Plus, it's as easy as it is special.
—*Sally Maloney, Dallas, Georgia*

- 1 package (9 ounces) refrigerated cheese tortellini
- 1 package (16 ounces) frozen corn, thawed *or*
     3-1/3 cups fresh corn
- 2 cups cherry tomatoes, quartered
- 1/4 cup thinly sliced green onions
- 1/4 cup minced fresh basil
- 2 tablespoons grated Parmesan cheese
- 4 teaspoons olive oil
- 1/4 teaspoon garlic powder
- 1/8 teaspoon pepper

1. In a Dutch oven, cook tortellini according to package
directions, adding the corn during the last 5 minutes of
cooking. Drain and rinse in cold water.

2. In a large serving bowl, combine tortellini mixture and
remaining ingredients; toss to coat.

Nutrition Facts: 1-3/4 cups equals 366 calories, 12 g fat (4 g saturated
fat), 30 mg cholesterol, 286 mg sodium, 57 g carbohydrate,
5 g fiber, 14 g protein.

What veggie is more synonymous
with the season than corn? Whether
eaten straight from the cob or used
in a variety of dishes, it's summer
produce's golden child.

SEASON: Peaks June-July

AT THE MARKET: Husks should be
bright green and fit snugly around the
ear of corn. Kernels should be plump
and in tight rows right to the tip of
the ear.

STORAGE: 1-2 days.

CHEESE TORTELLINI WITH TOMATOES
AND CORN NOTES: _____
_____
_____
_____
_____

Homemade Cream-Style Corn

Prep/Total Time: 30 min. • **Yield:** 4 servings.
My son-in-law isn't a creamed corn enthusiast. But ever since he tried mine, he asks me to make it. It's so much better than the canned variety—and nearly as easy.
—*Verl Diro, Rapid City, South Dakota*

4 medium ears sweet corn	1 tablespoon minced fresh cilantro
3/4 cup heavy whipping cream	1 teaspoon Italian seasoning
1 tablespoon butter	

1. Place corn in a Dutch oven; cover with water. Bring to a boil; cover and cook for 5-10 minutes or until tender. Drain. Cut corn from cobs.

2. In a large saucepan, bring the corn, cream and butter to a boil. Reduce heat; stir in cilantro and Italian seasoning. Simmer, uncovered, for 3-5 minutes to allow flavors to blend.

Nutrition Facts: 2/3 cup equals 257 calories, 20 g fat (12 g saturated fat), 69 mg cholesterol, 51 mg sodium, 18 g carbohydrate, 3 g fiber, 4 g protein.

HOMEMADE CREAM-STYLE CORN NOTES:

_____

_____

_____

_____

Lattice Corn Pie

Prep: 25 min. • **Bake:** 35 min. • **Yield:** 8 servings.
This unique side dish is full of old-fashioned goodness, with fresh, sweet corn and tender diced potatoes. Once you've tried this delicious pie, you'll never want to serve corn any other way!
—*Kathy Spang, Manheim, Pennsylvania*

1 cup diced peeled potatoes	1 teaspoon sugar
1/3 cup milk	1/2 teaspoon salt
2 eggs	1 package (15 ounces) refrigerated pie pastry
2 cups fresh *or* frozen corn, thawed	

1. Place potatoes in a small saucepan and cover with water. Bring to a boil. Reduce heat; cover and cook for 6-8 minutes or until tender. Drain and set aside.

2. In a blender, combine the milk, eggs, corn, sugar and salt; cover and process until blended.

3. Line a 9-in. pie plate with bottom pastry; trim pastry even with edge of plate. Spoon potatoes into crust; top with corn mixture (crust will be full). Roll out remaining pastry; make a lattice crust. Seal and flute edges.

4. Bake at 375° for 35-40 minutes or until crust is golden brown and filling is bubbly.

Nutrition Facts: 1 piece equals 310 calories, 16 g fat (7 g saturated fat), 64 mg cholesterol, 373 mg sodium, 37 g carbohydrate, 1 g fiber, 5 g protein.

LATTICE CORN PIE NOTES: _____

_____

_____

_____

_____

Veggie Corn Cakes

Prep/Total Time: 30 min. • **Yield:** 7 servings.
These golden hot cakes are chock-full of corn and
vegetables, plus a zippy hint of hot pepper sauce.
—*Cindy Neville, Edinburgh, Indiana*

1 cup all-purpose flour
1 cup cornmeal
Sugar substitute equivalent to 2 teaspoons sugar
2 teaspoons baking powder
1/2 teaspoon salt
1 egg
1-1/2 cups fat-free milk
1 cup frozen corn, thawed
1/4 cup chopped red onion
1/4 cup chopped green pepper
1/4 cup finely chopped roasted sweet red peppers
1/4 teaspoon hot pepper sauce
14 tablespoons salsa
7 tablespoons reduced-fat sour cream

1. In a large bowl, combine the first five ingredients. In
a small bowl, whisk the egg, milk, corn, onion, peppers
and hot pepper sauce; stir into dry ingredients until well
blended.

2. Heat a large nonstick griddle or skillet coated with
cooking spray; drop batter by 1/4 cupfuls onto griddle. Fry
until golden brown, about 3 minutes on each side. Serve
with salsa and sour cream.

Nutrition Facts: 2 corn cakes with 2 tablespoons salsa and 1
tablespoon sour cream equals 223 calories, 3 g fat (1 g saturated fat),
36 mg cholesterol, 498 mg sodium, 40 g carbohydrate, 4 g fiber, 8 g
protein. **Diabetic Exchanges:** 2-1/2 starch.

EDITOR'S NOTE: Recipe was tested with Splenda no-calorie sweetener.

Tarragon Corn on the Cob

Prep: 10 min. • **Grill:** 25 min. • **Yield:** 4 servings.
Nothing says summer like the fresh flavor of grilled corn, and
these seasoned ears show it off at its best.
—Brandy Jenkins, Greenwood, Mississippi

- 4 large ears sweet corn, husks removed
- 4 tarragon sprigs
- 1/3 cup butter, melted
- 4 teaspoons reduced-sodium soy sauce
- 2 teaspoons minced fresh tarragon *or* 1/2 teaspoon dried tarragon

1. Place each ear of corn with a tarragon sprig on a 14-in. x 12-in. piece of heavy-duty foil. Fold foil over corn and seal tightly. Grill corn, covered, over medium heat for 25-30 minutes or until tender, turning occasionally.

2. In a small bowl, combine the butter, soy sauce and minced tarragon. Open foil carefully to allow steam to escape; brush corn with butter mixture.

Nutrition Facts: 1 ear of corn equals 261 calories, 17 g fat (10 g saturated fat), 40 mg cholesterol, 331 mg sodium, 28 g carbohydrate, 4 g fiber, 5 g protein.

TARRAGON CORN ON THE COB NOTES: ____

Double Corn Cornbread

Prep: 15 min. • **Bake:** 40 min. + cooling • **Yield:** 1 loaf (6 slices).
Looking for a moist bread to dunk in a bowl of chowder or chili?
Try this tasty recipe. It's even safe for people who need to follow a
gluten-free diet. The bits of corn add delicious color and texture.
—Silvana Nardone, Brooklyn, New York

- 1 cup gluten-free all-purpose baking flour
- 1 cup cornmeal
- 1/4 cup sugar
- 1 tablespoon baking powder
- 1 teaspoon baking soda
- 1 teaspoon salt
- 2 eggs, lightly beaten
- 1 cup rice milk
- 1/4 cup canola oil
- 1 tablespoon cider vinegar
- 1 cup frozen corn, thawed

1. In a large bowl, combine the flour, cornmeal, sugar, baking powder, baking soda and salt. In a small bowl, whisk the eggs, rice milk, oil and vinegar. Stir into dry ingredients just until moistened; stir in corn.

2. Transfer to an 8-in x 4-in. loaf pan coated with cooking spray. Bake at 350° for 40-45 minutes or until top is lightly browned and a toothpick inserted near the center comes out clean. Cool on a wire rack.

Nutrition Facts: 1 slice equals 334 calories, 13 g fat (1 g saturated fat), 71 mg cholesterol, 842 mg sodium, 51 g carbohydrate, 4 g fiber, 7 g protein.

EDITOR'S NOTE: Read all ingredient labels for possible gluten content prior to use. Ingredient formulas can change, and production facilities vary among brands. If you're concerned that your brand may contain gluten, contact the company.

DOUBLE CORN CORNBREAD NOTES: _____

Curried Chicken Corn Chowder

Prep: 15 min. • **Cook:** 30 min.
Yield: 9 servings (2-1/4 quarts).
This recipe is close to one my mom used to make for us kids when the weather turned cold. Hers called for heavy cream, but I came up with a slimmer version that I think is pretty true to the original!
—*Kendra Doss, Kansas City, Missouri*

- 2 medium onions, chopped
- 2 celery ribs, chopped
- 1 tablespoon butter
- 3 cans (14-1/2 ounces *each*) reduced-sodium chicken broth
- 5 cups frozen corn
- 2 teaspoons curry powder
- 1/4 teaspoon salt
- 1/4 teaspoon pepper
- Dash cayenne pepper
- 1/2 cup all-purpose flour
- 1/2 cup 2% milk
- 3 cups cubed cooked chicken breast
- 1/3 cup minced fresh cilantro

1. In a Dutch oven, saute onions and celery in butter until tender. Stir in the broth, corn, curry, salt, pepper and cayenne. Bring to a boil. Reduce heat; cover and simmer for 15 minutes.

2. In a small bowl, whisk flour and milk until smooth. Whisk into the pan. Bring to a boil; cook and stir for 2 minutes or until thickened. Add chicken and cilantro; heat through.

Nutrition Facts: 1 cup equals 221 calories, 4 g fat (1 g saturated fat), 40 mg cholesterol, 517 mg sodium, 29 g carbohydrate, 3 g fiber, 20 g protein. **Diabetic Exchange:** 2 starch, 2 lean meat.

```
CURRIED CHICKEN CORN CHOWDER
NOTES:_____
_____
_____
_____
_____
_____
```

Corn Potato Pancakes

Prep/Total: 20 min. • **Yield:** about 1 dozen.
We usually prepare these tender pancakes when we have leftover mashed potatoes on hand. They are a great main or side dish.
—*Carolyn Wilson, Lyndon, Kansas*

- 2 cups mashed potatoes (with added milk and butter)
- 1/4 cup all-purpose flour
- 1/4 cup cream-style corn
- 1 egg, lightly beaten
- 3 tablespoons finely chopped onion
- 1 teaspoon minced fresh parsley
- 1/2 teaspoon salt
- 1/2 teaspoon minced garlic
- 1/8 teaspoon pepper
- 6 teaspoons canola oil, *divided*

1. In a large bowl, combine the first nine ingredients. In a large nonstick skillet, heat 2 teaspoons oil; drop four 1/4 cupfuls of batter into skillet. Cook for 1-2 minutes on each side or until golden brown. Repeat with remaining oil and pancake batter.

Nutrition Facts: 2 pancakes equals 160 calories, 8 g fat (2 g saturated fat), 43 mg cholesterol, 461 mg sodium, 18 g carbohydrate, 1 g fiber, 3 g protein. **Diabetic Exchanges:** 1-1/2 fat, 1 starch.

```
CORN POTATO PANCAKES NOTES:
_____
_____
_____
_____
_____
```

CUCUMBERS

Fresh Tomato & Cucumber Salad

Prep/Total Time: 20 min. • **Yield:** 6 servings.

This bright, fresh recipe is so easy to prepare. It helps us find a use for the many vegetables we accumulate from our garden and from friends who kindly share vegetables, too.

—*Jodie Gharbi, Shreveport, Louisiana*

- 1/4 cup lemon juice
- 1/4 cup olive oil
- 1 tablespoon minced fresh basil *or* 1 teaspoon dried basil
- 1 tablespoon white wine vinegar
- 1 garlic clove, minced
- 1 teaspoon minced fresh mint *or* 1/4 teaspoon dried mint
- 1/8 teaspoon kosher salt
- 1/8 teaspoon coarsely ground pepper
- 4 plum tomatoes, seeded and chopped
- 2 medium cucumbers, chopped
- 1/2 cup Greek olives, sliced
- 2 cups torn mixed salad greens
- 3/4 cup crumbled feta cheese
- 1/4 cup pine nuts, toasted

1. In a small bowl, whisk first eight ingredients; set aside.

2. In a large bowl, combine the tomatoes, cucumbers and olives. Drizzle with half of the dressing; toss to coat. Arrange salad greens on a large serving plate; spoon tomato mixture over top. Sprinkle with cheese and pine nuts and drizzle with remaining dressing.

Nutrition Facts: 1 cup equals 209 calories, 17 g fat (4 g saturated fat), 8 mg cholesterol, 366 mg sodium, 9 g carbohydrate, 3 g fiber, 6 g protein.

Nothing cools off a hot summer day like refreshing cucumbers. Whether pickled or tossed in a salad, cukes are definitely the darlings of summer.

SEASON: Peak midsummer.

AT THE MARKET: Select firm cucumbers with round ends. Avoid cucumbers with soft spots, bulging middles or withered ends.

STORAGE: Refrigerate unwashed for up to 1 week.

FRESH TOMATO & CUCUMBER SALAD
NOTES:_____
_____
_____
_____

Egg Salad & Cucumber Sandwiches

Prep/Total Time: 15 min. • **Yield:** 6 servings.

Cool, crisp cucumber adds a summery crunch to these tasty egg sandwiches with just a little kick. I sometimes substitute rye bread for sourdough and add celery.

—Kelly McCune, Westerville, Ohio

1/2 cup chopped red onion	1/4 teaspoon salt
1/2 cup mayonnaise	8 hard-cooked eggs, chopped
1/4 cup sour cream	1 large cucumber, sliced
2 tablespoons Dijon mustard	1 tablespoon dill weed
1/2 teaspoon pepper	12 slices sourdough bread, toasted

1. In a small bowl, combine the first six ingredients. Add eggs; stir gently to combine. In another bowl, toss cucumber and dill. Spread egg salad over six slices of toast; top with cucumbers and remaining toast.

Nutrition Facts: 1 sandwich equals 458 calories, 25 g fat (6 g saturated fat), 296 mg cholesterol, 823 mg sodium, 41 g carbohydrate, 2 g fiber, 17 g protein.

EGG SALAD & CUCUMBER SANDWICHES NOTES: _____
_____
_____
_____
_____

Cucumber Rolls

Prep/Total Time: 25 min. • **Yield:** 1 dozen.

The fresh flavors of cucumber and smoked salmon are delicious, but it's the presentation here that will stop guests in their tracks. There's no cooking with these beauties. Just assemble and watch them disappear!

—Heidi Hall, North St. Paul, Minnesota

1/2 cup cream cheese, softened	1 medium cucumber
1-1/2 teaspoons prepared horseradish	1 ounce smoked salmon *or* lox, cut into thin strips
1/4 teaspoon garlic powder	Kosher salt
1/4 teaspoon curry powder	Coarsely ground pepper
	Chives

1. In a small bowl, combine the cream cheese, horseradish, garlic powder and curry; set aside.

2. With a vegetable peeler or metal cheese slicer, cut 12 very thin slices down the length of the cucumber; pat dry. Spread about 1 teaspoon cream cheese mixture down the center of each cucumber slice. Roll up.

3. Arrange salmon on top of rolls; sprinkle lightly with salt and pepper. Garnish with chives.

Nutrition Facts: 1 appetizer (calculated without salt, pepper and chives) equals 41 calories, 3 g fat (2 g saturated fat), 11 mg cholesterol, 78 mg sodium, 1 g carbohydrate, trace fiber, 1 g protein. **Diabetic Exchange:** 1/2 fat.

CUCUMBER ROLLS NOTES: _____
_____
_____
_____
_____

Minty Watermelon Cucumber Salad

Prep/Total Time: 20 min. • **Yield:** 16 servings (3/4 cup each).
Capturing fantastic flavors of summer, this refreshing, beautiful salad will be the talk of any picnic or potluck.
—*Roblynn Hunnisett, Guelph, Ontario*

- 8 cups cubed seedless watermelon
- 2 medium English cucumbers, halved lengthwise and sliced
- 6 green onions, chopped
- 1/4 cup minced fresh mint
- 1/4 cup olive oil
- 1/4 cup balsamic vinegar
- 1/2 teaspoon salt
- 1/2 teaspoon pepper

1. In a large bowl, combine the watermelon, cucumbers, onions and mint. In a small bowl, whisk the oil, vinegar, salt and pepper. Pour over watermelon mixture; toss to coat. Serve immediately or cover and refrigerate for up to 2 hours.

Nutrition Facts: 3/4 cup equals 60 calories, 3 g fat (trace saturated fat), 0 cholesterol, 78 mg sodium, 9 g carbohydrate, 1 g fiber, 1 g protein. **Diabetic Exchanges:** 1/2 fruit, 1/2 fat.

MINTY WATERMELON CUCUMBER SALAD NOTES:_____

Chilled Salmon with Cucumber-Dill Sauce

Prep: 20 min. • **Cook:** 10 min. + chilling • **Yield:** 4 servings.
A friend from Boston shared this traditional New England dish. During the warmer months, it's a nice change of pace from the traditional, heavy cookout food.
—*Sheri Sidwell, Alton, Illinois*

- 1-1/2 cups water
- 1 cup white wine *or* chicken broth
- 4 green onions, sliced
- 10 whole peppercorns
- 4 salmon fillets (5 ounces *each*)

DILL SAUCE:
- 1/2 cup reduced-fat sour cream
- 1/4 cup chopped peeled cucumber
- 4-1/2 teaspoons snipped fresh dill *or* 1-1/2 teaspoons dill weed
- 2 teaspoons prepared horseradish
- 1-1/2 teaspoons lemon juice
- 1/8 teaspoon salt
- 1/8 teaspoon pepper

1. In a large skillet, combine the water, wine, onions and peppercorns. Bring to a boil. Reduce heat; carefully add the salmon. Cover and cook for 5-7 minutes or until fish flakes easily with a fork.

2. With a spatula, carefully remove salmon; discard cooking liquid. Cool salmon for 10 minutes; refrigerate until chilled. In a small bowl, combine the sauce ingredients. Serve with salmon.

Nutrition Facts: 1 fillet with 8 teaspoons sauce equals 316 calories, 18 g fat (5 g saturated fat), 94 mg cholesterol, 186 mg sodium, 3 g carbohydrate, trace fiber, 30 g protein.

CHILLED SALMON WITH CUCUMBER-DILL SAUCE NOTES:_____

Cucumber Couscous Salad

Prep/Total Time: 25 min. • **Yield:** 8 servings.

Chicken or grilled salmon are perfect alongside this refreshing salad. Its combination of cucumber and dill tastes great, and couscous makes it a hearty side dish.

—Evelyn Lewis, Independence, Missouri

1-1/4 cups water	1/2 cup buttermilk
1 cup uncooked couscous	1/4 cup reduced-fat plain yogurt
2 medium cucumbers, peeled, quartered lengthwise and sliced	2 tablespoons minced fresh dill
1 cup chopped sweet red pepper	2 tablespoons white vinegar
1/4 cup thinly sliced green onions	1 tablespoon olive oil
	1/2 teaspoon salt
	1/4 teaspoon pepper

1. In a small saucepan, bring water to a boil. Stir in couscous. Remove from the heat; cover and let stand for 5 minutes. Fluff with a fork. Cool to room temperature.

2. In a large bowl, combine the couscous, cucumbers, red pepper and onions. Whisk together the buttermilk, yogurt, dill, vinegar, oil, salt and pepper. Pour over couscous mixture. Cover and refrigerate for at least 1 hour.

Nutrition Facts: 2/3 cup equals 126 calories, 2 g fat (trace saturated fat), 1 mg cholesterol, 172 mg sodium, 22 g carbohydrate, 2 g fiber, 5 g protein.
Diabetic Exchanges: 1 starch, 1 vegetable, 1/2 fat.

CUCUMBER COUSCOUS SALAD TIP:
Couscous is a grain product usually made from semolina shaped into tiny beads with origins in the Middle East and North Africa. You can find it in the rice or pasta section of the grocery store. —Taste of Home

Cool as a Cucumber Soup

Prep/Total Time: 15 min. • **Yield:** 7 servings.

This chilled soup makes a wonderful appetizer or side on a hot summer day. Bright bursts of dill provide a pleasant contrast to the milder flavor of cucumber.

—Deirdre Dee Cox, Milwaukee, Wisconsin

1 pound cucumbers, peeled, seeded and sliced	1 garlic clove, minced
1/2 teaspoon salt	4-1/2 teaspoons snipped fresh dill
1-1/2 cups fat-free plain yogurt	Additional chopped green onion and snipped fresh dill
1 green onion, coarsely chopped	

1. In a colander set over a bowl, toss cucumbers with salt. Let stand for 30 minutes. Squeeze and pat dry.

2. Place the cucumbers, yogurt, onion and garlic in a food processor; cover and process until smooth. Stir in dill. Serve immediately in chilled bowls. Garnish with additional onion and dill.

Nutrition Facts: 1/2 cup equals 31 calories, trace fat (trace saturated fat), 1 mg cholesterol, 199 mg sodium, 6 g carbohydrate, 1 g fiber, 3 g protein.
Diabetic Exchanges: 1/2 fat-free milk.

COOL AS A CUCUMBER SOUP NOTES:

Cucumber Punch

Prep: 10 min. + chilling • **Yield:** 25 servings (4-3/4 quarts).
I first tasted this at an event—it was the most unusual yet
delicious beverage I'd ever tasted. I've served it numerous times
since and always get requests for the recipe.
—*Renee Olson, Kendrick, Idaho*

2	medium cucumbers	2	liters diet ginger ale, chilled
3	cups water		
1	can (12 ounces) frozen lemonade concentrate, thawed	4-1/2	cups diet grapefruit *or* citrus soda, chilled

1. With a zester or fork, score cucumbers lengthwise;
cut widthwise into thin slices. In a large pitcher, combine
water and lemonade concentrate; add cucumbers. Cover and
refrigerate overnight.

2. Just before serving, transfer cucumber mixture to a
punch bowl; stir in ginger ale and grapefruit soda.

Nutrition Facts: 3/4 cup equals 29 calories, trace fat (trace saturated
fat), 0 cholesterol, 15 mg sodium, 7 g carbohydrate, trace fiber, trace
protein. **Diabetic Exchange:** 1/2 starch.

CUCUMBER PUNCH NOTES: _____
_____
_____
_____
_____

Smoked Salmon Cucumber Canapes

Prep/Total Time: 25 min. • **Yield:** 3-1/2 dozen.
This is one appetizer I'm always asked to bring to parties.
It's make-ahead convenient but looks like I fussed.
—*Judy Grebetz, Racine, Wisconsin*

2	medium cucumbers, peeled	1	tablespoon capers, drained
4	ounces smoked salmon, flaked	1	tablespoon minced fresh parsley
2	tablespoons lemon juice	1/2	teaspoon Dijon mustard
1	tablespoon finely chopped onion	1/8	teaspoon pepper

1. Cut cucumbers in half lengthwise; remove and discard
seeds. In a small bowl, combine the remaining ingredients.
Spoon into cucumber halves.

2. Wrap in plastic wrap. Refrigerate for 3-4 hours or until
filling is firm. Cut into 1/2-in. slices.

Nutrition Facts: 1 serving equals 6 calories, trace fat (trace saturated
fat), 1 mg cholesterol, 27 mg sodium, 1 g carbohydrate, trace fiber,
1 g protein. **Diabetic Exchanges:** 1 free food.

SMOKED SALMON CUCUMBER CANAPES
NOTES:_____
_____
_____
_____

Cucumber & Spinach Tortellini Salad

Prep: 15 min. • **Cook:** 10 min. + cooling • **Yield:** 6 servings.
Pretty and packed with nutrition, this fresh-tasting salad makes
a company-special light meal or side dish! I also add diced purple
onion and red bell pepper...or substitute diced cooked chicken and
bow-tie pasta for the tortellini.
—*Emily Hanson, Logan, Utah*

CUCUMBER & SPINACH TORTELLINI
SALAD NOTES: _____
_____
_____
_____
_____
_____

1   package (9 ounces) refrigerated cheese tortellini
1/2 cup sugar
1/4 cup red wine vinegar
1/4 cup olive oil
1   tablespoon sesame seeds, toasted
1   tablespoon grated onion
1/2 teaspoon salt
1/4 teaspoon paprika
1   package (6 ounces) fresh baby spinach
2   cups sliced cucumbers
1   can (11 ounces) mandarin oranges, drained
1/4 cup honey-roasted sliced almonds
1/4 cup real bacon bits

1. Cook tortellini according to package directions.
Meanwhile, for dressing, in a small heavy saucepan, combine
the sugar, vinegar and oil. Cook and stir over low heat just
until sugar is dissolved. Remove from the heat. Stir in the
sesame seeds, onion, salt and paprika; set aside.

2. Drain tortellini and rinse with cold water. In a large
bowl, combine the tortellini, spinach, cucumbers, oranges,
almonds and bacon. Pour dressing over salad; toss to coat.
Serve immediately.

Nutrition Facts: 1-1/2 cup equals 359 calories, 17 g fat (4 g saturated
fat), 22 mg cholesterol, 591 mg sodium, 45 g carbohydrate, 3 g fiber,
10 g protein.

KOHLRABI

Don't pass by this little guy at the farmers market. Despite its odd, sputnik-like appearance, this yummy relative of the cabbage family has a pleasantly mild, sweet flavor that's a knockout when added to stir-fry or soup or sliced and enjoyed as-is.

SEASON: Peaks in June-July.

AT THE MARKET: Select small (no larger than 3 in.), firm, pale green bulbs with tender skins. Leaves should appear fresh and crisp.

Storage: Refrigerate unwashed kohlrabi in an open plastic bag for up to 5 days. Refrigerate greens separately in a sealed plastic bag for up to 3 days.

Marinated Kohlrabi and Veggies

Prep: 25 min. + marinating • **Yield:** 2 servings.
I never worry about getting enough vegetables when this crisp and colorful salad is on the menu. My mother gave me the recipe for the eye-catching medley that always disappears in a hurry.
—*Lynn Blosser, Lynnwood, Washington*

- 1/2 cup fresh broccoli florets
- 1/2 cup fresh cauliflowerets
- 1 small carrot, sliced
- 2 tablespoons chopped peeled kohlrabi
- 2 tablespoons chopped celery
- 2 tablespoons sliced ripe olives
- 1 large radish, sliced
- 1 tablespoon chopped green pepper

MARINADE:

- 1/4 cup sugar
- 4-1/2 teaspoons white vinegar
- 1/4 teaspoon salt
- 1/4 teaspoon ground mustard
- 4-1/2 teaspoons canola oil
- 1 tablespoon finely chopped onion
- 1/8 teaspoon celery seed

Dash Italian seasoning

1. In a small bowl, combine the first eight ingredients; set aside.

2. In a small saucepan, combine the sugar, vinegar, salt and mustard; cook and stir over low heat just until sugar is dissolved. Pour into a bowl; cool slightly.

3. Add the oil, onion, celery seed and Italian seasoning; whisk until well combined. Pour over vegetables and toss to coat. Cover and refrigerate for 4 hours or overnight. Serve with a slotted spoon.

Nutrition Facts: 3/4 cup equals 228 calories, 11 g fat (1 g saturated fat), 0 cholesterol, 399 mg sodium, 32 g carbohydrate, 3 g fiber, 2 g protein.

MARINATED KOHLRABI AND VEGGIES
NOTES:_____
_____
_____
_____

Creamed Kohlrabi

Prep/Total Time: 30 min. • **Yield:** 6 servings.
This might look like potato salad, but it's actually kohlrabi cubes covered in a white, velvety sauce and accented with chives.
—*Lorraine Foss, Puyallup, Washington*

4 cups cubed peeled kohlrabies (about 6 medium)	1/2 teaspoon salt
	1/4 teaspoon pepper
2 tablespoons butter	Dash paprika
2 tablespoons all-purpose flour	1 egg yolk, lightly beaten
2 cups whole milk	Minced chives and additional paprika

1. Place kohlrabies in a large saucepan; add 1 in. of water. Bring to a boil. Reduce heat; cover and simmer for 6-8 minutes or until crisp-tender.

2. Meanwhile, in a small saucepan, melt butter. Stir in flour until smooth; gradually add milk. Bring to a boil. Stir in the salt, pepper and paprika. Gradually stir a small amount of hot mixture into egg yolk; return all to the pan, stirring constantly. Bring to a gentle boil; cook and stir for 2 minutes.

3. Drain kohlrabies and place in a serving bowl; add sauce and stir to coat. Sprinkle with chives and additional paprika.

Nutrition Facts: 2/3 cup equals 125 calories, 7 g fat (4 g saturated fat), 52 mg cholesterol, 276 mg sodium, 11 g carbohydrate, 3 g fiber, 5 g protein.
Diabetic Exchanges: 1-1/2 fat, 1 vegetable, 1/2 starch.

CREAMED KOHLRABI NOTES: _____
_____
_____
_____
_____

Hot Vegetable Plate

Prep: 15 min. • **Cook:** 15 min. • **Yield:** 8 servings.
A creamy mustard sauce adds spark to an interesting lineup of vegetables in this side dish. You'll always receive compliments with this special presentation.
—*Julie Polakowski, West Allis, Wisconsin*

1 medium kohlrabi	MUSTARD SAUCE:
1 medium turnip	1/4 cup butter, cubed
1 small rutabaga	2 tablespoons all-purpose flour
4 medium carrots, halved crosswise	1/4 teaspoon salt, optional
4 medium leeks (white portion only), sliced	Pinch pepper
12 fresh cauliflowerets	1 cup milk
	1 to 2 teaspoons Dijon mustard

1. Peel kohlrabi, turnip and rutabaga; cut into 1/4-in. slices. Halve the kohlrabi and turnip slices; quarter the rutabaga slices. Place all vegetables in a large saucepan and cover with water; cook until crisp-tender.

2. Meanwhile, melt butter in a small saucepan; stir in flour. Bring to a boil; cook and stir for 2 minutes. Add salt if desired and pepper. Gradually add milk; cook and stir until mixture boils. Reduce heat; cook and stir for 1 minute or until thickened. Remove from the heat; stir in mustard.

3. Drain vegetables; serve with warm mustard sauce.

Nutrition Facts: 1 cup equals 152 calories, 6 g fat (0 saturated fat), 1 mg cholesterol, 146 mg sodium, 22 g carbohydrate, 0 fiber, 4 g protein.
Diabetic Exchanges: 1 starch, 1 vegetable, 1 fat.

HOT VEGETABLE PLATE NOTES: _____
_____
_____
_____
_____

SAY HELLO TO KOHLRABI.
Don't let its odd appearance make you shy away. Here's how to peel, cut and use this versatile veggies.

STEP ONE: Wash kohlrabi and trim greens with kitchen shears. With a paring knife, work around the bulb to remove remaining leaf pieces, woody portions and peel.

STEP TWO: Slice off one end of the bulb so that it sits flat on the cutting board. Cut as directed in the recipe.

Kohlrabi with Honey Butter

Prep/Total Time: 20 min. • **Yield:** 4 servings.

If you're not acquainted with kohlrabi, this recipe will serve as a pleasant introduction. Honey and lemon lend a sweet, citrusy taste to the turnip-like veggie. Even after several years, this versatile side dish remains one of my family's favorites.

—*Wanda Holoubek, Salina, Kansas*

- 1 pound kohlrabi (4 to 5 small), peeled and cut into 1/4-inch strips
- 1 medium carrot, cut into 1/8-inch strips
- 1 tablespoon minced chives
- 1 tablespoon lemon juice
- 1 tablespoon butter, melted
- 2 teaspoons honey
- 1/4 teaspoon grated lemon peel
- 1/8 teaspoon pepper
- 4 lemon slices

1. In a large skillet, bring 1 in. of water, kohlrabi and carrot to a boil. Reduce heat; cover and simmer for 6-10 minutes or until crisp-tender.

2. In a small bowl, combine the chives, lemon juice, butter, honey, lemon peel and pepper; mix well. Drain vegetables and transfer to a serving bowl. Add honey butter and toss to coat. Garnish with lemon slices.

Nutrition Facts: One serving (1/2 cup) equals 77 calories, 3 g fat (2 g saturated fat), 8 mg cholesterol, 62 mg sodium, 12 g carbohydrate, 5 g fiber, 2 g protein. **Diabetic Exchanges:** 2 vegetable, 1/2 fat.

KOHLRABI WITH HONEY BUTTER
NOTES:_____
_____
_____
_____

Kohlrabi & Carrot Bake

Prep: 35 min. • **Bake:** 20 min. • **Yield:** 6 servings.
We love kohlrabi from our garden, but it can be difficult to find
recipes that use the unusual veggie. Here's one that's wonderful!
—*Dianne Bettin, Truman, Minnesota*

- 3 medium kohlrabies, peeled and sliced
- 4 medium carrots, sliced
- 1/4 cup chopped onion
- 3 tablespoons butter, *divided*
- 2 tablespoons all-purpose flour
- 1/2 teaspoon salt

Dash pepper

- 1-1/2 cups 2% milk
- 1/4 cup minced fresh parsley
- 1 tablespoon lemon juice
- 3/4 cup soft bread crumbs

1. Place kohlrabies and carrots in a large saucepan and
cover with water. Bring to a boil. Reduce heat; cover and
cook for 15-20 minutes or until tender. Drain well; set aside.

2. In a large skillet, saute onion in 2 tablespoons butter
until tender. Stir in the flour, salt and pepper until blended.
Gradually whisk in milk. Bring to a boil; cook and stir for
2 minutes or until thickened.

3. Remove from the heat. Stir in the vegetable mixture,
parsley and lemon juice. Transfer to a shallow 2-qt. baking
dish coated with cooking spray.

4. In a small skillet, melt remaining butter over medium
heat. Add bread crumbs; cook and stir for 2-3 minutes or
until lightly browned. Sprinkle over vegetable mixture.

5. Bake, uncovered, at 350° for 20-25 minutes or until
heated through.

Nutrition Facts: 3/4 cup equals 141 calories, 7 g fat (4 g saturated fat),
20 mg cholesterol, 347 mg sodium, 16 g carbohydrate, 4 g fiber,
4 g protein.

PEPPERS

From sweet and versatile bells to hot and sassy jalapenos, garden-fresh peppers add color, zest and nutrition to an array of summer dishes.

SEASON: Peaks mid-summer.

AT THE MARKET: Look for peppers with firm, smooth, glossy skin. Avoid peppers that are shriveled or have soft spots.

STORAGE: Refrigerate unwashed for up to 5 days.

Roasted Red Pepper Soup

Prep: 45 min. • **Cook:** 30 min. • **Yield:** 12 servings (3 quarts).

I love oven-roasted peppers, especially when I transform them into this silky soup seasoned with garlic and thyme.
—*Kathy Rairigh, Milford, Indiana*

- 2 pounds sweet red peppers, cut into 1-inch pieces (about 6 medium)
- 1 large onion, sliced
- 2 medium carrots, sliced
- 1 jalapeno pepper, quartered and seeded
- 2 tablespoons olive oil
- 5 garlic cloves, minced
- 2 tablespoons whole fresh thyme leaves plus 1 teaspoon minced fresh thyme, *divided*
- 4 cups vegetable broth *or* water
- 4 cups chicken broth
- 2 cups cubed peeled potatoes
- 2 cups cubed peeled sweet potato
- 2 cups cubed peeled butternut squash
- 1 teaspoon salt
- 1/8 teaspoon pepper

1. Place the red peppers, onion, carrots and jalapeno in two greased 15-in. x 10-in. x 1-in. baking pans; drizzle with oil and toss to coat. Bake at 425° for 25-30 minutes or until tender, stirring occasionally. Add garlic and whole thyme leaves; bake 5 minutes longer.

2. Meanwhile, in a Dutch oven, combine vegetable broth, chicken broth, potatoes, sweet potato, squash, salt, pepper and minced thyme. Bring to a boil. Reduce heat; cover and simmer for 15 minutes or until vegetables are tender.

3. Add roasted pepper mixture; cook 5 minutes longer. Cool slightly. In a blender, process soup in batches until smooth. Return all to the pan and heat through.

Nutrition Facts: 1 cup equals 113 calories, 3 g fat (trace saturated fat), 2 mg cholesterol, 862 mg sodium, 21 g carbohydrate, 4 g fiber, 3 g protein.

EDITOR'S NOTE: We recommend wearing disposable gloves when cutting hot peppers. Avoid touching your face.

ROASTED RED PEPPER SOUP NOTES:

Roasted Potatoes and Peppers

Prep: 10 min. • **Bake:** 40 min. • **Yield:** 8 servings.
Creamy garlic salad dressing really perks up the flavor in this simple, roasted side dish. It's a family favorite but also a hit with guests.
—*Joan Hallford, North Richland Hills, Texas*

2 pounds small red potatoes, quartered	1 medium red onion, coarsely chopped
1 medium green pepper, coarsely chopped	1/2 cup creamy garlic salad dressing
1 medium sweet red pepper, coarsely chopped	

1. In a 15-in. x 10-in. x 1-in. baking pan coated with cooking spray, combine the potatoes, peppers and onion. Drizzle with dressing and toss to coat.

2. Bake at 400° for 40-45 minutes or until potatoes are tender, stirring occasionally.

Nutrition Facts: 3/4 cup equals 149 calories, 6 g fat (1 g saturated fat), 0 cholesterol, 188 mg sodium, 22 g carbohydrate, 3 g fiber, 3 g protein.
Diabetic Exchange: 1-1/2 starch, 1 fat.

ROASTED POTATOES AND PEPPERS

NOTES:_____

_____

_____

_____

Grilled Stuffed Jalapenos

Prep/Total Time: 30 min. • **Yield:** 10 appetizers.
These cheese-stuffed jalapenos are always popular when my husband and I host a tapas (appetizers) party. The fresh and spicy bites are a welcomed alternative to the usual deep-fried version.
—*Mary Potter, Sterling Heights, Michigan*

4 ounces cream cheese, softened	1/2 teaspoon chili powder
1/2 cup shredded Monterey Jack cheese	1/4 teaspoon salt
1/2 teaspoon garlic powder	1/4 teaspoon smoked paprika *or* paprika
1/2 teaspoon ground cumin	10 jalapeno peppers

1. In a small bowl, combine the first seven ingredients. Cut a lengthwise slit down each pepper, leaving the stem intact; remove membranes and seeds. Fill each pepper with 1 tablespoon cheese mixture.

2. Prepare the grill for indirect heat. Place the peppers in a disposable foil pan. Grill, covered, over indirect medium heat for 8-10 minutes or until peppers are tender and cheese is melted. Serve warm.

Nutrition Facts: 1 stuffed pepper equals 66 calories, 6 g fat (4 g saturated fat), 18 mg cholesterol, 125 mg sodium, 1 g carbohydrate, trace fiber, 2 g protein.

EDITOR'S NOTE: We recommend wearing disposable gloves when cutting hot peppers. Avoid touching your face.

GRILLED STUFFED JALAPENOS NOTES:

_____

_____

_____

_____

Quinoa-Stuffed Peppers

Prep: 35 min. • **Bake:** 35 min. • **Yield:** 4 servings.
Quinoa adds yummy texture, corn lends sweetness and color, and red pepper flakes ratchet up the heat in these tender stuffed peppers. Whole wheat rolls or breadsticks and a pitcher of iced tea make for a standout supper.
—*Joyce Moynihan, Lakeville, Minnesota*

- 1 can (14-1/2 ounces) diced tomatoes, undrained
- 1 cup water
- 1/2 cup quinoa, rinsed
- 4 large green peppers
- 3/4 pound lean ground beef (90% lean)
- 1 large onion, finely chopped
- 3 teaspoons dried parsley flakes
- 2 teaspoons paprika
- 1/2 teaspoon salt
- 1/4 to 1/2 teaspoon crushed red pepper flakes
- 1/4 teaspoon pepper
- 3 garlic cloves, minced
- 2 cans (8 ounces *each*) no-salt-added tomato sauce, *divided*
- 3/4 cup frozen corn, thawed
- 1/2 cup shredded reduced-fat cheddar cheese

1. Drain diced tomatoes reserving juice; set aside. In a small saucepan, bring water to a boil. Add the quinoa. Reduce heat; cover and simmer for 12-15 minutes or until liquid is absorbed.

2. Meanwhile, cut peppers in half lengthwise and remove seeds. In a Dutch oven, cook peppers in boiling water for 3-5 minutes. Drain and rinse in cold water; invert onto paper towels.

3. In a large skillet, cook beef, onion, parsley, paprika, salt, red pepper flakes and pepper over medium heat until meat is no longer pink. Add garlic; cook 1 minute longer. Stir in one can tomato sauce, corn, quinoa and tomatoes; heat through.

4. Spoon into pepper halves. Place in a 13-in. x 9-in. baking dish coated with cooking spray. Combine the reserved tomato juice and remaining tomato sauce; pour over peppers.

5. Cover and bake at 350° for 30-35 minutes or until peppers are tender. Sprinkle with cheese; bake 5 minutes longer or until cheese is melted.

Nutrition Facts: 2 stuffed pepper halves equals 386 calories, 11 g fat (5 g saturated fat), 52 mg cholesterol, 622 mg sodium, 47 g carbohydrate, 9 g fiber, 26 g protein.

EDITOR'S NOTE: Find quinoa in the cereal, rice or organic food aisle.

Peasant Peppers

Prep: 15 min. • **Bake:** 45 min. • **Yield:** 5 servings.
My mother-in-law, who lives in Italy, taught me to make this
simple casserole. It's considered wholesome peasant fare, but
I've never tasted peppers as delicious!
—*Robyn Scollo, Fairport, New York*

3 large green peppers, thinly sliced	1-1/2 teaspoons salt
3 large sweet red peppers, thinly sliced	1 teaspoon pepper
2 tablespoons olive oil	1/2 cup soft bread crumbs

1. Place peppers in two 15-in. x 10-in. x 1-in. baking pans. Drizzle with oil and sprinkle with salt and pepper; toss to coat.

2. Bake at 400° for 30-35 minutes until tender and skins are slightly blackened. Sprinkle with bread crumbs. Bake 15-20 minutes longer or until lightly browned.

Nutrition Facts: 3/4 cup equals 106 calories, 6 g fat (1 g saturated fat), 0 cholesterol, 746 mg sodium, 13 g carbohydrate, 4 g fiber, 2 g protein.

PEASANT PEPPERS NOTES: _____
_____
_____
_____
_____
_____

Three-Pepper Coleslaw

Prep: 20 min. + chilling • **Yield:** 8 servings.
There are never any leftovers when I make this dish for a picnic,
barbecue or any other social gathering.
—*Priscilla Gilbert, Indian Harbour Beach, Florida*

1 package (10 ounces) angel hair coleslaw mix	3 green onions, chopped
1 medium sweet red pepper, finely chopped	1/4 cup white wine vinegar
1 medium green pepper, finely chopped	2 tablespoons lime juice
1 to 2 jalapeno peppers, seeded and finely chopped	2 teaspoons canola oil
	1 teaspoon sugar
	1/2 teaspoon salt
	1/4 teaspoon pepper

1. Place the first five ingredients in a large serving bowl. In a small bowl, whisk the remaining ingredients. Pour over coleslaw mixture; toss to coat. Cover and refrigerate for at least 30 minutes before serving.

Nutrition Facts: 3/4 cup equals 36 calories, 1 g fat (trace saturated fat), 0 cholesterol, 158 mg sodium, 6 g carbohydrate, 2 g fiber, 1 g protein. **Diabetic Exchange:** 1 vegetable.

EDITOR'S NOTE: We recommend wearing disposable gloves when cutting hot peppers. Avoid touching your face.

THREE-PEPPER COLESLAW NOTES: _____
_____
_____
_____
_____

Roasted Pepper Tart

Prep: 20 min. + chilling • **Bake:** 40 min. + cooling
Yield: 12 servings.
For a summer picnic, I whisked this tart out of the oven, wrapped it in foil and headed out the door. My friends were delighted at its pretty appearance and fresh taste.
—*Marian Platt, Sequim, Washington*

1-1/2 cups all-purpose flour
1/8 teaspoon salt
1/2 cup cold butter, cubed
3 to 4 tablespoons water
3 medium sweet red peppers, halved and seeded
2 medium green bell peppers, halved and seeded
1/3 cup olive oil
2 garlic cloves, minced
4-1/2 teaspoons minced fresh oregano
2 cups (8 ounces) shredded Monterey Jack cheese, *divided*
1 can (2-1/4 ounces) sliced ripe olives, drained

1. In a large bowl, combine flour and salt; cut in butter until crumbly. Gradually add water, tossing with a fork until dough forms a ball. Cover and refrigerate for 1 hour.

2. Broil peppers 4 in. from the heat until skins are blistered and blackened, about 10 minutes. Immediately place peppers in a bowl; cover and let stand for 15-20 minutes. Peel off and discard charred skin. Coarsely chop peppers; place in a bowl. Add oil, garlic and oregano; toss to coat. Set aside.

3. Roll out dough to fit a 12-in. pizza pan. Transfer to pan. Prick dough thoroughly with a fork. Bake at 350° for 30-35 minutes or until lightly browned and crust begins pulling away from edges of pan. Cool completely.

4. Sprinkle 1 cup cheese over crust. Sprinkle with pepper mixture and remaining cheese. Arrange olives around edge. Bake at 350° for 10-15 minutes or until cheese is melted. Serve immediately.

Nutrition Facts: 1 serving (1 slice) equals 268 calories, 20 g fat (9 g saturated fat), 37 mg cholesterol, 251 mg sodium, 16 g carbohydrate, 2 g fiber, 7 g protein.

ROASTED PEPPER TART NOTES: _____

Grilled Stuffed Peppers

Prep: 30 min. **Grill:** 30 min. • **Yield:** 6 servings.
After hearing the recipe described at a local Italian restaurant, I decided to try to make these peppers at home. Everyone enjoyed the pretty green "shells" brimming with a hearty filling.
—*Carol Gaus, Elk Grove Village, Illinois*

3 large green peppers
1 large tomato, peeled, seeded and chopped
1 cup (4 ounces) shredded part-skim mozzarella cheese
1/4 cup grated Parmesan cheese
2 tablespoons minced fresh basil
2 teaspoons dried oregano
1-1/2 pounds bulk Italian sausage
Additional shredded part-skim mozzarella cheese

1. Cut peppers in half lengthwise; remove stems and seeds. Set aside. In a large bowl, combine the tomato, cheeses, basil and oregano. Crumble sausage over mixture and mix well. Spoon into pepper halves.

2. Prepare grill for indirect heat, using a drip pan. Place peppers over drip pan. Grill, covered, over indirect medium heat for 30-35 minutes or until sausage is no longer pink and peppers are tender. Sprinkle with additional cheese.

Nutrition Facts: 1 stuffed pepper half equals 479 calories, 40 g fat (15 g saturated fat), 100 mg cholesterol, 972 mg sodium, 7 g carbohydrate, 2 g fiber, 23 g protein.

GRILLED STUFFED PEPPERS NOTES:

COLOR ME DELICIOUS.
Did you know that all peppers start out green and only change color as they mature? You can eat peppers at whatever stage you prefer, but you'll reap better taste and more nutrition if you wait for them to fully ripen.

late summer
to FALL

CANNING AND
PRESERVING YOUR HARVEST

The assortment of late summer and fall produce is as varied as the splashes of colors now visible in the ever-changing landscape. Bright blue skies, a break from the humidity and a bounty of ripe-for-the-picking veggies and fruits make this season something to savor.

apples & PEARS

Johnny Appleseed was on to something when he planted apple orchards across the countryside—people eat nearly 20 pounds of apples each year! Like apples, pears are highly versatile, appearing in pies, chutneys, sauces and salads. Get inspired to enjoy these juicy beauties.

SEASON: Apples peak August-October; Pears peaks July-September.

AT THE MARKET: Select apples that are firm and have a smooth, unblemished skin. Select plump pears. In some varieties, the skin color will change as the pear ripens. Select firm pears for baking. For eating, select pears that give slightly when gently pressed.

STORAGE: Apples, refrigerate unwashed for up to 6 weeks; Pears, refrigerate unwashed ripe pears for 3-5 days.

High-Rise Apple Pancake

Prep: 15 min. • **Bake:** 20 min. • **Yield:** 2 servings.
If you want to fix something special for a weekend breakfast or Sunday brunch, whip up this delicious pancake filled with warm cinnamon-sugar apple slices.
—*Wanda J. Nelson, Woodruff, Wisconsin*

- 1/4 cup all-purpose flour
- 1/4 cup 2% milk
- 1 egg, lightly beaten
- 1-1/2 teaspoons plus 2 tablespoons sugar, *divided*
- 1/8 teaspoon salt
- 1-1/2 teaspoons plus 2 tablespoons butter, *divided*
- 3 cups chopped peeled apples
- 1/8 teaspoon ground cinnamon

1. In a small bowl, whisk the flour, milk, egg, 1 -1/2 teaspoons sugar and salt until smooth. Place 1-1/2 teaspoons butter in a 7-in. pie plate; place in a 400° oven for 2-3 minutes or until melted. Pour batter into pan. Bake for 18-20 minutes or until the edges are lightly browned.

2. Meanwhile, in a saucepan, melt the remaining butter over medium heat. Saute the apples, cinnamon and remaining sugar until apples are tender. Spoon into pancake. Serve immediately.

Nutrition Facts: 1/2 each equals 390 calories, 18 g fat, (10 g saturated fat), 147 mg cholesterol, 339 mg sodium, 54 g carbohydrate, 4 g fiber, 6 g protein.

HIGH-RISE APPLE PANCAKE NOTES:

Berry Apple Pie

Prep: 30 min. • **Bake:** 45 min. + cooling • **Yield:** 8 servings.
Our active family is full of big eaters, so I'm thankful for our raspberry patch, our apple orchard and pie recipes like this one. You can substitute frozen berries for fresh.
—*Heidi Jo Keranen, Bruno, Minnesota*

- 1 cup sugar
- 3 tablespoons quick-cooking tapioca
- 3 cups coarsely chopped peeled tart apples
- 3 cups fresh *or* frozen raspberries
- Pastry for double-crust pie (9 inches)
- 2 tablespoons butter

1. In a large bowl, combine the sugar and tapioca. Add the apples and raspberries; toss to coat. Let stand for 15 minutes. Meanwhile, line a 9-in. pie plate with bottom crust; trim pastry even with edge.

2. Spoon filling into crust; dot with butter. Roll out remaining pastry to fit top of pie; place over filling. Trim, seal and flute edges. Cut slits in pastry.

3. Bake at 375° for 45-55 minutes or until crust is golden brown and apples are tender. Cool on a wire rack.

Nutrition Facts: 1 piece equals 419 calories, 17 g fat (8 g saturated fat), 18 mg cholesterol, 220 mg sodium, 65 g carbohydrate, 4 g fiber, 3 g protein.

BERRY APPLE PIE NOTES:
_____
_____
_____
_____

Gorgonzola Pear Salad

Prep: 15 min. • **Bake:** 25 min. • **Yield:** 12 servings.
Tired of tossed salads? Here's an irresistible variation featuring pears that makes an attractive and tasty first course. The cheese and pecans are nice additions. You'll appreciate how easy it is.
—*Melinda Singer, Tarzana, California*

- 6 medium pears, quartered and cored
- 1/3 cup olive oil
- 1 teaspoon salt
- 12 cups spring mix salad greens
- 4 plum tomatoes, seeded and chopped
- 2 cups crumbled Gorgonzola cheese
- 1 cup pecan halves, toasted
- 1-1/2 cups balsamic vinaigrette

1. Place pears in an ungreased 13-in. x 9-in. baking dish. Drizzle with oil and sprinkle with salt. Bake, uncovered, at 400° for 25-30 minutes, basting occasionally with cooking juices.

2. In a large salad bowl, combine the greens, tomatoes, cheese and pecans. Drizzle with dressing and toss to coat. Divide among 12 serving plates; top each with two pear pieces.

Nutrition Facts: 1 cup equals 303 calories, 23 g fat (6 g saturated fat), 17 mg cholesterol, 716 mg sodium, 21 g carbohydrate, 6 g fiber, 6 g protein.

GORGONZOLA PEAR SALAD NOTES:
_____
_____
_____
_____

SQUASH-APPLE BAKE NOTES: _____
_____
_____
_____

Squash-Apple Bake

Prep: 15 min. • **Bake:** 50 min. • **Yield:** 4-6 servings.
This is my mother-in-law's recipe, but I've made it so often I feel as though it's my own! Squash and apples are representative of New England in the fall and taste even better when baked together.
—*Judith Hawes, Chelmsford, Massachusetts*

1 medium buttercup *or* butternut squash (about 1-1/4 pounds), peeled and cut into 3/4-inch slices	1/2 cup packed brown sugar
	1 tablespoon all-purpose flour
	1/4 cup butter, melted
2 medium apples, peeled and cut into wedges	1/2 teaspoon salt
	1/2 teaspoon ground mace

1. Arrange squash in a 2-qt. baking dish. Top with apple wedges. Combine the remaining ingredients; spoon the mixture over apples.

2. Bake, uncovered, at 350° for 50-60 minutes or until apples and squash are tender.

Nutrition Facts: 1 serving (3/4 cup) equals 198 calories, 8 g fat (5 g saturated fat), 20 mg cholesterol, 284 mg sodium, 34 g carbohydrate, 3 g fiber, 1 g protein.

Almond Pear Chutney

Prep: 15 min. • **Cook:** 30 min. • **Yield:** 3 cups.
My sweet, chunky chutney—flavored with orange, almond and ginger—is great with chicken, turkey or pork. You can prepare it a couple of days in advance and use it to dress up any plain weekday supper.
—*Michaela Rosenthal, Woodland Hills, California*

4 cups chopped peeled ripe pears	1/4 teaspoon ground cinnamon
1 small unpeeled navel orange, halved and thinly sliced	1/3 cup coarsely chopped unblanched almonds, toasted
1/2 cup water	2 tablespoons chopped crystallized ginger
2 teaspoons lemon juice	
1-1/2 cups sugar	

1. In a large saucepan, combine the pears, orange, water and lemon juice. Bring to a boil, stirring constantly. Reduce heat; simmer, uncovered, for 10 minutes. Stir in the sugar and cinnamon. Bring to a boil. Reduce heat; simmer, uncovered, for 15-20 minutes or until thickened, stirring occasionally.

2. Remove from the heat; stir in almonds and ginger. Serve warm or cold. May be refrigerated for up to 1 week.

Nutrition Facts: 1/4 cup equals 165 calories, 2 g fat (trace saturated fat), 0 cholesterol, 3 mg sodium, 37 g carbohydrate, 2 g fiber, 1 g protein.

ALMOND PEAR CHUTNEY NOTES: _____
_____
_____
_____
_____

Apple Dumplings with Caramel Sauce

Prep: 30 min. + chilling • **Bake:** 50 min. • **Yield:** 2 servings.
Of all my autumn recipes, apple dumplings are a hands-down favorite. A rich, homemade caramel sauce tops them off.
—*Lois Stache, Brillion, Wisconsin*

2/3 cup all-purpose flour
2 teaspoons sugar
1/2 teaspoon baking powder
1/8 teaspoon salt
1/4 cup cold butter, cubed
1/4 cup milk
2 medium apples, peeled and cored
4 teaspoons brown sugar
1/4 teaspoon ground cinnamon
4 teaspoons butter

SAUCE:
2 teaspoons all-purpose flour
1/2 cup water
1/3 cup sugar
1/3 cup packed brown sugar
3 tablespoons butter
Dash salt

1. In a small bowl, combine the flour, sugar, baking powder and salt; cut in cold butter until crumbly. Gradually add milk, tossing with a fork until dough forms a ball; divide dough in half. Cover and refrigerate for 1 hour or until easy to handle.

2. On a well-floured surface, roll each portion of dough into an 8-in. square. Cut apples in half horizontally; place an apple bottom on each square. Place brown sugar and cinnamon in the core of each bottom; dot each with 2 teaspoons butter. Replace apple tops.

3. Gently bring up corners of pastry to center, pinch edges to seal. Place in a greased 8-in. baking dish. Bake, uncovered, at 350° for 15 minutes.

4. Meanwhile, in a small saucepan, combine flour and water until smooth. Add sugars, butter and salt. Bring to a boil; cook and stir until smooth and blended. Pour over dumplings.

5. Bake 35-40 minutes longer or until apples are tender and pastry is golden brown. Serve warm.

Nutrition Facts: 1 dumpling equals 979 calories, 49 g fat, (31 g saturated fat), 128 mg cholesterol, 688 mg sodium, 134 g carbohydrate, 3 g fiber, 6 g protein.

All-Day Apple Butter

Prep: 20 min. **Cook:** 11 hours • **Yield:** 4 pints.
I make several batches of this simple and delicious apple butter to freeze in jars. Depending on the sweetness of the apples used, you can adjust the sugar to taste.
—*Betty Ruenholl, Syracuse, Nebraska*

5-1/2	pounds apples, peeled and finely chopped	2	to 3 teaspoons ground cinnamon
4	cups sugar	1/4	teaspoon ground cloves
		1/4	teaspoon salt

1. Place apples in a 3-qt. slow cooker. Combine sugar, cinnamon, cloves and salt; pour over apples and mix well. Cover and cook on high for 1 hour. Reduce heat to low; cover and cook for 9-11 hours or until thickened and dark brown, stirring occasionally (stir more frequently as it thickens to prevent sticking).

2. Uncover and cook on low 1 hour longer. If desired, stir with a wire whisk until smooth. Spoon into freezer containers, leaving 1/2-in. headspace. Cover and refrigerate or freeze.

Nutrition Facts: 1 serving (2 tablespoons) equals 68 calories, trace fat (trace saturated fat), 0 cholesterol, 9 mg sodium, 17 g carbohydrate, 1 g fiber, trace protein.

ALL-DAY APPLE BUTTER NOTES:

_____
_____
_____
_____

BUMBLEBERRY PIE NOTES:

_____
_____
_____
_____
_____

Bumbleberry Pie

Prep: 20 min. • **Bake:** 55 min. + cooling • **Yield:** 8 servings.
What a delightful ending to any meal! Apple, raspberries and rhubarb work in unison to create this fresh-flavored pie.
—*Judy Parker, Albuquerque, New Mexico*

1-3/4	cups sugar	1	medium tart apple, peeled and chopped
5	tablespoons quick-cooking tapioca	1	cup fresh *or* frozen raspberries
3	cups chopped fresh *or* frozen rhubarb, thawed		Pastry for double-crust pie (9 inches)

1. In a large bowl, combine sugar and tapioca. Stir in the rhubarb, apple and raspberries; toss gently to coat. Let stand for 15 minutes.

2. Line a 9-in. pie plate with the bottom pastry; trim to 1 in. beyond edge of plate. Spoon filling into crust. Roll out remaining pastry to fit top of pie. Cut slits in pastry. Place pastry over filling; trim, seal and flute edges. Cover edges loosely with foil.

3. Bake at 375° for 25 minutes. Remove foil and bake 30-35 minutes longer or until crust is golden brown and filling is bubbly. Cool on a wire rack.

Nutrition Facts: 1 piece equals 459 calories, 14 g fat (6 g saturated fat), 10 mg cholesterol, 202 mg sodium, 82 g carbohydrate, 2 g fiber, 3 g protein.

EDITOR'S NOTE: If using frozen rhubarb, measure rhubarb while still frozen, then thaw completely. Drain in a colander, but do not press liquid out.

Pear Custard Pie

Prep: 10 min. • **Bake:** 45 min. + chilling • **Yield:** 6 servings.
My daughter CJ baked a pear pie for us once, and I've made it several times since then. We like it so much that I contribute it to bake sales!
—*Barbara Rea, Glenshaw, Pennsylvania*

1 sheet refrigerated pie pastry	1/4 cup all-purpose flour
3 medium ripe pears, peeled and thinly sliced	2 eggs, lightly beaten
	1 cup heavy whipping cream
1 cup sugar	1 teaspoon vanilla extract

1. Unroll pastry into a 9-in. pie plate; flute edges. Place the pears in pastry. In a small bowl, combine sugar and flour. Stir in the eggs, cream and vanilla. Pour over pears. Bake at 375° for 45-50 minutes or until a knife inserted near the center comes out clean.

2. Cool on a wire rack. Cover; refrigerate for at least 2 hours.

Nutrition Facts: 1 piece equals 518 calories, 26 g fat (14 g saturated fat), 132 mg cholesterol, 173 mg sodium, 69 g carbohydrate, 3 g fiber, 5 g protein.

PEAR CUSTARD PIE NOTES: _____
_____
_____
_____
_____

Cinnamon-Apple Pork Chops

Prep/Total Time: 25 min. • **Yield:** 4 servings.
I found this autumn favorite online years ago. It took just one bite to make it a dinnertime staple. The ingredients are easy to keep on hand and one-pan cleanup is a bonus.
—*Christina Price, Wheeling, West Virginia*

4 boneless pork loin chops (4 ounces *each*)	1/2 teaspoon ground nutmeg
2 tablespoons reduced-fat butter, *divided*	1/4 teaspoon salt
3 tablespoons brown sugar	4 medium tart apples, thinly sliced
1 teaspoon ground cinnamon	2 tablespoons chopped pecans

1. In a large skillet over medium heat, cook the pork chops in 1 tablespoon butter for 4-5 minutes on each side or until a thermometer reads 160°. Meanwhile, in a small bowl, combine the brown sugar, cinnamon, nutmeg and salt.

2. Remove chops and keep warm. Add the apples, pecans, brown sugar mixture and remaining butter to the pan; cook and stir until apples are tender. Serve with chops.

Nutrition Facts: 1 each equals 316 calories, 12 g fat (4 g saturated fat), 62 mg cholesterol, 232 mg sodium, 31 g carbohydrate, 4 g fiber, 22 g protein. **Diabetic Exchanges:** 3 lean meat, 1 starch, 1 fruit, 1 fat.

EDITOR'S NOTE: This recipe was tested with Land O'Lakes light stick butter.

CINNAMON-APPLE PORK CHOPS NOTES:
_____
_____
_____
_____

Almond Butter-Stuffed Pears

Prep: 1 hour • **Bake:** 30 min. • **Yield:** 12 servings.
A formal dinner calls for an elegant dessert like these stuffed pears. A mild nutty filling pairs well with the tender, sweet fruit.
—*Taste of Home Test Kitchen*

- 2 cups unblanched whole almonds, toasted
- 1/4 teaspoon salt
- 2 tablespoons canola oil
- 2 cups pear juice
- 3 cups sweet white wine, *divided*
- 1/4 cup packed brown sugar
- 1 vanilla bean, split
- 12 medium pears

1. Combine almonds and salt in a food processor. Cover and process until almonds are finely chopped. Add oil; cover and process until blended. Set aside.

2. In a large saucepan, combine the pear juice, 1 cup wine, brown sugar and vanilla bean. Bring to a boil. Remove from the heat; remove vanilla bean. With a sharp knife, scrape the bean to remove the seeds; stir into sauce. Discard vanilla bean. Return to a boil; cook, uncovered, over medium heat for 50-55 minutes or until the mixture coats the back of a metal spoon.

3. Meanwhile, slice 1 in. off the top of each pear and set aside. Core pears, leaving bottoms intact. Fill with reserved almond mixture. Place pears in a shallow roasting pan; replace tops. Add remaining wine. Bake, uncovered, at 400° for 30-35 minutes or until pears are tender, basting occasionally. Serve with sauce.

Nutrition Facts: 1 each equals 309 calories, 15 g fat (1 g saturated fat), 0 cholesterol, 62 mg sodium, 42 g carbohydrate, 8 g fiber, 6 g protein.

```
ALMOND BUTTER-STUFFED PEARS
NOTES:_____
    _____
    _____
    _____
```

Ham with Apple Raisin Sauce

Prep: 10 min. • **Bake:** 1-3/4 hours + standing • **Yield:** 16 servings.
Since I ran across this recipe several years ago, I've used it often for special dinners. What I really like is the ease of preparation. You don't have a lot of cleanup because everything is done right there in the bag.
—*Sandy Olberding, Spencer, Iowa*

- 1 tablespoon all-purpose flour
- 1 large oven roasting bag
- 4 medium tart apples, peeled and chopped
- 2 cups apple juice
- 1 cup raisins
- 1/2 cup packed brown sugar
- 1 teaspoon ground cinnamon
- 1 boneless fully cooked ham (about 6 pounds)

1. Shake flour in the oven roasting bag. Place in an ungreased 13-in. x 9-in. baking pan. Place the apples, apple juice, raisins, brown sugar and cinnamon in the bag; mix well. Place ham in bag. Close bag. Cut six 1/2-in. slits in top of bag.

2. Bake ham at 325° for 1-3/4 to 2 hours or until a thermometer reads 140°. Let ham stand for 10 minutes before slicing. Serve with sauce.

Nutrition Facts: 6 ounce weight equals 266 calories, 6 g fat (2 g saturated fat), 86 mg cholesterol, 1,769 mg sodium, 22 g carbohydrate, 1 g fiber, 32 g protein.

```
HAM WITH APPLE RAISIN SAUCE
NOTES:_____
    _____
    _____
    _____
```

DOWN TO THE CORE.
To core a pear, slice off the top, as indicated in the recipe, and insert an apple corer to within 1 in. of the pear's bottom. Twist the corer to cut around the core, then slowly pull it out of the pear. Don't have an apple corer? A melon baller will do the trick.

BEETS

No matter how you serve these sweet beauties—boiled, roasted, baked or pickled—you can't beat beets for flavor, nutrition and that gorgeous scarlet color. Don't waste the greens! Steam 'em, then toss them with a little lemon and butter.

SEASON: June through October; peaks June-August.

AT THE MARKET: Select firm, deep red beets that have unwilted green tips and smooth, unblemished and unbroken skin. Small and medium-sized beets are the most tender.

STORAGE: Remove greens 2 inches from beets. Refrigerate greens separately in a sealed plastic bag for up to 3 days. Refrigerate uncooked beets in an open plastic bag for about 2 weeks.

Beet Salad with Orange-Walnut Dressing

Prep: 20 min. • **Bake:** 40 min. + cooling • **Yield:** 12 servings.
Light and refreshing, this salad goes nicely with the heavier dishes we tend to enjoy during the cooler months.
—*Marian Platt, Sequim, Washington*

- 1 pound fresh beets
- 6 cups torn Bibb *or* Boston lettuce
- 3 medium navel oranges, peeled and sectioned
- 2 cups torn curly endive
- 2 cups watercress
- 2/3 cup chopped walnuts, toasted

DRESSING:
- 1/2 cup canola oil
- 1/3 cup orange juice
- 3 tablespoons white wine vinegar
- 1 green onion, finely chopped
- 1 tablespoon lemon juice
- 1 tablespoon Dijon mustard
- 1/2 teaspoon salt
- 1/8 teaspoon white pepper

1. Place beets in a 13-in. x 9-in. baking dish; add 1 in. of water. Cover and bake at 400° for 40-45 minutes or until tender. Cool; peel and julienne.

2. In a serving bowl, combine the lettuce, oranges, endive and watercress. Add beets and walnuts.

3. In a small bowl, whisk the oil, orange juice, vinegar, onion, lemon juice, mustard, salt and pepper. Drizzle over salad; toss gently to coat.

Nutrition Facts: 1-1/2 cups equals 255 calories, 14 g fat (1 g saturated fat), 0 cholesterol, 274 mg sodium, 28 g carbohydrate, 18 g fiber, 9 g protein.

```
BEET SALAD WITH ORANGE-WALNUT
DRESSING NOTES:
_____
_____
_____
```

Maple Horseradish Beets

Prep: 50 min. • **Cook:** 10 min. • **Yield:** 6 servings.
Even people who say they don't like beets will think this simple treatment is a winner. An easy glaze gives them great taste...and a little zip.
—*Leslie Palmer, Swampscott, Massachusetts*

1-3/4	pounds fresh beets	2	tablespoons cider vinegar
1	tablespoon canola oil		
2	tablespoons butter	1/4	teaspoon salt
1/4	cup maple syrup	1/4	teaspoon pepper
3	tablespoons prepared horseradish		

1. Peel beets and cut into wedges. Place in a 15-in. x 10-in. x 1-in. baking pan; drizzle with oil and toss to coat. Bake at 400° for 40-50 minutes or until tender.

2. In a small saucepan, melt butter. Stir in the maple syrup, horseradish, vinegar, salt and pepper. Bring to a boil. Carefully stir in beets; cook for 5-6 minutes or until liquid is slightly thickened, gently stirring occasionally.

Nutrition Facts: 3/4 cup equals 152 calories, 6 g fat (3 g saturated fat), 10 mg cholesterol, 252 mg sodium, 23 g carbohydrate, 3 g fiber, 2 g protein.
Diabetic Exchanges: 2 vegetable, 1 fat, 1/2 starch.

MAPLE HORSERADISH BEETS NOTES:
_____
_____
_____
_____

Gingered Orange Beets

Prep: 10 min. • **Bake:** 70 min. • **Yield:** 4 servings.
My husband was pleasantly surprised when he tried my new twist on beets. The orange and ginger are a surprising complement, making this particular vegetable a wonderful addition to any menu.
—*Marion Tipton, Phoenix, Arizona*

1-1/2	pounds whole fresh beets (about 4 medium), trimmed and cleaned	1	tablespoon thawed orange juice concentrate
6	tablespoons olive oil, *divided*	1-1/2	teaspoons grated orange peel, *divided*
1/4	teaspoon salt	1/2	teaspoon minced fresh gingerroot
1/4	teaspoon white pepper	1	medium navel orange, peeled, sectioned and chopped
1	tablespoon rice vinegar	1/3	cup pecan halves, toasted

1. Brush beets with 4 tablespoons oil; sprinkle with salt and pepper. Wrap loosely in foil; place on a baking sheet. Bake at 425° for 70-75 minutes or until fork-tender. Cool slightly.

2. In a small bowl, whisk vinegar, orange juice concentrate, 1 teaspoon orange peel, ginger and remaining oil; set the bowl aside.

3. Peel beets and cut into wedges; place in a serving bowl. Add the orange sections and pecans. Drizzle with orange sauce and toss to coat. Sprinkle with remaining orange peel.

Nutrition Facts: 1 cup equals 342 calories, 27 g fat (3 g saturated fat), 0 cholesterol, 279 mg sodium, 25 g carbohydrate, 5 g fiber, 4 g protein.

GINGERED ORANGE BEETS NOTES:
_____
_____
_____
_____

Beets in Orange Sauce

Prep: 15 min. • **Cook:** 35 min. • **Yield:** 8 servings.
To ensure your family eats their veggies, we suggest you top beets
with an irresistible orange glaze.
—*Taste of Home Test Kitchen*

8	whole fresh beets	1	cup orange juice
1/4	cup sugar	1	medium navel orange, halved and sliced, optional
2	teaspoons cornstarch		
Dash pepper		1/2	teaspoon grated orange peel

1. Place beets in a large saucepan; cover with water.
Bring to a boil. Reduce heat; cover and cook for 25-30
minutes or until tender. Drain and cool slightly. Peel and
slice; place in a serving bowl and keep warm.

2. In a small saucepan, combine the sugar, cornstarch and
pepper; stir in orange juice until smooth. Bring to a boil;
cook and stir for 2 minutes or until thickened. Remove
from the heat; stir in orange slices if desired and peel.
Pour over beets.

Nutrition Facts: 1 cup equals 63 calories, trace fat (trace saturated fat),
0 cholesterol, 39 mg sodium, 15 g carbohydrate, 1 g fiber, 1 g protein.

EDITOR'S NOTE: A 15-ounce can of sliced beets may be substituted
for the fresh beets. Drain canned beets. Omit first step of the recipe.

```
BEETS IN ORANGE SAUCE NOTES:
_____
_____
_____
```

Roasted Beet and Clementine Salad

Prep: 20 min. • **Cook:** 50 min. • **Yield:** 4 servings.
This special salad is beautiful with its jewel-toned colors.
Fresh fennel adds great texture to the smooth beets.
—*Marie Sheppard, Chicago, Illinois*

12	fresh baby beets	1/2	teaspoon minced fresh thyme *or* 1/8 teaspoon dried thyme
1/2	cup canola oil, *divided*		
1	egg white	1/4	teaspoon salt
1/4	teaspoon pepper	4	lettuce leaves
1/4	cup hazelnuts	2	clementines, peeled and sectioned
3	tablespoons red wine vinegar		
2	teaspoons finely chopped shallot	4	teaspoons finely chopped fennel bulb

1. Place beets on a double thickness of heavy-duty foil (about
18 in. x 12 in.). Drizzle with 2 tablespoons oil. Fold foil around
beets and seal tightly. Place on a baking sheet. Bake at 400°
for 40-50 minutes or until tender. Cool.

2. Meanwhile, in a small bowl, combine egg white and pepper;
add hazelnuts and toss to coat. Transfer to a 9-in. square baking
pan coated with cooking spray. Bake for 10-12 minutes or until
golden brown, stirring twice. Cool on a wire rack.

3. In a small bowl, combine the vinegar, shallot, thyme and
salt. Gradually whisk in remaining oil.

4. Peel and thinly slice beets. Line four individual salad
bowls with the lettuce; top with the beet and clementine
slices. Sprinkle salads with fennel and hazelnuts; drizzle with
dressing. Serve immediately.

Nutrition Facts: 1 each equals 368 calories, 35 g fat (3 g saturated fat),
0 cholesterol, 195 mg sodium, 14 g carbohydrate, 3 g fiber, 4 g protein.

```
ROASTED BEET AND CLEMENTINE
SALAD NOTES: _____
_____
_____
```

Spring Greens with Beets and Goat Cheese

Prep: 10 min. • **Cook:** 10 min. • **Yield:** 8 servings.
I love to put small variations on this salad, depending on what I have on hand, but this version is my absolute favorite. I just fell in love with the flavor combinations.
—*Kristin Kossak, Bozeman, Montana*

- 2/3 cup pecan halves
- 3 tablespoons balsamic vinegar, *divided*
- 1 tablespoon water
- 1 tablespoon sugar
- 1/4 cup olive oil
- 2 tablespoons maple syrup
- 1 teaspoon stone-ground mustard
- 1/8 teaspoon salt
- 1 package (5 ounces) spring mix salad greens
- 8 medium beets, cooked and sliced
- 1 cup crumbled goat cheese

1. In a large heavy skillet, cook the pecans, 1 tablespoon vinegar and water over medium heat until nuts are toasted, about 4 minutes. Sprinkle with sugar. Cook and stir for 2-4 minutes or until sugar is melted. Spread on foil to cool.

2. In a small bowl, whisk the oil, syrup, mustard, salt and remaining vinegar. Refrigerate until serving.

3. In a large bowl, combine salad greens and dressing; toss to coat. Divide among eight salad plates. Top with beets, goat cheese and glazed pecans.

Nutrition Facts: 3/4 cup equals 268 calories, 22 g fat (7 g saturated fat), 22 mg cholesterol, 299 mg sodium, 12 g carbohydrate, 2 g fiber, 8 g protein.

Harvest Green Salad

Prep: 25 min. • **Bake:** 1 hour + cooling • **Yield:** 6 servings.
This salad always gets rave reviews. Guests say that it fills them up without weighing them down.
—*Beth Royals, Richmond, Virginia*

- 3 whole medium fresh beets
- 1 large sweet potato, peeled and cubed
- 2 tablespoons water
- 1/2 cup reduced-fat balsamic vinaigrette
- 2 tablespoons jellied cranberry sauce
- 1 package (5 ounces) spring mix salad greens
- 1/2 cup dried cranberries
- 4 ounces crumbled Gorgonzola cheese

1. Wash beets; trim stem and leave root intact. Wrap beets in aluminum foil. Place on a baking sheet. Bake at 400° for 1 hour or until tender. Remove foil and cool.

2. In a microwave-safe bowl, combine the sweet potato and water. Cover and microwave on high for 4-5 minutes or until tender. Cool.

3. In a blender, combine vinaigrette and cranberry sauce; cover and process until smooth. Peel beets and cut into slices.

4. On six salad plates, arrange greens, beets and sweet potatoes. Sprinkle with cranberries and cheese. Drizzle with the dressing.

Nutrition Facts: 1 serving (1-1/8 cups) equals 187 calories, 9 g fat (4 g saturated fat), 17 mg cholesterol, 438 mg sodium, 23 g carbohydrate, 3 g fiber, 6 g protein. **Diabetic Exchanges:** 1 starch, 1 vegetable, 1 fat, 1/2 fruit.

EDITOR'S NOTE: This recipe was tested in a 1,100-watt microwave.

ONION BEET SALAD NOTES: _____
_____
_____
_____
_____

Onion Beet Salad

Prep: 30 min. • **Bake:** 1 hour + chilling • **Yield:** 9 servings.
Everyone loves the tangy dressing on these mouthwatering baked beets. I'm always asked to bring this pretty dish to family gatherings.
—*Barbara Van Lanen, Salinas, California*

12 whole fresh beets (about 2-1/2 pounds), peeled and halved
5 tablespoons olive oil, *divided*
1 large red onion, chopped
1/2 cup balsamic vinegar
1/3 cup red wine vinegar
1/4 cup sugar
1 teaspoon salt
1 teaspoon dried basil
1/2 teaspoon pepper

1. Place the beets in a large resealable plastic bag; add 2 tablespoons oil. Seal bag; shake to coat. Place an 18-in. x 12-in. piece of heavy-duty foil in a 15-in. x 10-in. x 1-in. baking pan. Arrange beets on foil; fold foil over beets and seal tightly. Bake at 400° for 1 to 1-1/4 hours or until beets are tender.

2. Cool to room temperature. Cut beets into cubes; place in a large bowl. Add onion. In a small bowl, whisk the vinegars, sugar, salt, basil, pepper and remaining oil.

3. Pour over beet mixture; gently toss to coat. Cover and refrigerate for at least 1 hour, stirring several times. Serve with a slotted spoon.

Nutrition Facts: 3/4 cup equals 135 calories, 8 g fat (1 g saturated fat), 0 cholesterol, 318 mg sodium, 17 g carbohydrate, 2 g fiber, 1 g protein.

Roasted Beet and Potato Salad

Prep: 20 min. • **Bake:** 35 min. • **Yield:** 9 servings.
You'll love the combination of beets and balsamic dressing in this lovely addition to your holiday meal!
—*Jennifer Fisher, Austin, Texas*

1-1/2 pounds small red potatoes, halved
2 medium red onions, cut into wedges
1/2 teaspoon salt, *divided*
2 tablespoons olive oil
1-1/2 pounds fresh beets, peeled and cut into wedges
2/3 cup reduced-sodium chicken broth *or* vegetable broth
1/3 cup balsamic vinegar
2 teaspoons brown sugar
2 teaspoons minced fresh thyme *or* 1/2 teaspoon dried thyme
1/2 teaspoon pepper
2 tablespoons minced fresh parsley

1. Place potatoes and onions in two 15-in. x 10-in. x 1-in. baking pans coated with cooking spray. Sprinkle with 1/4 teaspoon salt; drizzle with oil and toss to coat.

2. Place beets in pans with potatoes (do not stir). Bake, uncovered, at 425° for 35-40 minutes or until tender.

3. For dressing, in a small saucepan, combine the broth, vinegar, brown sugar, thyme, pepper and remaining salt. Bring to a boil. Reduce heat; simmer, uncovered, until reduced to 1/3 cup.

4. Transfer vegetables to a large bowl. Drizzle with dressing and toss to coat. Sprinkle with parsley.

Nutrition Facts: 3/4 cup equals 135 calories, 3 g fat (trace saturated fat), 0 cholesterol, 244 mg sodium, 24 g carbohydrate, 3 g fiber, 3 g protein. **Diabetic Exchanges:** 1 starch, 1 vegetable, 1/2 fat.

ROASTED BEET AND POTATO SALAD NOTES:_____
_____
_____
_____
_____

Warm Roasted Beet Salad

Prep: 30 min. • **Bake:** 40 min. • **Yield:** 6 servings.
Here is a recipe that lets beets shine. It's a hearty main dish salad
that is beautiful on the plate, too. I prefer to use
hazelnut oil in this salad if I can find it.
—*Jill Anderson, Sleepy Eye, Minnesota*

8 whole fresh beets

Cooking spray

1-1/2 cups orange juice

1 shallot, chopped

2 tablespoons olive oil

2 tablespoons balsamic vinegar

1 teaspoon minced fresh thyme *or* 1/4 teaspoon
dried thyme

1/2 teaspoon grated orange peel

1/8 teaspoon salt

1/8 teaspoon pepper

6 cups fresh arugula *or* baby spinach

3 tablespoons crumbled blue cheese

3 tablespoons chopped hazelnuts, toasted

1. Scrub beets and cut into wedges; place on a baking
sheet coated with cooking spray. Lightly coat beets with
additional cooking spray. Bake at 350° for 40-50 minutes or
until tender, turning occasionally.

2. Meanwhile, for dressing, place orange juice in a small
saucepan. Bring to a boil. Reduce heat; simmer, uncovered,
until liquid is syrupy and reduced to about 1/3 cup. Remove
from the heat. Whisk in the shallot, oil, vinegar, thyme,
orange peel, salt and pepper. Set aside to cool.

3. Just before serving, place arugula in a large bowl.
Drizzle with 1/4 cup dressing and toss to coat. Divide
mixture among six salad plates. Place beets in the same
bowl; add remaining dressing and toss to coat. Arrange on
plates. Sprinkle salads with blue cheese and hazelnuts.

Nutrition Facts: 1 serving equals 147 calories, 8 g fat (2 g saturated
fat), 3 mg cholesterol, 167 mg sodium, 17 g carbohydrate, 2 g fiber,
4 g protein. **Diabetic Exchanges:** 2 vegetable, 1-1/2 fat, 1/2 fruit.

WARM ROASTED BEET SALAD NOTES:
_____
_____
_____
_____

Grilled Broccoli & Cauliflower

Prep/Total Time: 20 min. • **Yield:** 2 servings.

Add this grilled side to just about any meat. For variation, add one large baking potato, or mix in asparagus for a veggie extravaganza.
—*Tara Delgado, Wauseon, Ohio.*

> 1   cup fresh broccoli florets
> 1   cup fresh cauliflowerets
> 1   small onion, cut into wedges
> Refrigerated butter-flavored spray
> 1/4   teaspoon garlic salt
> 1/8   teaspoon paprika
> 1/8   teaspoon pepper

1. In a large bowl, combine the broccoli, cauliflower and onion; spritz with butter-flavored spray. Sprinkle with the garlic salt, paprika and pepper; toss to coat. Place vegetables on a double thickness of heavy-duty foil (about 18-in. x 12-in.); fold foil around vegetables and seal tightly.

2. Grill, covered, over medium heat for 10-15 minutes or until vegetables are tender. Open foil carefully to allow steam to escape.

Nutrition Facts: 1 cup equals 47 calories, 1 g fat (trace saturated fat), 0 cholesterol, 262 mg sodium, 8 g carbohydrate, 3 g fiber, 2 g protein. **Diabetic Exchange:** 2 vegetable.

Broccoli and cauliflower pack a one-two punch when it comes to offering solid nutrition and recipe versatility. Enjoy them raw, baked, roasted, stir-fried—the possibilities are endless!

SEASON: October to March

AT THE MARKET: Select firm but tender stalks of broccoli with compact, dark green or slightly purplish florets. Select firm, solid white or creamy colored heads of cauliflower that are heavy for their size. Florets should be clean and tightly packed; surrounding jacket leaves should be fresh and green.

STORAGE: Broccoli, refrigerate unwashed in an open plastic bag for up to 4 days; Cauliflower, refrigerate unwashed in an open plastic bag for up to 5 days.

GRILLED BROCCOLI & CAULIFLOWER
NOTES:_____
_____
_____
_____
_____

Broccoli Egg Cups

Prep: 30 min. • **Bake:** 30 min. • **Yield:** 6 servings.
Serving brunch? This delicious egg bake is filled with crunchy bites of broccoli and served in ramekins. I promise your company will love it!
—Edna Hoffman, Hebron, Indiana

1	bunch broccoli, cut into florets	1	tablespoon minced fresh parsley
10	eggs	1/2	teaspoon salt
2	cups half-and-half cream	1/2	teaspoon minced fresh basil
1/4	cup shredded Swiss cheese	1/8	teaspoon cayenne pepper

1. Grease six 8-oz. ramekins; set aside.

2. In a large saucepan, bring 3 cups water to a boil. Add the broccoli; cover and boil for 3 minutes. Drain and immediately place broccoli in ice water. Drain and pat dry.

3. In a large bowl, whisk 4 eggs, cream, cheese, parsley, salt, basil and cayenne; pour into prepared dishes. Break an egg into each dish; arrange broccoli around each egg.

4. Bake at 350° for 30-35 minutes or until set.

Nutrition Facts: 1 serving equals 256 calories, 18 g fat (9 g saturated fat), 397 mg cholesterol, 378 mg sodium, 6 g carbohydrate, 1 g fiber, 16 g protein.

```
BROCCOLI EGG CUPS NOTES: _____
_____
_____
_____
_____
```

Wild Rice Crab Salad

Prep: 45 min. + chilling • **Yield:** 12 servings.
We have an abundance of wild rice in the northern part of Minnesota, and I use it in many recipes. This one uses fresh broccoli and cauliflower.
—LaVerna Mjones, Moorhead, Minnesota

1-1/2	cups uncooked wild rice	1/4	cup chopped onion
1	pound cooked fresh *or* canned crabmeat	1	bottle (16 ounces) ranch salad dressing
2	cups fresh broccoli florets	1	tablespoon sugar
2	cups fresh cauliflowerets	1/2	teaspoon salt
		1/4	teaspoon pepper

1. Cook rice according to package directions; drain and rinse in cold water.

2. In a large bowl, combine the rice, crab, broccoli, cauliflower and onion. Combine the salad dressing, sugar, salt and pepper; pour over salad and toss to coat. Cover; refrigerate for 4 hours before serving.

Nutrition Facts: 1 cup equals 337 calories, 22 g fat (3 g saturated fat), 44 mg cholesterol, 532 mg sodium, 23 g carbohydrate, 2 g fiber, 11 g protein.

```
WILD RICE CRAB SALAD NOTES: _____
_____
_____
_____
_____
```

Dilly Grilled Veggies

Prep/Total Time: 30 min. • **Yield:** 6 servings.
Use any combination of vegetables in this versatile side dish. I like to include broccoli, carrots, green peppers and onions, too!
—*Fran Scott, Birmingham, Michigan*

- 2 cups sliced fresh mushrooms
- 2 cups sliced fresh zucchini
- 2 cups fresh broccoli florets
- 1/2 medium sweet red pepper, cut into strips
- 2 tablespoons olive oil
- 2 tablespoons minced fresh dill *or* 2 teaspoons dill weed
- 1/8 teaspoon garlic salt
- 1/8 teaspoon pepper

1. Place vegetables on a double thickness of heavy-duty foil (about 18-in. square). Drizzle with oil; sprinkle with dill, garlic salt and pepper. Fold foil around vegetables and seal tightly.

2. Grill, covered, over medium heat for 15 minutes or until the vegetables are tender. Open foil carefully to allow steam to escape.

Nutrition Facts: 3/4 cup equals 61 calories, 5 g fat (1 g saturated fat), 0 cholesterol, 49 mg sodium, 4 g carbohydrate, 2 g fiber, 2 g protein.
Diabetic Exchanges: 1 vegetable, 1 fat.

DILLY GRILLED VEGGIES NOTES:
_____
_____
_____
_____
_____

Veggie Mac 'n' Cheese

Prep: 30 min. • **Bake:** 15 min. • **Yield:** 12 servings.
One taste of this creamy mac 'n' cheese and you'll know it didn't come from a box! Fresh veggies add crunch and color and will leave everyone saying, "More, please!"
—*Marsha Morrill, Brownsville, Oregon*

- 1-1/2 cups uncooked elbow macaroni
- 3 cups fresh broccoli florets
- 2 cups fresh cauliflowerets
- 3 large carrots, halved and thinly sliced
- 2 celery ribs, sliced
- 1 medium onion, chopped
- 1 tablespoon butter
- 1/4 cup all-purpose flour
- 1 cup 2% milk
- 1 cup chicken broth
- 3 cups (12 ounces) shredded sharp cheddar cheese
- 1 tablespoon Dijon mustard
- 1/4 teaspoon salt
- 1/8 teaspoon pepper
- 1/4 teaspoon paprika

1. Cook macaroni according to package directions, adding the broccoli, cauliflowerets, carrots and celery during the last 6 minutes. Drain; transfer to a greased 13-in. x 9-in. baking dish.

2. Meanwhile, in a Dutch oven, saute onion in butter until tender. Sprinkle with flour; stir until blended. Gradually stir in the milk and broth. Bring to a boil; cook and stir for 2 minutes or until thickened. Stir in the cheese, mustard, salt and pepper.

3. Pour over macaroni mixture; stir to coat. Sprinkle with paprika. Bake, uncovered, at 350° for 15-20 minutes or until heated through.

Nutrition Facts: 1 cup equals 189 calories, 10 g fat (7 g saturated fat), 35 mg cholesterol, 374 mg sodium, 16 g carbohydrate, 2 g fiber, 10 g protein.

VEGGIE MAC 'N' CHEESE NOTES:
_____
_____
_____
_____
_____

EAT YOUR BROCCOLI.
Americans have grown broccoli in their gardens for only about 200 years, and it wasn't until the 1920s that it was commercially available. At that time, your garden would've been considered exotic if it included the vitamin-packed veggie. Today, Americans consume an average of 4 pounds each of broccoli each year.

Lemon Broccoli with Garlic

Prep/Total Time: 20 min. • **Yield:** 6 servings.
Here is an easy recipe that's great for using up leftover broccoli. That's what Mom did, and I tend to do the same thing.
—*Linda Harrington, Hudson, New Hampshire*

1 large bunch broccoli, cut into florets	4 garlic cloves, minced
1/2 cup olive oil	1/4 teaspoon salt
1/4 cup lemon juice	1/8 teaspoon pepper

1. Place broccoli in a steamer basket; place in a large saucepan over 1 in. of water. Bring to a boil; cover and steam for 6-8 minutes or until crisp-tender.

2. Meanwhile, in a small bowl, combine the remaining ingredients. Immediately place broccoli in ice water. Drain and pat dry. Place in a large bowl. Pour oil mixture over broccoli; toss to coat. Refrigerate until serving.

Nutrition Facts: 2/3 cup equals 207 calories, 19 g fat (3 g saturated fat), 0 cholesterol, 140 mg sodium, 9 g carbohydrate, 5 g fiber, 5 g protein.

LEMON BROCCOLI WITH GARLIC
NOTES: _____
_____
_____
_____
_____

"Broccomole" Dip

Prep: 10 min. + chilling • **Yield:** 6 servings.
For a snack that's very much like guacamole—but without the avocados—try this dip. I grow and freeze broccoli, so this recipe is convenient to make.
—*Sue Gronholz, Beaver Dam, Wisconsin*

2 cups chopped fresh broccoli, cooked and chilled	1 tablespoon fat-free mayonnaise
1/4 cup reduced-fat sour cream	2 to 3 tablespoons lemon juice
1 to 2 tablespoons finely chopped onion	1/4 to 1/2 teaspoon chili powder
	Assorted fresh vegetables *or* tortilla chips

1. In a food processor, combine the first six ingredients; cover and process until smooth. Refrigerate for several hours. Serve with vegetables or tortilla chips.

Nutritional Analysis: 1 serving (3 tablespoons) equals 27 calories, 2 g fat (0 saturated fat), 5 mg cholesterol, 33 mg sodium, 3 g carbohydrate, 0 fiber, 2 g protein. **Diabetic Exchange:** 1 vegetable.

"BROCCOMOLE" DIP NOTES: _____
_____
_____
_____
_____

Broccoli Strawberry Salad

Prep/Total Time: 20 min. • **Yield:** 10 servings.

I got this speedy recipe from my friend Marilyn who brings this fresh-tasting salad to potlucks and cookouts. It's usually the first dish to be finished!
—*Emily Robertson, West Peoria, Illinois*

- 8 cups fresh broccoli florets
- 8 ounces Colby-Monterey Jack cheese, cut into 1/2-inch cubes
- 1 cup mayonnaise
- 2 tablespoons sugar
- 1 teaspoon cider vinegar
- 2 cups fresh strawberries, quartered
- 1/4 cup sliced almonds, toasted

1. In a large bowl, combine broccoli and cheese. In a small bowl, whisk the mayonnaise, sugar and vinegar. Pour over broccoli mixture and toss to coat. Gently stir in strawberries; sprinkle with almonds.

Nutrition Facts: 1 serving (1 cup) equals 297 calories, 26 g fat (7 g saturated fat), 30 mg cholesterol, 273 mg sodium, 9 g carbohydrate, 3 g fiber, 8 g protein.

BROCCOLI STRAWBERRY SALAD TIP:
When using fresh broccoli in your recipes, the best broccoli will have dark green tops with lighter green stems. Its nutritional value depletes the longer it's stored, so use it as soon as possible! —Taste of Home

Quinoa Vegetable Pilaf

Prep/Total Time: 30 min. • **Yield:** 2 servings.

If you've never tried quinoa, this colorful side dish makes a great introduction. The combination is wonderful.
—*Jill Heatwole, Pittsville, Maryland*

- 2 tablespoons finely chopped onion
- 2 tablespoons chopped carrot
- 1/2 teaspoon canola oil
- 1/4 cup uncooked jasmine rice
- 1/4 cup quinoa, rinsed
- 1 cup reduced-sodium chicken broth
- 1/8 teaspoon pepper
- 1/3 cup chopped fresh broccoli

1. In a small saucepan, saute the onion and carrot in oil until tender. Add the rice and quinoa; stir to coat. Stir in the broth and pepper.

2. Bring to a boil. Reduce heat; cover and simmer for 15-20 minutes or until liquid is absorbed, adding the broccoli during the last 3 minutes of cooking. Remove from the heat; let stand for 5 minutes. Fluff with a fork.

Nutrition Facts: 1 cup equals 193 calories, 3 g fat (trace saturated fat), 0 cholesterol, 300 mg sodium, 36 g carbohydrate, 2 g fiber, 6 g protein.

EDITOR'S NOTE: Look for quinoa in the cereal, rice or organic food aisle.

QUINOA VEGETABLE PILAF NOTES:
_____
_____
_____
_____
_____

brussels SPROUTS

Sure, Mom probably force-fed you the overcooked and mushy store-bought variety when you were a kid. But those can't hold a candle to homegrown sprouts. Rediscover Brussels sprouts' slightly nutty flavor and tender texture in these yummy dishes.

SEASON: September through May; peaks October-February.

AT THE MARKET: Select small, firm, tightly closed heads that have a bright green color.

STORAGE: Refrigerate unwashed in an open plastic bag for up to 3 days.

Pickled Veggie Salad

Prep: 20 min. • **Cook:** 10 min. + marinating • **Yield:** 14 servings.

One year I created this recipe to use up an overabundance of Brussels sprouts. My family asked for seconds, so now this tangy side is a staple on our Thanksgiving menu.
—*Bobbi Ballantine, Grove City, Pennsylvania*

- 1 pound fresh Brussels sprouts
- 1 cup sugar
- 3/4 cup white vinegar
- 1/2 pound sliced fresh mushrooms
- 1 small onion, chopped
- 2 garlic cloves, minced
- 1 tablespoon plus 1/4 cup canola oil, *divided*
- 1 can (8 ounces) sliced water chestnuts, drained
- 2 cans (2-1/4 ounces *each*) sliced ripe olives, drained
- 2 plum tomatoes, sliced
- 1 jar (2 ounces) diced pimientos, drained
- 1 tablespoon lemon juice

1. Cut an "X" in the core of each Brussels sprout. Place 1/2 in. of water in a large saucepan; add Brussels sprouts. Bring to a boil. Reduce heat; cover and simmer for 8-10 minutes or until tender.

2. Meanwhile, in a small saucepan, bring sugar and vinegar to a boil; cook and stir for 1 minute or until sugar is dissolved. Remove from the heat; cool slightly.

3. In a large skillet, saute the mushrooms, onion and garlic in 1 tablespoon oil until tender. Transfer to a large bowl. Add the water chestnuts, olives, tomatoes, pimientos and lemon juice.

4. Drain Brussels sprouts; cool slightly. Cut into quarters and add to vegetable mixture. Add sugar mixture and remaining oil; toss to coat. Cover and refrigerate overnight. Serve with a slotted spoon.

Nutrition Facts: 1/2 cup equals 114 calories, 5 g fat (trace saturated fat), 0 cholesterol, 90 mg sodium, 17 g carbohydrate, 2 g fiber, 2 g protein. **Diabetic Exchanges:** 1 vegetable, 1 fat, 1/2 starch.

PICKLED VEGGIE SALAD NOTES: _____
_____
_____
_____
_____

Brussels Sprouts with Golden Raisins

Prep/Total Time: 30 min. • **Yield:** 5 servings.
Take a break from ordinary steamed Brussels sprouts by combining them with raisins and a slightly tart dressing. Thinly slicing the sprouts makes them appeal to people who normally don't like the texture.
—*Michaela Rosenthal, Woodland Hills, California*

1	pound fresh Brussels sprouts, thinly sliced	1/8	teaspoon white pepper
1	tablespoon olive oil	1/3	cup golden raisins
2	tablespoons water	1	teaspoon white balsamic vinegar
1/4	teaspoon celery salt		

1. In a large skillet, saute Brussels sprouts in oil until crisp-tender. Add the water, celery salt and pepper. Reduce heat; cover and cook for 4-5 minutes or until tender. Stir in raisins and vinegar.

Nutrition Facts: 2/3 cup equals 93 calories, 3 g fat (trace saturated fat), 0 cholesterol, 98 mg sodium, 16 g carbohydrate, 4 g fiber, 3 g protein.
Diabetic Exchanges: 1 vegetable, 1/2 fruit, 1/2 fat.

BRUSSELS SPROUTS WITH GOLDEN
RAISINS NOTES: _____
_____
_____
_____

Balsamic-Glazed Brussels Sprouts

Prep/Total Time: 30 min. • **Yield:** 8 servings.
My relatives claim to hate Brussels sprouts, which I took as a challenge to come up with a recipe they'd love. When I served this at my Christmas buffet, there wasn't a sprout left in the bowl!
—*Carol Bess White, Portland, Oregon*

2	pounds fresh Brussels sprouts	2	tablespoons stone-ground mustard
1/2	pound bacon strips, cut into 1/2-inch pieces	1/2	teaspoon garlic powder
1	medium onion, sliced	1/8	teaspoon salt
1/4	cup white balsamic vinegar	1/2	cup soft bread crumbs

1. Cut an "X" in the core of each Brussels sprout. Place in a large saucepan; add 1 in. of water. Bring to a boil. Reduce heat; cover and simmer for 8-10 minutes or until crisp-tender.

2. Meanwhile, in a large ovenproof skillet, cook bacon over medium heat until crisp. Using a slotted spoon, remove to paper towels; drain, reserving 2 tablespoons drippings.

3. Saute onion in drippings until tender. Stir in the vinegar, mustard, garlic powder, salt, Brussels sprouts and bacon; cook 2-3 minutes longer.

4. Sprinkle with bread crumbs; broil 4-6 in. from the heat for 2-3 minutes or until golden brown.

Nutrition Facts: 3/4 cup equals 256 calories, 16 g fat (5 g saturated fat), 34 mg cholesterol, 823 mg sodium, 16 g carbohydrate, 5 g fiber, 15 g protein.

BALSAMIC-GLAZED BRUSSELS SPROUTS
NOTES:_____
_____
_____
_____
_____

Herbed Brussels Sprouts

Prep: 20 min. • **Bake:** 15 min. • **Yield:** 8 servings.
This is a delicious take on a seasonal standby. The sprouts
are so tasty that even children enjoy them.
—*Debbie Marrone, Warner Robins, Georgia*

  8 cups fresh Brussels sprouts (about 2-1/2
      pounds)
  1 cup sliced fresh mushrooms
1/4 cup packed brown sugar
1/4 cup cider vinegar
  2 tablespoons butter, melted
1/2 teaspoon salt
1/2 teaspoon dried tarragon
1/2 teaspoon dried marjoram
1/2 teaspoon pepper
1/4 cup chopped pimientos

1. Trim Brussels sprouts and cut an "X" in the core of each.
Place sprouts in a steamer basket; place in a large saucepan
over 1 in. of water. Bring to a boil; cover and steam for 9-11
minutes or until crisp-tender.

2. Transfer to a 13-in. x 9-in. baking dish coated with
cooking spray. Top with the mushrooms. In a small bowl,
combine the brown sugar, vinegar, butter, salt, tarragon,
marjoram and pepper. Drizzle over vegetables. Sprinkle with
the pimientos.

3. Bake, uncovered, at 350° for 15-20 minutes or until
vegetables are tender.

Nutrition Facts: 3/4 cup equals 94 calories, 3 g fat (2 g saturated fat),
8 mg cholesterol, 203 mg sodium, 16 g carbohydrate, 4 g fiber,
3 g protein. **Diabetic Exchanges:** 2 vegetable, 1/2 starch, 1/2 fat.

Buttery Carrots and Brussels Sprouts

Prep/Total Time: 20 min. • **Yield:** 8 servings

Every cook needs a traditional, standby recipe for Brussels sprouts—look no further. This one is fabulous and versatile.

—*Stacy Duffy, Chicago, Illinois*

1 pound carrots, cut into 1/4-inch slices	1 tablespoon lemon juice
3/4 pound Brussels sprouts, halved	2 teaspoons grated lemon peel
1/4 cup butter, cubed	1 teaspoon sugar
1 tablespoon minced fresh gingerroot	Salt and pepper to taste
	Minced fresh parsley, optional

1. In a large saucepan over medium heat, cook carrots and Brussels sprouts in boiling water for 8-10 minutes or until tender; drain.

2. In a small saucepan, melt butter. Add ginger; cook for 2 minutes. Add the lemon juice, peel, sugar, salt and pepper; pour over vegetables. Sprinkle with parsley if desired.

Nutrition Facts: 1 serving (3/4 cup) equals 96 calories, 6 g fat (4 g saturated fat), 15 mg cholesterol, 88 mg sodium, 10 g carbohydrate, 3 g fiber, 2 g protein.

```
BUTTERY CARROTS AND BRUSSELS
SPROUTS NOTES: _____
_____
_____
_____
```

```
MAPLE-DIJON GLAZED BRUSSELS SPROUTS
NOTES:_____
_____
_____
_____
_____
```

Maple-Dijon Glazed Brussels Sprouts

Prep: 20 min. • **Cook:** 20 min. • **Yield:** 6 servings.

Ordinary Brussels sprouts get jazzed up with a sweet, tangy sauce. It's best when prepared with local maple syrup. Even those who normally steer clear of sprouts will ask for seconds of these!

—*Holly Scarborough, Melbourne, Florida*

2 pounds fresh Brussels sprouts, trimmed	1/4 cup Dijon mustard
2 tablespoons butter	1/4 cup maple syrup
1/2 cup chicken broth	1/4 teaspoon pepper

1. Cut an "X" in the core of each Brussels sprout. In a large skillet, saute Brussels sprouts in butter for 4-5 minutes or until lightly browned.

2. Stir in the broth, mustard, syrup and pepper. Bring to a boil. Reduce heat; cover and simmer for 5 minutes. Uncover; cook and stir 8-10 minutes longer or until the Brussels sprouts are tender.

Nutrition Facts: 3/4 cup equals 145 calories, 4 g fat (2 g saturated fat), 10 mg cholesterol, 388 mg sodium, 25 g carbohydrate, 6 g fiber, 5 g protein. **Diabetic Exchanges:** 2 vegetable, 1 starch, 1 fat.

Brussels Sprouts with Bacon

Prep/Total Time: 30 min. • **Yield:** 12 servings
Bacon lends a wonderful salty flavor while balsamic vinegar adds a hint of spicy tang. Who knew Brussels sprouts could taste so good?
—*Paula Young, Tiffin, Ohio*

3 bacon strips	2 tablespoons water
1-1/4 pounds fresh *or* frozen Brussels sprouts, thawed, quartered	1/4 teaspoon salt
	1/8 teaspoon pepper
1 large onion, chopped	2 tablespoons balsamic vinegar

1. In a large skillet, cook bacon over medium heat until crisp. Remove to paper towels; drain, reserving 1 tablespoon drippings. Crumble bacon and set aside.

2. In the same pan, saute Brussels sprouts and onion in reserved drippings until crisp-tender. Add the water, salt and pepper. Bring to a boil. Reduce heat; cover and simmer for 4-5 minutes or until Brussels sprouts are tender. Stir in bacon and vinegar.

Nutrition Facts: 2/3 cup equals 90 calories, 4 g fat (1 g saturated fat), 6 mg cholesterol, 200 mg sodium, 11 g carbohydrate, 4 g fiber, 5 g protein. **Diabetic Exchanges:** 2 vegetable, 1 fat.

```
BRUSSELS SPROUTS WITH BACON
NOTES:_____
       _____
       _____
       _____
       _____
```

Fettuccine with Brussels Sprouts

Prep/Total Time: 25 min. • **Yield:** 4 servings.
To separate the leaves from the Brussels sprouts, cut off the stem end to loosen the leaves. Then separate them with your fingers.
—*Taste of Home Test Kitchen*

8 ounces uncooked fettuccine	1/2 teaspoon minced garlic
1 pound fresh Brussels sprouts, cored and separated into leaves	1 cup (4 ounces) shredded Parmesan cheese
1/2 cup chopped red onion	3/4 cup walnut halves, toasted
1/3 cup butter, cubed	

1. Cook the fettuccine according to package directions. Meanwhile, in a large skillet, saute Brussels sprouts and onion in butter until tender. Add garlic; cook 1 minute longer. Drain fettuccine; add to the skillet and toss to coat. Sprinkle with cheese and walnuts.

Nutrition Facts: 2 cups equals 592 calories, 35 g fat (14 g saturated fat), 55 mg cholesterol, 541 mg sodium, 55 g carbohydrate, 8 g fiber, 22 g protein.

```
FETTUCCINE WITH BRUSSELS SPROUTS
NOTES:_____
       _____
       _____
       _____
       _____
```

Winter Chowder

Prep/Total Time: 30 min. • **Yield:** 5 servings.

As a mother of three, it goes without saying that time is short but precious to me. I whipped up this fast and nutritious chowder one night, and my 7-year-old son said it was "Awesome!"

—*Brenda Turner, Schererville, Indiana*

3 medium potatoes, peeled and cut into 1/4-inch pieces	1/2 cup cubed fully cooked ham (1/4-inch pieces)
1/2 cup chopped onion	1 cup fresh *or* frozen Brussels sprouts, quartered
1 cup water	
3/4 teaspoon onion powder *or* onion salt	1-1/2 cups fat-free milk
1/2 teaspoon pepper	3/4 cup shredded reduced-fat Colby-Monterey Jack cheese, *divided*
1/8 teaspoon salt	
2 drops Louisiana-style hot sauce	

1. In a large saucepan, bring potatoes, onion and water to a boil. Reduce heat. Cover; cook for 10-12 minutes or until tender. Do not drain. Mash potatoes (mixture will not be smooth). Stir in onion salt, pepper, salt and hot sauce; set aside.

2. In a large nonstick skillet coated with cooking spray, saute ham and Brussels sprouts for 5-6 minutes or until sprouts are tender. Stir into the potato mixture. Add milk. Bring to a boil. Reduce heat; simmer, uncovered, for 5-6 minutes or until heated through, stirring occasionally.

3. Gradually stir in 1/2 cup cheese; cook for 2-3 minutes or until cheese is melted. Garnish with remaining cheese.

Nutrition Facts: 1 cup equals 403 calories, 7 g fat (3 g saturated fat), 21 mg cholesterol, 457 mg sodium, 66 g carbohydrate, 23 g fiber, 33 g protein.

WINTER CHOWDER TIP:
Before using Brussels sprouts in your recipes, remove any loose or yellowed outer leaves; trim stem end. And be sure to rinse them to remove any lingering dirt trapped in the leaves.
—Taste of Home

Lemon-Garlic Brussels Sprouts

Prep/Total Time: 30 min. • **Yield:** 2 servings.

Even lifelong Brussels sprouts haters love these! For a heartier dish, I sometimes add crumbled bacon.

—*Jan Roberts, San Pedro, California*

1/2 pound fresh Brussels sprouts	1/4 teaspoon garlic powder
1-1/2 teaspoons olive oil	Dash pepper
1-1/2 teaspoons lemon juice	1 tablespoon shredded Parmesan cheese
1/4 teaspoon salt	

1. Cut an "X" in the core of each Brussels sprout. Place in a shallow baking pan coated with cooking spray. Drizzle with oil and lemon juice; sprinkle with salt, garlic powder and pepper.

2. Bake, uncovered, at 400° for 20-25 minutes or until tender, stirring once. Sprinkle with cheese.

Nutrition Facts: 3/4 cup equals 91 calories, 4 g fat (1 g saturated fat), 2 mg cholesterol, 366 mg sodium, 11 g carbohydrate, 4 g fiber, 5 g protein. **Diabetic Exchanges:** 2 vegetable, 1 fat.

LEMON-GARLIC BRUSSELS SPROUTS NOTES:

CABBAGE

Sweet-and-Sour Red Cabbage

Prep: 20 min. • **Cook:** 1-1/4 hours • **Yield:** 8 servings.
My grandfather was German, so my grandmother prepared
many German dishes for him. This is one I like best.
—*Leonie Kenyon, Narragansett, Rhode Island*

- 1 medium onion, chopped
- 1/4 cup butter, cubed
- 1 medium head red cabbage, chopped (about 8 cups)
- 1 teaspoon salt
- 1/4 teaspoon pepper
- 2 medium tart apples, peeled and chopped
- 1/4 cup water
- 1/2 cup white vinegar
- 1/3 cup packed brown sugar

1. In a large saucepan, saute onion in butter until tender.
Stir in cabbage, salt and pepper. Reduce heat. Cover; simmer
for 10 minutes. Stir in apples and water. Cover; simmer 45
minutes longer or until cabbage and apples are tender.

2. Combine vinegar and brown sugar; stir into cabbage
mixture. Bring to a boil. Reduce heat; simmer, uncovered,
for 15 minutes or until cabbage and apples are glazed.

Nutrition Facts: 1 serving (3/4 cup) equals 136 calories, 6 g fat
(4 g saturated fat), 15 mg cholesterol, 369 mg sodium, 21 g
carbohydrate, 3 g fiber, 2 g protein.

From coleslaw to sauerkraut, cabbage
has clout. A member of the same
family that brings you broccoli and
Brussels sprouts, cabbage is packed
with vitamins K and C, iron and
folate—and it's inexpensive to boot!

SEASON: Late summer to early fall.

AT THE MARKET: Cabbage heads will
vary in size; for green cabbage, select
round, compact and solid heads. Red
cabbage heads are not as compact.

STORAGE: Refrigerate unwashed for
up to 2 weeks.

SWEET-AND-SOUR RED CABBAGE
NOTES:_____
_____
_____
_____
_____

Chicken and Asian Slaw

Prep/Total Time: 20 min. • **Yield:** 4 servings.
Sesame ginger salad dressing adds refreshing flavor to this pairing of broiled chicken and an exotic homemade coleslaw. This meal is always a hit, and it goes together so quickly.
—*Melissa Jelinek, Menomonee Falls, Wisconsin*

2 cups cubed fresh pineapple
2 cups sliced bok choy
2 cups shredded red cabbage

1/3 cup plus 1/4 cup sesame ginger salad dressing, divided
4 boneless skinless chicken breast halves (4 ounces *each*)

1. In a large bowl, combine the pineapple, bok choy, cabbage and 1/3 cup dressing; toss to coat. Chill until serving.

2. Brush chicken with remaining dressing; transfer to a 15-in. x 10-in. x 1-in. baking pan. Broil 4 in. from the heat for 4-5 minutes on each side or until a meat thermometer reads 170°.

3. Divide slaw among four bowls. Slice chicken; arrange over slaw. Serve immediately.

Nutrition Facts: 1 serving equals 302 calories, 13 g fat (3 g saturated fat), 63 mg cholesterol, 433 mg sodium, 21 g carbohydrate, 2 g fiber, 24 g protein.

CHICKEN AND ASIAN SLAW NOTES:

_____
_____
_____
_____

New England Boiled Dinner

Prep: 10 min. • **Cook:** 2 hours • **Yield:** 8-10 servings.
This has been a popular dinner among our family for a long time. When we moved to California, I'd make it often to remind us of New England. We're back home now and continue to enjoy this scrumptious dish.
—*Natalie Cook, Scarborough, Maine*

1 smoked boneless pork shoulder butt roast (2 to 2 1/2 pounds)
1 pound fresh carrots, sliced lengthwise and halved
8 medium red potatoes, peeled and halved

2 medium onions, cut into quarters
1 large head cabbage, cut into quarters
1 large turnip, peeled and cut into quarters
1 large rutabaga, peeled, halved and sliced

1. Place pork roast in a large Dutch oven; cover with water. Bring to a boil. Reduce heat; cover and simmer for 1 hour.

2. Add the remaining ingredients; return to a boil. Reduce the heat. Cover and simmer for 1 hour or until the vegetables are tender; drain.

Nutrition Facts: 1 serving equals 350 calories, 17 g fat (6 g saturated fat), 52 mg cholesterol, 1,120 mg sodium, 36 g carbohydrate, 9 g fiber, 17 g protein.

NEW ENGLAND BOILED DINNER NOTES:

_____
_____
_____
_____

Campers' Coleslaw

Prep: 20 min. + chilling • **Yield:** 12 servings.
Crispy and crunchy, this traditional, no-fuss slaw makes a refreshing side dish for summer picnics and parties.
—*Kim Wallace, Dennison, Ohio*

1-1/2	cups sugar	1	medium head cabbage, shredded
3/4	cup white vinegar		
3/4	cup olive oil	1	large onion, chopped
3	teaspoons salt		
1	teaspoon celery seed	1	medium green pepper, chopped

1. In a small saucepan, combine the first five ingredients. Bring to a boil; boil for 1-2 minutes or until sugar is dissolved. Remove from heat; cool to room temperature.

2. In a large bowl, combine the cabbage, onion, and pepper; add dressing and toss to coat. Refrigerate until chilled. Serve with a slotted spoon.

Nutrition Facts: 3/4 cup equals 121 calories, 6 g fat (1 g saturated fat), 0 cholesterol, 274 mg sodium, 17 g carbohydrate, 2 g fiber, 1 g protein. **Diabetic Exchanges:** 1 starch, 1 fat.

CAMPERS' COLESLAW NOTES:

_____
_____
_____
_____
_____

Colcannon Potatoes

Prep: 10 min. • **Cook:** 35 min. • **Yield:** 12-16 servings.
Every Irish family has its own version or this classic dish...my recipe comes from my father's family in Ireland. It's part of my St. Pat's menu, along with lamb chops, carrots and soda bread.
—*Marilou Robinson, Portland, Oregon*

2	pounds cabbage, shredded	1	cup chopped green onions
2	cups water		Salt and coarsely ground pepper to taste
4	pounds potatoes, peeled and quartered	1/4	cup butter, melted
2	cups milk		Crumbled cooked bacon and minced fresh parsley

1. In a large saucepan, bring cabbage and water to a boil. Reduce heat; cover and simmer for 10-12 minutes or until tender. Drain, reserving cooking liquid. Keep cabbage warm.

2. Place cooking liquid and potatoes in a large saucepan; add enough additional water to cover the potatoes. Bring to a boil. Reduce heat; cover and cook for 15-17 minutes or until tender. Drain and keep warm.

3. In a small saucepan, bring milk and onions to a boil; remove from the heat. In a large bowl, mash potatoes. Add milk mixture; beat until blended. Beat in the cabbage, salt and pepper. Drizzle with the melted butter, bacon and parsley.

Nutrition Facts: 3/4 cup calculated without salt and bacon equals 149 calories, 4 g fat (2 g saturated fat), 11 mg cholesterol, 50 mg sodium, 26 g carbohydrate, 3 g fiber, 4 g protein.

COLCANNON POTATOES NOTES: _____
_____
_____
_____
_____

Sausage Tortellini Soup

Prep: 10 min. • **Cook:** 30 min. • **Yield:** 10 servings.
Always searching for new and different soup recipes, I came across a similar one in an old church cookbook and changed a few ingredients to suit my family's tastes. Now it's one of our favorites.
—*Heather Persch, Hudsonville, Michigan*

1 pound bulk Italian sausage
2 cups water
2 cups chopped cabbage
1 can (14-1/2 ounces) Italian stewed tomatoes, undrained and cut up
1 can (14-1/2 ounces) beef broth
1 can (10-1/2 ounces) condensed French onion soup
1 package (9 ounces) refrigerated cheese tortellini
1/2 cup grated Parmesan cheese

1. In a large saucepan, cook sausage over medium heat until no longer pink; drain. Stir in the water, cabbage, tomatoes, broth and soup. Bring to a boil. Reduce heat; simmer, uncovered, for 8 minutes.

2. Stir in tortellini; cook 7-9 minutes longer or until pasta is tender. Sprinkle with cheese.

Nutrition Facts: 1 cup equals 199 calories, 10 g fat (4 g saturated fat), 34 mg cholesterol, 912 mg sodium, 17 g carbohydrate, 2 g fiber, 11 g protein.

SAUSAGE TORTELLINI SOUP NOTES:
_____
_____
_____
_____

Grilled Cabbage

Prep/Total Time: 30 min. • **Yield:** 8 servings.
I didn't really like cabbage, but when I fixed this recipe I couldn't believe how good it was. We threw some burgers on the grill and our dinner was complete. Now it's a regular whenever we're grilling out.
—*Elizabeth Wheeler, Thornville, Ohio*

1 medium head cabbage (about 1-1/2 pounds)
1/3 cup butter, softened
1/4 cup chopped onion
1/2 teaspoon garlic salt
1/4 teaspoon pepper

1. Cut cabbage into eight wedges; place on a double thickness of heavy-duty foil (about 24 in. x 12 in.). Spread cut sides with butter. Sprinkle with onion, garlic salt and pepper.

2. Fold foil around cabbage and seal tightly. Grill, covered, over medium heat for 20 minutes or until tender. Open foil carefully to allow steam to escape.

Nutrition Facts: 1 wedge equals 98 calories, 8 g fat (5 g saturated fat), 20 mg cholesterol, 188 mg sodium, 7 g carbohydrate, 3 g fiber, 2 g protein.
Diabetic Exchanges: 1-1/2 fat, 1 vegetable.

GRILLED CABBAGE NOTES:
_____
_____
_____
_____

CARROTS

Chilled Squash and Carrot Soup

Prep: 30 min. + chilling • **Yield:** 4 servings.
This smooth soup is colorful as well as nutritious and filling. Served chilled, it makes an elegant first course when entertaining. It's also good served warm.
—*Elaine Sabacky, Litchfield, Minnesota*

1-1/2	pounds butternut squash, peeled, seeded and cubed (about 3 cups)
1	can (14-1/2 ounces) chicken *or* vegetable broth
2	medium carrots, sliced
1	medium onion, chopped
1/4	teaspoon salt
1/2	cup fat-free evaporated milk
3	tablespoons reduced-fat sour cream

1. In a large saucepan, combine the squash, broth, carrots, onion and salt. Bring to a boil. Reduce heat; cover and simmer for 15-20 minutes or until vegetables are very tender. Remove from the heat; cool.

2. In a blender or food processor, puree squash mixture in batches. Transfer to a bowl, stir in milk. Cover and chill until serving. Garnish with sour cream.

Nutrition Facts: 1-1/4 cup equals 127 calories, 1 g fat (1 g saturated fat), 5 mg cholesterol, 637 mg sodium, 25 g carbohydrate, 5 g fiber, 6 g protein. **Diabetic Exchanges:** 2 vegetable, 1 starch.

Good for the eyes and the skin, carrots boast a hefty dose of vitamin A and more beta carotene than any other veggie. But we're pretty sure it's that satisfying crunch that makes carrots a garden favorite among rabbits and people alike.

SEASON: Year round; harvested mid to late summer.

AT THE MARKET: Select crisp, firm, smooth, well-shaped carrots with deep orange color.

STORAGE: Trim tops and roots when present. Refrigerate unwashed, unpeeled carrots in a sealed plastic bag for 1 to 2 weeks.

```
CHILLED SQUASH AND CARROT SOUP
NOTES:_____
    _____
    _____
    _____
```

Whipped Carrots with Cranberries

Prep/Total Time: 30 min. • **Yield:** 4 servings.
The buttery texture and sweetness of cranberries and brown sugar make this a great addition to Thanksgiving turkey.
—*Margie Haen, Menomonee Falls, Wisconsin*

1	pound sliced fresh carrots	1/2	teaspoon ground ginger
3	tablespoons butter	1/4	teaspoon salt
1	tablespoon brown sugar	1/4	cup dried cranberries

1. Place 2 in. of water in a small saucepan; add carrots. Bring to a boil. Reduce heat; cover and simmer for 15-20 minutes or until tender. Drain.

2. Place carrots in a food processor; add the butter, brown sugar, ginger and salt. Cover and process until smooth. Transfer to a serving bowl; stir in cranberries.

Nutrition Facts: 1/3 cup equals 158 calories, 9 g fat (5 g saturated fat), 23 mg cholesterol, 288 mg sodium, 21 g carbohydrate, 4 g fiber, 1 g protein.

WHIPPED CARROTS WITH CRANBERRIES
NOTES:_____
_____
_____
_____

Cream Cheese Carrot Muffins

Prep: 25 min. • **Bake:** 20 min. • **Yield:** 1 dozen.
I revised a pumpkin bread recipe to make these delicious spiced muffins. Pureed canned carrots and a cream cheese filling make them so moist.
—*Francy Schneidecker, Tillamook, Oregon*

1-3/4	cups fresh sliced carrots, cooked	1	egg
1-3/4	cups all-purpose flour	1/3	cup canola oil
1	cup sugar		FILLING:
1-1/4	teaspoons baking soda	1	package (8 ounces) cream cheese, softened
1/2	teaspoon salt		
1/2	teaspoon ground cinnamon	1	egg
1/8	teaspoon *each* ground allspice, cloves and nutmeg	1/4	cup sugar

1. Place carrots in a food processor; cover and process until smooth. In a large bowl, combine the flour, sugar, baking soda, salt and spices. In a small bowl, whisk the pureed carrots, egg and oil; stir into the dry ingredients just until moistened.

2. Fill 12 greased muffin cups one-third full. In a small bowl, beat the filling ingredients until smooth. Drop by tablespoonfuls into the center of each muffin. Top with remaining batter.

3. Bake at 350° for 20-25 minutes or until a toothpick inserted near center comes out clean. Cool for 5 minutes before removing from pan to a wire rack. Serve warm. Refrigerate leftovers.

Nutrition Facts: 1 muffin equals 288 calories, 14 g fat (5 g saturated fat), 56 mg cholesterol, 370 mg sodium, 37 g carbohydrate, 1 g fiber, 5 g protein.

CREAM CHEESE CARROT MUFFINS
NOTES:_____
_____
_____

Gingered Orange Carrots

Prep/Total Time: 25 min. • **Yield:** 6 servings.
This attractive side dish looks lovely served alongside poultry, pork or beef. Every time my guests taste the deliciously spiced carrots, they ask for the recipe.
—*Laurie Hicks, Troy, Montana*

8 medium carrots, cut into 1/4-inch slices
2 medium onions, halved and thinly sliced
1/4 teaspoon ground ginger
2 tablespoons butter
1/4 cup orange juice
1/4 cup red currant jelly
1/4 teaspoon salt
1 tablespoon minced fresh parsley

1. In a large skillet, saute the carrots, onions and ginger in butter for 8-10 minutes or until crisp-tender.

2. Add the orange juice, jelly and salt. Cook and stir for 2-3 minutes or until sauce is slightly thickened. Sprinkle with parsley. Serve with a slotted spoon.

Nutrition Facts: 2/3 cup equals 125 calories, 4 g fat (2 g saturated fat), 10 mg cholesterol, 183 mg sodium, 22 g carbohydrate, 3 g fiber, 2 g protein. **Diabetic Exchanges:** 2 vegetable, 1 fat, 1/2 starch.

GINGERED ORANGE CARROTS NOTES:

Carrot Oatmeal Cookies

Prep: 30 min. + chilling • **Bake:** 10 min./batch • **Yield:** 6 dozen.
Cookies made from carrots? You bet! These carrot-flecked cookies my mom made when I was younger now get a thumbs-up from my kids.
—*Candace Zaugg, Eagar, Arizona*

1 cup butter, softened
1 cup shortening
1-1/2 cups sugar
1-1/2 cups packed brown sugar
4 eggs
2 teaspoons vanilla extract
2 cups shredded carrots
4 cups quick-cooking oats
3-1/2 cups all-purpose flour
2 teaspoons baking soda
2 teaspoons salt
1 cup chopped walnuts
1 cup miniature semisweet chocolate chips

1. In a large bowl, cream the butter, shortening and sugars until light and fluffy. Beat in eggs and vanilla. Beat in carrots. Combine the oats, flour, baking soda and salt; gradually add to creamed mixture and mix well. Stir in walnuts and chocolate chips. Cover and refrigerate for at least 4 hours.

2. Drop by rounded tablespoonfuls 3 in. apart onto baking sheets coated with cooking spray. Bake at 375° for 10-13 minutes or until lightly browned. Cool for 2 minutes before removing to wire racks.

Nutrition Facts: 1 cookie equals 147 calories, 8 g fat (3 g saturated fat), 19 mg cholesterol, 133 mg sodium, 18 g carbohydrate, 1 g fiber, 2 g protein. **Diabetic Exchanges:** 1-1/2 fat, 1 starch.

CARROT OATMEAL COOKIES NOTES:

EVEN STEVEN.
When cooking fresh carrots, cut the pieces as close to the same size as possible so they cook evenly. Cutting diagonally will expose more surface and allow the carrot to cook more quickly.

Mini Carrot Cake Tortes

Prep: 50 min. • **Bake:** 25 min. + cooling
Yield: 15 mini tortes.
"How cute!" is what you'll hear from guests when they spy
these darling individual tortes. A rich cream cheese frosting
is sandwiched between layers of moist cake.
—*Beatriz Marciano, Rockville, Maryland*

2 English Breakfast *or* other black tea bags
1 cup boiling water
1-1/2 cups sugar
1 cup canola oil
4 eggs
1/2 cup honey
1 tablespoon maple syrup
2 teaspoons vanilla extract
3 cups all-purpose flour
2 teaspoons ground cinnamon
1 teaspoon baking powder
1 teaspoon baking soda
1/4 teaspoon ground cloves
2 cups shredded carrots
1 cup chopped walnuts
1 cup raisins
FROSTING:
1 package (8 ounces) cream cheese, softened
1/2 cup butter, softened
1 teaspoon vanilla extract
3-3/4 cups confectioners' sugar
Toasted chopped walnuts, optional

MINI CARROT CAKE TORTES NOTES:

1. Place tea bags in a small bowl; add boiling water. Cover and steep for 3-5 minutes. Discard tea bags; set tea aside. Line a 15-in. x 10-in. x 1-in. baking pan with parchment paper and coat the paper with cooking spray; set aside.

2. In a large bowl, beat the sugar, oil, eggs, tea, honey, syrup and vanilla until well blended. Combine the flour, cinnamon, baking powder, baking soda and cloves; gradually beat into sugar mixture until blended. Stir in carrots, nuts and raisins. Transfer to prepared pan (pan will be full).

3. Bake at 350° for 25-30 minutes or until a toothpick inserted near the center comes out clean. Cool in pan on a wire rack; remove from pan and discard paper.

4. For frosting, in a large bowl, beat cream cheese and butter until light and fluffy. Beat in vanilla. Gradually beat in confectioners' sugar until smooth.

5. Using a metal 3-in. round cutter, cut 15 circles from cake. Cut each circle in half horizontally; place the cake bottoms on a parchment paper-lined baking sheet. Pipe frosting over each. Top with the remaining cake layers and frosting; sprinkle with walnuts if desired. Store tortes in the refrigerator.

Nutrition Facts: 1 torte (calculated without toasted nuts) equals 565 calories, 27 g fat (9 g saturated fat), 73 mg cholesterol, 183 mg sodium, 80 g carbohydrate, 2 g fiber, 6 g protein.

Vegetable Ribbons

Prep/Total Time: 15 min. • **Yield:** 4 servings.
Simple elegance best describes this fresh-tasting farm dish.
It's a great use of the late summer harvest.
—*Patty Singstock, Racine, Wisconsin*

- 3 medium carrots, peeled
- 2 medium zucchini
- 2 tablespoons butter
- 3/4 cup reduced-sodium chicken broth
- 2 tablespoons minced fresh parsley, *divided*

1. Using a vegetable peeler, cut the vegetables lengthwise into very thin strips.

2. In a large skillet over medium heat, melt butter. Add broth. Bring to a boil; cook until liquid is reduced to 1/3 cup. Add the vegetable strips and 1 tablespoon parsley; cook and stir for 2 minutes or just until crisp-tender. Sprinkle with remaining parsley. Serve with a slotted spoon.

Nutrition Facts: 3/4 cup equals 88 calories, 6 g fat (4 g saturated fat), 15 mg cholesterol, 190 mg sodium, 8 g carbohydrate, 2 g fiber, 2 g protein.
Diabetic Exchanges: 1 vegetable, 1 fat.

VEGETABLE RIBBONS NOTES: _____
_____
_____
_____
_____

Marmalade Candied Carrots

Prep/Total Time: 30 min. • **Yield:** 8 servings.
Orange marmalade lends a citrusy sweet flavor to crisp-tender carrots.
People say it really dresses up this classic veggie.
—*Heather Clemmons, Supply, North Carolina*

- 2 pounds fresh baby carrots
- 2/3 cup orange marmalade
- 3 tablespoons packed brown sugar
- 2 tablespoons butter
- 1/2 cup chopped pecans, toasted
- 1 teaspoon rum extract

1. Place carrots in a steamer basket; place in a large saucepan over 1 in. of water. Bring to a boil; cover and steam for 12-15 minutes or until crisp-tender.

2. Meanwhile, in a small saucepan, combine the marmalade, brown sugar and butter; cook and stir over medium heat until mixture is thickened and reduced to about 1/2 cup. Stir in pecans and extract.

3. Place carrots in a large bowl; drizzle with glaze and stir gently to coat.

Nutrition Facts: 3/4 cup equals 211 calories, 8 g fat (2 g saturated fat), 8 mg cholesterol, 115 mg sodium, 35 g carbohydrate, 4 g fiber, 2 g protein.

MARMALADE CANDIED CARROTS NOTES:
_____
_____
_____

Gingered Carrots & Parsnips

Prep/Total Time: 30 min. • **Yield:** 3 servings.
Ginger adds a marvelous taste to these root vegetables.
The flavorful side will be a hit on any buffet table.
—Marie Rizzio, Interlochen, Michigan

3 medium parsnips, peeled and sliced

4 medium carrots, peeled and sliced

2 tablespoons honey

1 teaspoon butter

1/2 teaspoon ground ginger

Dash salt

2 tablespoons chopped pecans, toasted

1. Place 1 in. of water in a small saucepan; add parsnips. Bring to a boil. Reduce heat; cover and simmer for 1 minute. Stir in carrots; cover and simmer 6-8 minutes longer or until vegetables are crisp-tender. Drain and set aside.

2. In same pan, combine the honey, butter, ginger and salt. Stir in vegetables; heat through. Sprinkle with pecans.

Nutrition Facts: 3/4 cup equals 173 calories, 5 g fat (1 g saturated fat), 3 mg cholesterol, 121 mg sodium, 32 g carbohydrate, 6 g fiber, 2 g protein. **Diabetic Exchanges:** 1-1/2 starch, 1 vegetable, 1 fat.

GINGERED CARROTS & PARSNIPS
NOTES:_____
_____
_____
_____
_____

Carrot Sausage Stew

Prep/Total Time: 30 min. • **Yield:** 2 servings.
Here's a delicious stew that gets special flavor from turnips and sausage. Serve it alongside slices of crusty bread—perfect for mopping up any remaining broth!
—Carma Blosser, Livermore, Colorado

1/2 pound bulk pork sausage

2 medium potatoes, peeled and cubed

2 medium carrots, sliced lengthwise and cut into 2-inch pieces

1 medium turnip, peeled and cubed

1/2 medium onion, chopped

3-1/2 cups water

1/4 teaspoon salt

1/8 teaspoon pepper

1 cup stewed tomatoes

1. In a large saucepan, cook sausage over medium heat until no longer pink; drain. Add the potatoes, carrots, turnip, onion, water, salt and pepper. Bring to a boil. Reduce heat; cover and simmer for 15-20 minutes or until vegetables are tender. Stir in tomatoes; heat through.

Nutrition Facts: 1-3/4 cup equals 445 calories, 21 g fat (8 g saturated fat), 41 mg cholesterol, 1,069 mg sodium, 53 g carbohydrate, 7 g fiber, 13 g protein.

CARROT SAUSAGE STEW NOTES: _____
_____
_____
_____
_____

Honey Mustard Carrots

Prep/Total Time: 20 min. • **Yield:** 10 servings.
A homemade honey mustard dressing makes fresh carrots shine.
—*Trisha Kruse, Eagle, Idaho*

4 packages (10 ounces *each*) julienned carrots	1/4 cup honey mustard
1/2 cup honey	4 teaspoons butter
	1/2 teaspoon salt

1. Place 1 in. of water in a large saucepan; add carrots. Bring to a boil. Reduce heat; cover and simmer for 3-4 minutes or until crisp-tender. Drain and set aside.

2. In a small saucepan, combine the remaining ingredients. Bring to a boil; cook and stir for 2-3 minutes or until slightly thickened. Pour over carrots; heat through.

Nutrition Facts: 1/2 cup equals 125 calories, 2 g fat (1 g saturated fat), 4 mg cholesterol, 259 mg sodium, 28 g carbohydrate, 3 g fiber, 1 g protein.
Diabetic Exchanges: 2 vegetable, 1 starch, 1/2 fat.

HONEY MUSTARD CARROTS TIP:
To julienne carrots, slice four sides of a clean, peeled carrot to create a rectangle. Cut the rectangle lengthwise into 1/8-in. slices. Then stack the 1/8-in. slices and cut them into 1/8-inch strips. —Taste of Home

CARROT BRAN MUFFINS NOTES:

Carrot Bran Muffins

Prep: 20 min. • **Bake:** 25 min. • **Yield:** 1 dozen.
With their golden brown tops, pretty flecks of orange and bursts of raisin sweetness, these bran muffins are anything but ordinary!
—*Taste of Home Test Kitchen*

1-1/2 cups all-purpose flour	1/2 teaspoon baking soda
1 cup wheat bran	1/2 teaspoon salt
1/2 cup packed brown sugar	2 eggs
1 1/2 teaspoons ground cinnamon	3/4 cup buttermilk
1-1/4 teaspoons baking powder	1/2 cup canola oil
	2 tablespoons molasses
	1-1/2 cups grated carrots
	1 cup raisins

1. In a large bowl, combine the first seven ingredients. Combine the eggs, buttermilk, oil and molasses; stir into dry ingredients just until moistened. Fold in carrots and raisins.

2. Fill greased or paper-lined muffin cups three-fourths full. Bake at 350° for 25-30 minutes or until a toothpick inserted near the center comes out clean. Cool for 5 minutes before removing from pan to a wire rack. Serve warm.

Nutrition Facts: 1 serving (1 each) equals 252 calories, 10 g fat (2 g saturated fat), 36 mg cholesterol, 231 mg sodium, 38 g carbohydrate, 3 g fiber, 5 g protein.

CRANBERRIES

It wouldn't be Thanksgiving without cranberries. But don't reserve the tart, scarlet berries for just the holidays. Let them mingle with other fruits and dress them up in pies, appetizers and sides.

SEASON: October-December.

AT THE MARKET: Select berries that are plump; avoid those that are bruised, mushy or moldy.

STORAGE: Sort and discard any crushed, mushy or moldy fruit. Refrigerate berries in a sealed bag for up to 2 months. To freeze, place fresh cranberries on a cookie sheet and put them in the freezer until frozen (about an hour and a half). Then place in freezer bags.

Cranberry-Cherry Nut Pie

Prep: 20 min. • **Bake:** 40 min. + cooling • **Yield:** 8 servings.
This delightful, stress-free pie using a basic pie crust pastry combines cranberries with convenient cherry pie filling for a fresh, fun flavor.
—*Taste of Home Test Kitchen*

Pastry for double-crust pie (9 inches)
- 1 can (21 ounces) cherry pie filling
- 2 cups fresh *or* frozen cranberries, thawed
- 3/4 cup sugar
- 1/2 cup chopped walnuts
- 2 tablespoons cornstarch
- 1 teaspoon vanilla extract
- 1/2 teaspoon ground cinnamon
- 1/8 teaspoon ground allspice
- 2 tablespoons butter
- 1 teaspoon 2% milk
- 1 tablespoon coarse sugar

1. Line a 9-in. pie plate with the bottom pastry; trim to 1 in. beyond edge of plate. In a large bowl, combine the pie filling, cranberries, sugar, walnuts, cornstarch, vanilla, cinnamon and allspice. Spoon into crust. Dot with butter.

2. Roll out remaining pastry to fit top of pie. Cut vents using decorative cookie cutters. Place pastry over filling; trim, seal and flute edges. Brush with milk; sprinkle with coarse sugar.

3. Bake at 375° for 40-45 minutes or until crust is golden brown and filling is bubbly. Cover edges with foil during the last 30 minutes to prevent overbrowning if necessary. Cool on a wire rack.

Nutrition Facts: 1 piece equals 498 calories, 22 g fat (8 g saturated fat), 18 mg cholesterol, 235 mg sodium, 73 g carbohydrate, 2 g fiber, 4 g protein.

CRANBERRY-CHERRY NUT PIE NOTES:

Maple-Honey Cranberry Sauce

Prep/Total Time: 25 min. • **Yield:** 2 cups.
This recipe is simple, quick and a family favorite. I'll often make a double batch for us to use on meats, spread on toast or even garnish desserts.
—*Rebecca Israel, Mansfield, Pennsylvania*

2 cups fresh *or* frozen cranberries
1/2 cup maple syrup
1/2 cup honey
1 tablespoon grated orange peel

1. In a large saucepan, combine the cranberries, syrup, honey and orange peel. Cook over medium heat until the berries pop, about 15 minutes. Cover and store in the refrigerator.

Nutrition Facts: 2 tablespoons equals 64 calories, trace fat (trace saturated fat), 0 cholesterol, 2 mg sodium, 17 g carbohydrate, 1 g fiber, trace protein. **Diabetic Exchange:** 1 starch.

MAPLE-HONEY CRANBERRY SAUCE
NOTES:_____
_____
_____
_____

Cranberry Apple Tart

Prep: 15 min. • **Bake:** 35 min. • **Yield:** 12-16 servings.
You'll love the tangy sweetness of this quick but elegant-looking dessert. Pastry leaf shapes add a special touch.
—*Suzanne Strocsher, Bothell, Washington*

Pastry for double-crust pie (9 inches)
2 cups fresh *or* frozen cranberries, coarsely chopped
2 medium tart apples, peeled and coarsely chopped
1-1/4 cups packed brown sugar
2 tablespoons all-purpose flour
1/2 teaspoon ground cinnamon
1 to 2 tablespoons butter

1. On a lightly floured surface, roll half of the pastry into a 13-in. circle. Press onto the bottom and up the sides of an ungreased 11 in. fluted tart pan with removable bottom or press onto bottom and 1 in. up the sides of a 10-in. springform pan.

2. In a large bowl, combine the cranberries, apples, brown sugar, flour and cinnamon; pour into crust. Dot with butter. Cut leaf shapes from the remaining pastry. Place over filling.

3. Place tart pan on a baking sheet. Bake at 425° for 35-40 minutes or until filling is hot and bubbly and crust is golden. Cool on a wire rack. Serve warm.

Nutrition Facts: 1 piece equals 208 calories, 8 g fat (3 g saturated fat), 7 mg cholesterol, 114 mg sodium, 34 g carbohydrate, 1 g fiber, 1 g protein.

CRANBERRY APPLE TART NOTES:
_____
_____
_____
_____

Cranberry Apple Crumble

Prep: 15 min. • **Bake:** 55 min. • **Yield:** 6 servings.
When I first took this fruity dessert to my family's Thanksgiving dinner, it quickly became a tradition. Now, we'll enjoy it for breakfast, lunch, dinner and snack time!
—*Teri Roberts, Hilliard, Ohio*

- 3 cups chopped peeled apples
- 2 cups fresh *or* frozen cranberries, thawed
- 3/4 cup sugar
- 1 cup old-fashioned *or* quick-cooking oats
- 3/4 cup packed brown sugar
- 1/3 cup all-purpose flour
- 1/2 cup butter, melted
- 1/2 cup chopped pecans, optional

1. In a greased 8-in. square baking dish, combine apples and cranberries; sprinkle with sugar. In another bowl, combine the oats, brown sugar, flour and butter; sprinkle over cranberry mixture. Top with pecans if desired.

2. Bake, uncovered, at 350° for 55-60 minutes or until browned and bubbly. Serve warm.

Nutrition Facts: 1 cup equals 456 calories, 16 g fat (10 g saturated fat), 41 mg cholesterol, 166 mg sodium, 78 g carbohydrate, 4 g fiber, 3 g protein.

CRANBERRY APPLE CRUMBLE NOTES:
_____
_____
_____
_____

Cranberry Fluff

Prep: 20 min. + chilling • **Yield:** 10 servings.
This tangy pink fluff gets "crunch" from chopped apples and nuts. It's terrific as a salad or dessert, and it keeps well in the refrigerator. I serve any leftovers with sandwiches the next day.
—*Tena Huckleby, Greeneville, Tennessee*

- 4 cups fresh *or* frozen cranberries
- 3 cups miniature marshmallows
- 3/4 cup sugar
- 2 cups finely chopped apples
- 1/2 cup green grapes, quartered
- 1/2 cup chopped walnuts
- 1/4 teaspoon salt
- 1 cup heavy whipping cream, whipped

1. Place the cranberries in a food processor; cover and process until finely chopped. Transfer cranberries to a large bowl; stir in the marshmallows and sugar. Cover and refrigerate overnight.

2. Just before serving, stir in the apples, grapes, walnuts and salt. Fold in whipped cream.

Nutrition Facts: 3/4 cup equals 280 calories, 13 g fat (6 g saturated fat), 33 mg cholesterol, 77 mg sodium, 43 g carbohydrate, 5 g fiber, 2 g protein.

CRANBERRY FLUFF NOTES: _____
_____
_____
_____
_____

Zippy Cranberry Appetizer

Prep: 20 min. + chilling • **Yield:** 2-1/2 cups.
Tart cranberry flavor blends nicely with mustard and horseradish in this out-of-the-ordinary cracker spread. It's quick to fix, too.
—*Marie Hattrup, The Dalles, Oregon*

1/2 cup sugar
1/2 cup packed brown sugar
1 cup water
1 package (12 ounces) fresh *or* frozen cranberries
1 to 3 tablespoons prepared horseradish
1 tablespoon Dijon mustard
1 package (8 ounces) cream cheese, softened
Assorted crackers

1. In a large saucepan, bring sugars and water to a boil over medium heat. Stir in the cranberries; return to a boil. Cook for 10 minutes or until mixture is thickened, stirring occasionally. Cool.

2. Stir in horseradish and mustard. Transfer to a large bowl; refrigerate until chilled. Just before serving, spread cream cheese over crackers; top with cranberry mixture.

Nutrition Facts: 1/4 cup equals 178 calories, 8 g fat (5 g saturated fat), 25 mg cholesterol, 114 mg sodium, 26 g carbohydrate, 1 g fiber, 2 g protein.

ZIPPY CRANBERRY APPETIZER NOTES:
_____
_____
_____
_____
_____
_____

EGGPLANT

Eggplant Parmesan is just one of many delish dishes you can make with the oblong fruit. Bonus points: The fruits come in different colors, which make them striking when grown in your own garden.

SEASON: Peaks July-September.

AT THE MARKET: Select firm and heavy eggplant that has a uniformly smooth color and glossy, taut skin. It should be free from blemishes and rust spots with intact green caps and mold-free stems.

STORAGE: Refrigerate unwashed in an open plastic bag for up to 3 days.

Rustic Roasted Vegetable Tart

Prep: 45 min. • **Bake:** 20 min. • **Yield:** 8 servings.
No one will miss the meat in this appealing tart. The flaky, rustic-style crust holds an assortment of flavorful veggies simply seasoned with garlic and olive oil.
—*Marie Rizzio, Interlochen, Michigan*

- 1 small eggplant, cut into 1-inch pieces
- 1 large zucchini, cut into 1/4-inch slices
- 4 plum tomatoes, chopped
- 1 medium sweet red pepper, cut into 1-inch pieces
- 4 tablespoons olive oil, *divided*
- 4 garlic cloves, minced
- 1/2 teaspoon salt
- 1/8 teaspoon pepper
- 1 sheet refrigerated pie pastry
- 1 tablespoon cornmeal
- 2 tablespoons shredded Parmesan cheese

Minced fresh basil, optional

1. In a large bowl, combine the vegetables, 3 tablespoons oil, garlic, salt and pepper. Transfer to an ungreased 15-in. x 10-in. x 1-in. baking pan. Bake at 450° for 25-30 minutes or until vegetables are tender and moisture has evaporated, stirring every 10 minutes.

2. On a lightly floured surface, roll pastry into a 13-in. circle. Sprinkle cornmeal over a greased 14-in. pizza pan; place pastry on prepared pan. Spoon vegetable mixture over pastry to within 1-1/2 in. of edges. Fold up edges of pastry over filling, leaving center uncovered. Brush pastry with remaining oil.

3. Bake at 450° for 20-25 minutes or until crust is golden brown. Sprinkle with cheese. Cut into wedges. Garnish with basil if desired.

Nutrition Facts: 1 wedge equals 219 calories, 14 g fat (4 g saturated fat), 6 mg cholesterol, 277 mg sodium, 21 g carbohydrate, 2 g fiber, 3 g protein.

RUSTIC ROASTED VEGETABLE TART
NOTES:_____
_____
_____
_____
_____

Spicy Grilled Eggplant

Prep/Total Time: 20 min. • **Yield:** 10 servings.
This versatile recipe goes well with grilled meats or sliced up and tossed with pasta. Thanks to the Cajun seasoning, it gets more attention than an ordinary side dish.
—*Greg Fontenot, The Woodlands, Texas*

2 small eggplants, cut into 1/2-inch slices	2 tablespoons lime juice
1/4 cup olive oil	1 tablespoon Cajun seasoning

1. Brush the eggplant slices with oil on both sides. Drizzle with the lime juice; sprinkle with the Cajun seasoning. Let stand for 5 minutes.

2. Grill eggplant, covered, over medium heat or broil 4 in. from the heat for 4-5 minutes on each side or until tender.

Nutrition Facts: 2 each equals 70 calories, 6 g fat (1 g saturated fat), 0 cholesterol, 164 mg sodium, 5 g carbohydrate, 3 g fiber, 1 g protein.
Diabetic Exchanges: 1 vegetable, 1 fat.

SPICY GRILLED EGGPLANT NOTES:

Grilled Eggplant Pepper Sandwiches

Prep: 50 min. • **Grill:** 15 min. • **Yield:** 4 servings.
I love eggplant! These savory, filling sandwiches give the vegetable new meaning. One bite, and you're hooked.
—*Paula Marchesi, Lenhartsville, Pennsylvania*

1/2 cup pitted ripe olives	1 teaspoon pepper
2 to 3 tablespoons balsamic vinegar	1/2 teaspoon salt
1 garlic clove, minced	1 large eggplant, cut lengthwise into 1/2-inch slices
1/8 teaspoon salt	2 large sweet red peppers, quartered
Dash pepper	8 slices firm white bread (1/2 inch thick)
1/4 cup olive oil	1/4 cup fresh basil leaves, thinly sliced
SANDWICHES:	
1/4 cup olive oil	
3 garlic cloves, minced	

1. Place the first five ingredients in a food processor; cover and process until pureed. While processing, gradually add oil in a steady stream; process until blended. Set aside.

2. For sandwiches, in a small bowl, combine the oil, garlic, pepper and salt; brush over eggplant and red peppers. Prepare grill for indirect heat, using a drip pan. Arrange vegetables on a grilling grid; place on a grill rack over drip pan.

3. Grill, covered, over indirect medium heat for 10-12 minutes or until tender. Remove and keep warm. Grill bread over medium heat for 1-2 minutes on each side or until toasted.

4. Spread olive mixture over toast. Top four slices with vegetables and basil; top with remaining toast.

Nutrition Facts: 1 sandwich equals 463 calories, 31 g fat (4 g saturated fat), 0 cholesterol, 844 mg sodium, 44 g carbohydrate, 8 g fiber, 7 g protein.

EDITOR'S NOTE: If you do not have a grilling grid, use a disposable foil pan. Poke holes in the bottom of the pan with a meat fork to allow liquid to drain.

GRILLED EGGPLANT PEPPER SANDWICHES NOTES:

Eggplant au Gratin

Prep: 20 min. + cooling • **Bake:** 20 min. • **Yield:** 2 servings.
A delicious late summer meal, this tasty bake features layers
of sliced eggplant topped with spaghetti sauce
and two kinds of cheese.
—*Jane Shapton, Irvine, California*

1 small eggplant
(about 1/2 pound) ,
peeled and cut into
1/4-inch slices
1 tablespoon olive oil
3/4 cup spaghetti sauce

3/4 cup shredded
part-skim
mozzarella cheese
2 tablespoons
shredded Parmesan
cheese

1. Brush both sides of eggplant slices with oil. Place on an ungreased baking sheet. Bake at 400° for 8 minutes. Turn and bake 7-8 minutes longer or until lightly browned and tender. Cool on a wire rack.

2. Place one eggplant slice in each of two 10-oz. ramekins coated with cooking spray. Top each with 2 tablespoons spaghetti sauce and 2 tablespoons mozzarella cheese. Repeat layers twice. Sprinkle with Parmesan cheese. Bake, uncovered, at 350° for 20-25 minutes or until bubbly and cheese is melted.

Nutrition Facts: 3/4 cup equals 287 calories, 18 g fat (7 g saturated fat), 30 mg cholesterol, 750 mg sodium, 16 g carbohydrate, 4 g fiber, 15 g protein.

EGGPLANT AU GRATIN NOTES:

Open-Faced Veggie Sandwiches

Prep: 25 min. • **Bake:** 20 min. • **Yield:** 4 servings.
Make the most of your garden's veggies with this summery sandwich! I jazz up the hearty, fresh-tasting bite with a tasty dressing and Muenster cheese.
—*Virginia Lawson, Cortez, Colorado*

2 tablespoons olive oil
3 garlic cloves, minced
1/2 teaspoon salt
1/2 teaspoon dried oregano
1/2 teaspoon dried basil
1 medium eggplant, thinly sliced
2 medium zucchini, halved and sliced
1 large onion, sliced
1 medium sweet red pepper, sliced
1 medium green pepper, sliced
1/4 cup mayonnaise
2 tablespoons balsamic vinegar
1 teaspoon Dijon mustard
4 slices Italian bread (1/2 inch thick), toasted
1 medium tomato, thinly sliced
4 slices Muenster cheese

1. In a large bowl, combine the oil, garlic, salt, oregano and basil. Add vegetables and toss to coat. Transfer to two 15-in. x 10-in. x 1-in. baking pans.

2. Bake, uncovered, at 425° for 15-20 minutes or until lightly browned, stirring occasionally.

3. Combine the mayonnaise, vinegar and mustard; spread over toast. Place on a baking sheet. Top with vegetable mixture, tomato and cheese. Broil 6-8 in. from the heat for 2-3 minutes or until cheese is melted.

Nutrition Facts: 1 sandwich equals 390 calories, 25 g fat (7 g saturated fat), 25 mg cholesterol, 688 mg sodium, 32 g carbohydrate, 8 g fiber, 11 g protein.

OPEN-FACED VEGGIE SANDWICHES
NOTES:

VEGGIE EXPERIMENTS.
Thomas Jefferson, who experimented with many varieties of plants in his Virginia garden, is credited with introducing eggplant to North America. To enhance its flavor, try pairing it with allspice, basil, garlic, oregano, sage or thyme.

HONEY

Nature's sweetest gift, honey has good reason to be nicknamed "liquid gold." Not only is it delicious in tea and spread on toast, honey is a natural energy source, promotes a robust immune system and acts as a natural health remedy.

SEASON: Honey is generally harvested in late summer to early fall but is available year-round.

AT THE MARKET: Honey's color ranges from almost clear to dark brown. In general, the darker the honey, the stronger the flavor. Honey is sold in many forms. Liquid or strained honey tends to be the most popular form, but you'll also find comb honey—honey still in the comb, cut into chunks—creamed honey and chunk honey, a combination of liquid and comb honey.

STORAGE: Store in a tightly covered container in a cool location away from direct sunlight. Honey has an indefinite shelf life.

Honey Lemon Muffins

Prep/Total Time: 30 min. • **Yield:** 10 muffins.

Honey's subtle sweetness comes through in every bite of these moist little muffins, providing the perfect counterpoint to the bright tartness of lemon.
—*Rachel Hart, Wildomar, California*

- 1 cup all-purpose flour
- 1/2 cup whole wheat flour
- 1 teaspoon baking powder
- 1/4 teaspoon baking soda
- 1/4 teaspoon salt
- 1 egg
- 1/2 cup honey
- 1/4 cup lemon juice
- 1/4 cup butter, melted
- 1/2 teaspoon grated lemon peel

DRIZZLE:
- 1/4 cup confectioners' sugar
- 1 teaspoon lemon juice

Additional grated lemon peel

1. In a large bowl, combine the flours, baking powder, baking soda and salt. In another bowl, combine the egg, honey, lemon juice, butter and lemon peel. Stir into dry ingredients just until moistened.

2. Coat muffin cups with cooking spray or use paper liners; fill one-half full with batter.

3. Bake at 375° for 15-18 minutes or until a toothpick inserted near the center comes out clean. Cool for 5 minutes before removing from pan to a wire rack.

4. In a small bowl, combine confectioners' sugar and lemon juice; drizzle over warm muffins. Sprinkle with additional lemon peel.

Nutrition Facts: 1 muffin equals 178 calories, 5 g fat (3 g saturated fat), 33 mg cholesterol, 171 mg sodium, 31 g carbohydrate, 1 g fiber, 3 g protein. **Diabetic Exchanges:** 2 starch, 1 fat.

HONEY LEMON MUFFINS NOTES: _____

Lemon Quencher

Prep: 15 min. + chilling • **Yield:** 8 servings.
Tart and refreshing, this minty lemon drink is sweetened with just a touch of honey. It makes a lovely summer cooler any time of day.
—*Clara Coulston, Washington Court House, Ohio*

5 cups water, *divided*	2 teaspoons grated lemon peel
10 fresh mint leaves	Ice cubes
1 cup lemon juice	Mint sprigs and lemon peel strips, optional
2/3 cup honey	

1. In a blender, combine 1 cup water and mint leaves; cover and process for 1 minute. Strain mixture into a pitcher, discarding mint. Add the lemon juice, honey, lemon peel and remaining water; stir until blended. Cover and refrigerate for at least 2 hours.

2. Serve in chilled glasses over ice. Garnish with mint sprigs and lemon peel if desired.

Nutrition Facts: 3/4 cup equals 96 calories, trace fat (trace saturated fat), 0 cholesterol, 2 mg sodium, 27 g carbohydrate, trace fiber, trace protein. **Diabetic Exchange:** 2 starch.

LEMON QUENCHER NOTES: _____
_____
_____
_____
_____

Honey Baked Apples

Prep: 10 min. • **Bake:** 45 min. • **Yield:** 2 servings.
My baked apple recipe is very old-fashioned but tried and true. It's definitely a comfort food.
—*Rachel Hamilton, Greenville, Pennsylvania*

2 medium tart apples	1/4 cup packed brown sugar
1/4 cup dried cranberries	1 tablespoon honey
2/3 cup water	
Vanilla ice cream	

1. Core apples, leaving bottoms intact. Peel the top third of each apple; place in a greased 8-in. x 4-in. glass loaf pan. Fill each with cranberries.

2. In a small saucepan, combine the water, brown sugar and honey; cook and stir over medium heat until sugar is dissolved. Pour over apples.

3. Bake, uncovered, at 350° for 45-55 minutes or until tender, basting occasionally with pan juices. Serve with ice cream.

Nutrition Facts: 1 each equals 253 calories, trace fat (trace saturated fat), 0 cholesterol, 13 mg sodium, 67 g carbohydrate, 4 g fiber, trace protein.

HONEY BAKED APPLES NOTES: _____
_____
_____
_____
_____

AWW...HONEY, HONEY! Did you know honey is the only food that includes all the substances necessary to sustain life—including water? It's true! Honey is 80% sugars and 20% water, and it never spoils. Over time, it may crystallize, but that's natural. To reliquify honey, simply place the jar in a container of warm water for a few minutes until smooth. —Taste of Home

Pistachio Butter

Prep/Total Time: 10 min. + chilling • **Yield:** 1-1/2 cups.
This spread is easy, elegant and yummy.
I like to scoop portions into small yet sturdy foil pans, cover them with clear plastic wrap and add a cheery ribbon before handing out as presents to family and friends.
—Marilyn Kayton, Naperville, Illinois

1 cup butter, softened
1/4 cup honey
1 tablespoon peach *or* apricot gelatin powder
1/4 cup chopped pistachios

1. In a small bowl, beat butter, honey and gelatin powder until smooth. Stir in pistachios. Transfer to small airtight containers. Cover and refrigerate for up to 1 month.

Nutrition Facts: 1 serving (1 tablespoon) equals 87 calories, 8 g fat (5 g saturated fat), 20 mg cholesterol, 84 mg sodium, 4 g carbohydrate, trace fiber, trace protein.

PISTACHIO BUTTER NOTES: _____
_____
_____
_____
_____
_____

Sweet Honey Almond Butter

Prep/Total Time: 10 min. • **Yield:** 2 cups.
Sweetened with honey, my homemade butter makes a wonderful accompaniment to fresh-from-the-oven bread.
—Evelyn Harris, Waynesboro, Virginia

1 cup butter, softened
3/4 cup honey
3/4 cup confectioners' sugar
3/4 cup finely ground almonds
1/4 to 1/2 teaspoon almond extract

1. In a bowl, combine all ingredients; mix well. Store in the refrigerator.

Nutrition Facts: 1 serving (2 tablespoons) equals 197 calories, 14 g fat (7 g saturated fat), 31 mg cholesterol, 116 mg sodium, 20 g carbohydrate, 1 g fiber, 1 g protein.

SWEET HONEY ALMOND BUTTER NOTES: _____
_____
_____
_____
_____
_____

Spiced Honey Butter

Prep/Total Time: 5 min. • **Yield:** 3/4 cups.
This is such delicious butter spread for afternoon tea or with a dessert bread. It is so easy to mix together, and you'll receive many compliments.
—Mary Bates, Cleveland, Ohio

1/2 cup butter, softened
1/4 cup honey
1 teaspoon grated orange peel
1/2 teaspoon ground cinnamon

1. In a small bowl, combine all ingredients. Serve immediately. Refrigerate leftovers.

Nutrition Facts: 1 serving (1 tablespoon) equals 89 calories, 8 g fat (5 g saturated fat), 20 mg cholesterol, 77 mg sodium, 6 g carbohydrate, trace fiber, trace protein.

SPICED HONEY BUTTER NOTES: _____
_____
_____
_____
_____
_____

SWEET SIDEKICKS.
Homemade honey butters
pair wonderfully with freshly
baked muffins and breads.
This tantalizing trio features
Honey Almond Butter (top left),
Pistachio Butter (top right) and
Spiced Honey Butter (bottom).

Honey Sweet Corn

Prep/Total Time: 15 min. • **Yield:** 6 servings.
There's nothing that says summer quite like fresh sweet corn.
Honey butter makes these ears even sweeter.
—*Nancy Kreiser, Lebanon, Pennsylvania*

6 medium ears sweet corn	1 teaspoon honey
1/4 cup butter, melted	Ground pepper, optional

1. Place corn in a Dutch oven, cover with water. Bring to a boil; cover and cook for 5-10 minutes or until tender. Drain. In a small bowl, combine butter and honey; brush over corn. Sprinkle with pepper if desired.

Nutrition Facts: 1 ear of corn equals 148 calories, 9 g fat (5 g saturated fat), 20 mg cholesterol, 67 mg sodium, 18 g carbohydrate, 2 g fiber, 3 g protein.

HONEY SWEET CORN NOTES:
_____
_____
_____
_____

Salmon with Pecan-Honey Sauce

Prep/Total Time: 20 min. • **Yield:** 6 servings.
If you're looking for an easy dish to serve to company, try this elegant entree. Flaky salmon fillets are draped with a sweet pecan glaze.
—*Buffy Sias, Whitehorse, Yukon*

6 salmon fillets (6 ounces *each*)	3/4 cup butter, *divided*
1/4 teaspoon salt	1 cup coarsely chopped pecans, toasted
1/4 teaspoon pepper	1 cup honey
1/4 cup vegetable oil	

1. Sprinkle salmon with salt and pepper. In a large skillet, cook salmon in oil and 6 tablespoons butter for 10-12 minutes or until fish flakes easily with a fork.

2. Meanwhile, in a small saucepan, cook pecans and honey in remaining butter over medium-low heat for 8-10 minutes or until bubbly. Serve with salmon.

Nutrition Facts: 1 each equals 642 calories, 49 g fat (17 g saturated fat), 78 mg cholesterol, 349 mg sodium, 49 g carbohydrate, 2 g fiber, 8 g protein.

SALMON WITH PECAN-HONEY SAUCE
NOTES:_____
_____
_____
_____
_____

Honey-Balsamic Goat Cheese Dip

Prep/Total Time: 10 min. • **Yield:** 8 servings.
This is so easy and delicious, you can't stop eating it. Best of all,
you can find both the honey and the goat cheese at your
local farmers market.
—*Joni Hilton, Rocklin, California*

- 1 cup crumbled goat cheese
- 1/3 cup fat-free mayonnaise
- 2 tablespoons honey
- 1 tablespoon balsamic vinegar
- 1 medium apple, sliced
- 8 slices French bread (1/4 inch thick)

1. In a small bowl, beat the goat cheese, mayonnaise, honey and vinegar until smooth. Serve with apple and bread slices.

Nutrition Facts: 1 each equals 101 calories, 5 g fat (3 g saturated fat), 12 mg cholesterol, 189 mg sodium, 12 g carbohydrate, 1 g fiber, 4 g protein.

HONEY-BALSAMIC GOAT CHEESE DIP
NOTES:_____
_____
_____
_____
_____

Honey Oatmeal Bread

Prep: 10 min. • **Bake:** 45 min. + cooling • **Yield:** 1 loaf.
Of all the breads I make, this is my husband's favorite. The subtle
honey and oat flavor makes it perfect for toast or sandwiches...or as a
side with a hot bowl of soup.
—*Marilyn Smith, Green Bay, Wisconsin*

- 1/2 cup water (80° to 90°)
- 1 tablespoon canola oil
- 4 teaspoons honey
- 1/4 teaspoon salt
- 1/4 cup quick-cooking oats
- 1-1/4 cups bread flour
- 2-1/4 teaspoons bread machine *or* quick-rise yeast

1. In a small bread machine pan, place all ingredients in order suggested by manufacturer. Select basic bread setting.

2. Bake according to bread machine directions (check dough after 5 minutes of mixing; add 1 to 2 tablespoons of water or flour if needed).

Nutrition Facts: 2 slices equals 203 calories, 4 g fat (trace saturated fat), 0 cholesterol, 149 mg sodium, 37 g carbohydrate, 2 g fiber, 7 g protein.

HONEY OATMEAL BREAD NOTES: _____
_____
_____
_____

peaches, plums & NECTARINES

Grilled Peaches 'n' Berries

Prep/Total Time: 30 min. • **Yield:** 2 servings.

Simple ingredients of brown sugar, butter and lemon juice release the flavors of the peaches and blueberries when they are grilled in a foil pouch.

—*Sharon Bickett, Chester, South Carolina.*

2	medium ripe peaches, halved and pitted
1/2	cup fresh blueberries
1	tablespoon brown sugar
2	teaspoons lemon juice
4	teaspoons butter

1. Place two peach halves, cut side up, on each of two double thicknesses of heavy-duty foil (12 in. square). Sprinkle each with blueberries, brown sugar and lemon juice; dot with butter. Fold foil around peaches and seal tightly.

2. Grill, covered, over medium-low heat for 18-20 minutes or until tender. Open foil carefully to allow steam to escape.

Nutrition Facts: 1 serving equals 156 calories, 8 g fat (5 g saturated fat), 20 mg cholesterol, 57 mg sodium, 23 g carbohydrate, 2 g fiber, 1 g protein. **Diabetic Exchanges:** 1 fruit, 1 fat, 1/2 starch.

Sometimes called "stone fruits" for their stone-like pit that's surrounded by a fleshy interior, peaches, plums and nectarines are among summer's sweetest pleasures.

SEASON: Necatarines & peaches, May-November; Plums, June-November.

AT THE MARKET: Select plump fruit. Avoid any fruit with bruises, soft spots or cuts. Ripe fruit will give slightly when gently pressed and have a sweet aroma.

STORAGE: Refrigerate ripe fruit for 3-5 days.

GRILLED PEACHES 'N' BERRIES
NOTES:_____
_____
_____
_____
_____

Chilled Peach Soup

Prep: 10 min. + chilling • **Yield:** 2 servings.
Welcome in summer with the fresh, creamy taste of this chilled soup. Top with toasted almonds to enjoy a crunchy kick with your light, tasty soup.
—Lane McLoud, Siloam Springs, Arkansas

1-1/2	cups chopped peeled fresh peaches	1/8	teaspoon almond extract
1/2	cup plain yogurt	2	tablespoons sliced almonds, toasted
1/2	teaspoon lemon juice		

1. In a blender, combine the peaches, yogurt, lemon juice and extract; cover and process until smooth. Refrigerate until chilled. Sprinkle with almonds just before serving.

Nutrition Facts: 3/4 cup equals 123 calories, 5 g fat (2 g saturated fat), 8 mg cholesterol, 28 mg sodium, 16 g carbohydrate, 3 g fiber, 5 g protein.
Diabetic Exchanges: 1 fruit, 1 fat.

CHILLED PEACH SOUP NOTES:

_____
_____
_____
_____

Ginger Plum Tart

Prep: 15 min. • **Bake:** 20 min. + cooling • **Yield:** 8 servings.
Looking for a quick and easy dessert that's pretty as a picture? Try this mouthwatering tart. For an extra-special effect, crown it with a scoop of low-fat ice cream, yogurt or a dollop of reduced-fat whipped topping.
—Taste of Home Test Kitchen

	Pastry for single-crust pie (9 inches)	1	tablespoon cornstarch
3-1/2	cups sliced unpeeled fresh plums	2	teaspoons finely chopped crystallized ginger
3	tablespoons plus 1 teaspoon coarse sugar, *divided*	1	egg white
		1	tablespoon water

1. Roll pastry into a 12-in. circle. Transfer to a large baking sheet lined with parchment paper. In a large bowl, combine plums, 3 tablespoons sugar and cornstarch. Arrange plums in a pinwheel pattern over pastry to within 2 in. of edges; sprinkle with ginger. Fold edges of pastry over plums.

2. Beat egg white and water; brush over pastry. Sprinkle with remaining sugar. Bake at 400° for 20-25 minutes or until crust is lightly browned. Cool for 15 minutes before removing from pan to a serving platter.

Nutrition Facts: 1 piece equals 190 calories, 7 g fat (3 g saturated fat), 5 mg cholesterol, 108 mg sodium, 30 g carbohydrate, 1 g fiber, 2 g protein.
Diabetic Exchanges: 1-1/2 starch, 1 fat, 1/2 fruit.

GINGER PLUM TART NOTES: _____

_____
_____
_____
_____

Fruit Bruschetta

Prep/Total Time: 20 min. • **Yield:** 32 servings.
This fantastic fruit bruschetta is a tasty twist from the traditional tomato variety and can be served as an appetizer or a dessert.
—*Taste of Home Test Kitchen*

- 1 French bread baguette (1 pound)
- 2 tablespoons olive oil
- 1-1/2 cups chopped fresh strawberries
- 3/4 cup chopped peeled fresh peaches
- 1-1/2 teaspoons minced fresh mint
- 1/2 cup Mascarpone cheese

1. Cut baguette into 32 slices, about 1/2 in. thick; place on ungreased baking sheets. Brush with oil. Broil 6-8 in. from the heat for 1-2 minutes or until lightly toasted.

2. In a small bowl, combine the strawberries, peaches and mint. Spread each slice of bread with cheese; top with fruit mixture. Broil for 1-2 minutes or until cheese is slightly melted. Serve immediately.

Nutrition Facts: 2 slices equals 154 calories, 8 g fat (4 g saturated fat), 18 mg cholesterol, 188 mg sodium, 17 g carbohydrate, 1 g fiber, 4 g protein.

FRUIT BRUSCHETTA NOTES: _____
_____
_____
_____
_____
_____

Peach-Glazed Salmon

Prep: 10 min. + marinating • **Grill:** 15 min. • **Yield:** 8 servings.
A local restaurant used fresh peaches to garnish a salmon dish, which gave me this idea for grilling the fish we catch. It's a beautiful presentation and quick to prepare.
—*Valerie Dawley Horner, Juneau, Alaska*

- 1 cup butter, cubed
- 1 cup peach preserves
- 1 tablespoon lime juice
- 1 garlic clove, minced
- 1/2 teaspoon prepared mustard
- 2 salmon fillets (1 pound *each*)
- 1/2 cup chopped peeled fresh peaches *or* frozen unsweetened sliced peaches, thawed

1. In a microwave-safe bowl, combine butter and preserves. Cover and microwave on high for 45-60 seconds. Stir in the lime juice, garlic and mustard until blended. Cool. Set aside 1 cup for basting and serving.

2. Place salmon fillets in a large resealable plastic bag; add remaining peach mixture. Seal bag and turn to coat. Marinate for 20 minutes.

3. Drain and discard marinade. Using long-handled tongs, moisten a paper towel with cooking oil and lightly coat the grill rack. Place salmon skin side down on grill rack.

4. Grill, covered, over medium heat for 5 minutes. Spoon half of reserved peach mixture over salmon. Grill 10-15 minutes longer or until fish flakes easily with a fork, basting frequently. Serve with sliced peaches and the remaining peach mixture.

Nutrition Facts: 4 ounce weight equals 360 calories, 23 g fat (12 g saturated fat), 79 mg cholesterol, 210 mg sodium, 28 g carbohydrate, trace fiber, 12 g protein.

EDITOR'S NOTE: This recipe was tested in a 1,100-watt microwave.

PEACH-GLAZED SALMON NOTES:
_____
_____
_____
_____

"A-PEELING" POINTERS.
When a recipe calls for peeled peaches, begin by placing the peaches in a large pot of boiling water for 10-20 seconds or until the skin splits. Remove with a slotted spoon. Immediately place in an ice water bath to cool the peaches and stop the cooking process. Then, use a paring knife to remove the skin, which should easily peel off.

Nectarine and Beet Salad

Prep/Total Time: 10 min. • **Yield:** 8 servings.
Nectarines paired with beets and feta cheese make a scrumptious new blend for a mixed green salad. The combination of ingredients may seem an unlikely group, but I guarantee it will become a favorite.
—*Nicole Werner, Cleveland, Ohio*

2 packages (5 ounces *each*) spring mix salad greens
2 cups sliced fresh nectarines
1 can (13-1/4 ounces) sliced beets, drained
1/2 cup balsamic vinaigrette
1/2 cup crumbled feta cheese

1. In a large salad bowl, combine the greens, nectarines and beets. Drizzle with dressing and toss gently to coat. Sprinkle with cheese.

Nutrition Facts: 1 cup equals 85 calories, 4 g fat (1 g saturated fat), 4 mg cholesterol, 293 mg sodium, 11 g carbohydrate, 2 g fiber, 3 g protein. **Diabetic Exchanges:** 2 vegetable, 1/2 fat.

NECTARINE AND BEET SALAD NOTES:
_____
_____
_____
_____

Fresh Peach Salsa

Prep/Total Time: 15 min. • **Yield:** 4 cups.
We like this fresh and fruity salsa with chips or even draped over grilled chicken or fish. Since it comes together in a food processor, it really takes almost no time to make.
—*Shawna Laufer, Ft. Myers, Florida*

4 medium peaches, peeled and pitted
2 large tomatoes, cut into wedges and seeded
1/2 sweet onion, cut into wedges
1/2 cup fresh cilantro leaves
2 garlic cloves, peeled and crushed
2 cans (4 ounces *each*) chopped green chilies
4 teaspoons cider vinegar
1 teaspoon lime juice
1/4 teaspoon pepper
Baked tortilla chip scoops

1. In a food processor, combine the first five ingredients; cover and pulse until coarsely chopped. Add the chilies, vinegar, lime juice and pepper; cover and pulse just until blended. Transfer to a serving bowl; chill until serving. Serve with chips.

Nutrition Facts: 1/4 cup (calculated without chips) equals 20 calories, trace fat (trace saturated fat), 0 cholesterol, 58 mg sodium, 5 g carbohydrate, 1 g fiber, 1 g protein. **Diabetic Exchange:** Free food.

FRESH PEACH SALSA NOTES: _____
_____
_____
_____
_____

Nectarine-Cherry Compote

Prep: 15 min. • **Bake:** 35 min. • **Yield:** 8 servings.
I sometimes use half a vanilla bean in this dessert. Just scrape the seeds into the baking dish and tuck the pod under the fruit. Either way, this fruity treat is a standout!
—Maria Breiner, Schwenksville, Pennsylvania

6 tablespoons sugar
2 tablespoons rum, optional
1 teaspoon cornstarch
1 teaspoon vanilla extract

4 medium nectarines, halved
1 pound fresh sweet cherries, pitted
Vanilla ice cream

1. In a small bowl, combine the sugar, rum if desired, cornstarch and vanilla. Transfer to a greased 13-in. x 9-in. baking dish. Place nectarine halves cut side down over sugar mixture. Sprinkle with cherries.

2. Bake, uncovered, at 375° for 35-40 minutes or until bubbly and fruit is tender. Serve warm with ice cream.

Nutrition Facts: 1 serving (calculated without ice cream) equals 111 calories, 1 g fat (trace saturated fat), 0 cholesterol, trace sodium, 27 g carbohydrate, 3 g fiber, 1 g protein. **Diabetic Exchanges:** 1 fruit, 1/2 starch.

NECTARINE-CHERRY COMPOTE TIP:
A compote is a recipe consisting of some sort of fruit that has been stewed in a syrup of sugar and other flavorings. Most commonly it is made from stone fruits, berries, apples, pears or even rhubarb. —Taste of Home

Plum Chicken Wraps

Prep/Total Time: 20 min. • **Yield:** 4 servings.
Dinner's a wrap with this easy, nutritious recipe loaded with the fruity flavors of pineapple and plum. It makes a sweet-and-sour chicken handheld that's hard to beat.
—Jennifer Michalicek, Phoenix, Arizona

1 can (8 ounces) unsweetened crushed pineapple, drained
1/3 cup plum sauce
1 tablespoon rice vinegar
1/2 teaspoon sesame oil
2 cups cubed cooked chicken breast

1/2 cup chopped green onions
1/4 cup salted cashews
2 medium fresh plums, sliced
12 Boston or Bibb lettuce leaves

1. In a large saucepan, combine the pineapple, plum sauce, vinegar and oil. Cook and stir over medium heat for 5 minutes.

2. Stir in the chicken, green onions and cashews; heat through. Remove from the heat; stir in plums. Place 1/3 cup chicken mixture on each lettuce leaf. Fold lettuce over filling.

Nutrition Facts: 3 filled wraps equals 298 calories, 8 g fat (2 g saturated fat), 54 mg cholesterol, 237 mg sodium, 32 g carbohydrate, 2 g fiber, 23 g protein. **Diabetic Exchanges:** 3 lean meat, 1-1/2 fruit, 1 fat, 1/2 starch.

PLUM CHICKEN WRAPS NOTES: _____

POTATOES

Golden Potato Salad

Prep: 25 min. • **Cook:** 15 min. + cooling • **Yield:** 10 servings.
What's a cookout without potato salad...incomplete! I think my version will become a summer staple at your house, too.
—*Linda Behrman, North Merrick, New York*

- 2-1/2 pounds Yukon Gold potatoes, peeled and cut into 1/2-inch cubes
- 1 medium sweet red pepper, chopped
- 1 small red onion, chopped
- 1/2 cup shredded carrot
- 1 cup mayonnaise
- 2 tablespoons olive oil
- 2 tablespoons balsamic vinegar
- 2 tablespoons spicy brown mustard
- 1 tablespoon mustard seed
- 3 teaspoons snipped fresh dill, *divided*
- 1-1/2 teaspoons sugar
- 3/4 teaspoon salt
- 1/2 teaspoon pepper

1. Place potatoes in a large saucepan and cover with water. Bring to a boil. Reduce heat; cover and simmer for 10-15 minutes or until tender. Drain; cool for 15 minutes.

2. In a large bowl, combine the red pepper, onion, carrot and potatoes.

3. In a small bowl, whisk the mayonnaise, oil, vinegar, mustard, mustard seed, 2 teaspoons dill, sugar, salt and pepper. Pour over potato mixture; gently toss to coat. Sprinkle with remaining dill. Refrigerate until serving.

Nutrition Facts: 3/4 cup equals 269 calories, 21 g fat (3 g saturated fat), 8 mg cholesterol, 345 mg sodium, 18 g carbohydrate, 2 g fiber, 2 g protein.

Mashed, baked, grilled or broiled— any way you prepare them, potatoes are a versatile and economical staple to any pantry. Get inspired by the tasty spuds showcased here.

SEASON: Year-round; generally harvested in the fall.

AT THE MARKET: Select well-shaped, firm potatoes that are free from cuts, decay, blemishes or green discoloration under the skin.

STORAGE: Keep potatoes in a dark, cool, dry, well-ventilated area for up to 2 months. Do not store with onions or in the refrigerator.

GOLDEN POTATO SALAD NOTES:
_____
_____
_____
_____

Potatoes with Mushrooms 'n' Peas

Prep/Total Time: 15 min. • **Yield:** 2 servings.
I love this "remarkably easy dish" I prepare in my microwave, especially in summer. The buttery flavor and tender veggies make this the perfect side dish to virtually any entree.
—Tamara Hanson, Big Lake, Minnesota

2 medium red potatoes, cut into 1-inch cubes	1/8 teaspoon pepper
1 tablespoon butter, cubed	1 cup sliced baby portobello mushrooms
1/4 teaspoon salt	1/2 cup fresh sugar snap peas

1. In a 1-qt. microwave-safe dish, combine the potatoes, butter, salt and pepper. Cover and microwave on high for 4 minutes or until crisp-tender. Stir in mushrooms and peas; cover and cook 2-3 minutes longer or until vegetables are tender.

Nutrition Facts: 3/4 cup equals 158 calories, 6 g fat (4 g saturated fat), 15 mg cholesterol, 345 mg sodium, 22 g carbohydrate, 4 g fiber, 5 g protein.
Diabetic Exchanges: 1 starch, 1 vegetable, 1 fat.

EDITOR'S NOTE: This recipe was tested in a 1,100-watt microwave.

POTATOES WITH MUSHROOMS 'N' PEAS
NOTES:_____
_____
_____
_____

Garden Cheddar Frittata

Prep: 30 min. • **Bake:** 15 min. • **Yield:** 6 servings.
I've made the frittata with goat cheese, too, and it's delicious. You can also use other vegetables if you like.
—Eva Amuso, Cheshire, Massachusetts

2 small potatoes, peeled and cut into 1/2-inch cubes	1/4 cup chopped onion
8 eggs, lightly beaten	1 tablespoon butter
2 tablespoons water	1 tablespoon olive oil
1/4 teaspoon salt	2 medium Roma tomatoes, thinly sliced
1/8 teaspoon garlic powder	1 cup (4 ounces) shredded sharp cheddar cheese
1/8 teaspoon chili powder	
1/8 teaspoon pepper	Minced chives and additional shredded cheddar cheese
1 small zucchini, chopped	

1. Place potatoes in small saucepan and cover with water. Bring to a boil. Reduce heat; cover and simmer for 5 minutes. Drain. In a large bowl, whisk the eggs, water, salt, garlic powder, chili powder and pepper; set aside.

2. In a 10-in. ovenproof skillet saute the zucchini, onion and potatoes in butter and oil until tender. Reduce heat. Pour 1-1/2 cups egg mixture into skillet. Arrange half of the tomatoes over top; sprinkle with 1/2 cup cheese. Top with remaining egg mixture, tomatoes and cheese.

3. Bake, uncovered, at 425° for 14-18 minutes or until eggs are completely set. Let stand for 5 minutes. Sprinkle with the chives and additional cheddar cheese. Cut into wedges.

Nutrition Facts: 1 wedge (calculated without chives and additional cheese) equals 251 calories, 16 g fat (8 g saturated fat), 307 mg cholesterol, 325 mg sodium, 13 g carbohydrate, 2 g fiber, 14 g protein.

GARDEN CHEDDAR FRITTATA NOTES:
_____
_____
_____
_____

BAKED VEGGIE CHIPS NOTES: _____
_____
_____
_____
_____

Baked Veggie Chips

Prep/Total Time: 30 min. • **Yield:** 3-1/2 cups.
Colorful roasted root vegetables are a fun, festive snack or side. These perfectly seasoned chips are so tasty they don't even need dip!
—*Christine Schenher, San Clemente, California*

1/2	pound fresh beets (about 2 medium)	2	tablespoons grated Parmesan cheese
1	medium potato	1/2	teaspoon salt
1	medium sweet potato	1/2	teaspoon garlic powder
1	medium parsnip	1/2	teaspoon dried oregano
2	tablespoons canola oil		Dash pepper

1. Peel vegetables and cut into 1/8-inch slices. Place in a large bowl. Drizzle with oil. Combine the remaining ingredients; sprinkle over vegetables and toss to coat.

2. Arrange in a single layer on racks in two ungreased 15-in. x 10-in. x 1-in. baking pans. Bake at 375° for 15-20 minutes or until golden brown, turning once.

Nutrition Facts: 1/2 cup equals 108 calories, 5 g fat (1 g saturated fat), 1 mg cholesterol, 220 mg sodium, 15 g carbohydrate, 2 g fiber, 2 g protein.

Sweet Potato Pie & Maple Praline Sauce

Prep: 20 min. **Bake:** 1 hour + cooling • **Yield:** 10 servings.
A delicious pie with a mouthwatering sauce, this one will have your guests talking. I use leftover sauce as an ice cream topping or as a dessert sauce for pound cake.
—*Rosemary Johnson, Irondale, Alabama*

Pastry for single-crust pie (9 inches)
1-1/4 cups sugar, *divided*
  1 cup chopped pecans
  1 teaspoon ground cinnamon
  4 eggs, lightly beaten
  1 cup mashed sweet potatoes
3/4 cup buttermilk
1/4 cup butter, melted
1/4 cup maple syrup
  1 teaspoon maple flavoring
1/4 teaspoon ground cloves

MAPLE PRALINE SAUCE:
1/2 cup butter, cubed
1/2 cup chopped pecans
1/2 cup sugar
1/2 cup maple syrup
  1 teaspoon maple flavoring
1/4 cup sour cream

1. Line a 9-in. deep-dish pie plate with pastry; trim and flute edges. In a small bowl, combine 1/4 cup sugar, pecans and cinnamon; sprinkle evenly into pastry shell. Set aside.

2. In a large bowl, combine the eggs, sweet potatoes, buttermilk, butter, syrup, maple flavoring, cloves and remaining sugar. Pour over pecan layer.

3. Bake at 350° for 60-70 minutes or until a knife inserted near the center comes out clean. Cover edges with foil during the last 15 minutes to prevent overbrowning if necessary. Cool on a wire rack.

4. For sauce, in a small heavy skillet, melt the butter. Add pecans; cook over medium heat until toasted, about 4 minutes. Add the sugar, syrup and maple flavoring; cook and stir for 2-4 minutes or until sugar is dissolved. Remove from the heat; stir in sour cream. Serve with pie.

Nutrition Facts: 1 serving with 8 teaspoons sauce equals 616 calories, 35 g fat (14 g saturated fat), 129 mg cholesterol, 237 mg sodium, 71 g carbohydrate, 3 g fiber, 6 g protein.

SWEET POTATO PIE & MAPLE PRALINE SAUCE NOTES:_____
_____
_____
_____
_____
_____

SWEET AS PIE.
The sweet potato is particularly popular in the southern region of the United States. An excellent source of vitamin A and a good source of potassium and vitamins C and B6, sweet potatoes' smooth, velvety texture and pretty orange color make for one terrific pie, too!

Elegant Roasted Potatoes

Prep: 20 min. • **Bake:** 40 min. • **Yield:** 6 servings.
Here is an excellent way to provide an easy, nutrition-packed side dish with any meal. It's a personal favorite since I grow these vegetables in my garden.
—*Kathy Rairigh, Milford, Indiana*

1 pound small red potatoes, quartered	1 teaspoon minced fresh oregano
1-1/2 cups cut fresh green beans (2-inch pieces)	1 teaspoon minced fresh thyme
1 medium sweet red pepper, julienned	1/2 teaspoon salt
1 tablespoon olive oil	1/4 teaspoon pepper
1 teaspoon garlic powder	2 cups chopped Swiss chard

1. In a large bowl, combine the first nine ingredients. Transfer to a greased 15-in. x 10-in. x 1-in. baking pan.

2. Bake, uncovered, at 425° for 25 minutes, stirring once. Add Swiss chard. Bake 15-20 minutes longer or until potatoes are tender, stirring once.

Nutrition Facts: 2/3 cup equals 92 calories, 2 g fat (trace saturated fat), 0 cholesterol, 229 mg sodium, 16 g carbohydrate, 3 g fiber, 2 g protein. **Diabetic Exchange:** 1 starch.

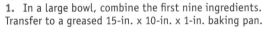

ELEGANT ROASTED POTATOES NOTES:

Italian Beef Stew

Prep: 20 min. • **Cook:** 1 hour • **Yield:** 2 servings.
Looking for a heartwarming meal-in-one on a nippy autumn evening? Try this hearty stew. Cubed steak makes it quick and economical.
—*Margaret Peschke, Hadley, New York*

3/4 pound beef cubed steak, chopped	1/2 small sweet red pepper, chopped
1 cup water	1 tablespoon reduced-sodium onion soup mix
1 can (8 ounces) tomato sauce	1/2 teaspoon Italian seasoning
1 small potato, peeled and cubed	1/4 teaspoon garlic powder
1/2 cup sliced fresh carrot	1/2 cup frozen peas
1/2 small onion, cut into thin wedges	

1. In a large saucepan coated with cooking spray, brown the meat over medium heat for 5 minutes. Stir in the water, tomato sauce, potato, carrot, onion, red pepper, soup mix, Italian seasoning and garlic powder. Bring to a boil. Reduce heat; simmer, uncovered, for 45 minutes.

2. Stir in the peas; simmer 15 minutes longer or until vegetables are tender.

Nutrition Facts: 1-3/4 cups equals 360 calories, 6 g fat (2 g saturated fat), 96 mg cholesterol, 784 mg sodium, 32 g carbohydrate, 6 g fiber, 44 g protein.

ITALIAN BEEF STEW NOTES: _____

Mashed Potatoes 'n' Brussels Sprouts

Prep: 30 min. • **Cook:** 20 min. • **Yield:** 6-8 servings.
If you're tired of eating the same old mashed white potatoes, try this tasty recipe. These potatoes are fluffy and delicious.
—*Raymonde Hebert Bernier, Saint-Hyacinthe, Quebec*

3 pounds potatoes (about 9 medium), peeled and quartered
2 cups fresh *or* frozen Brussels sprouts
2 garlic cloves, peeled
1/2 cup half-and-half cream
2 tablespoons butter
2 teaspoons chicken bouillon granules
1 teaspoon salt
1/4 teaspoon dried basil
1/8 teaspoon pepper

1. Place potatoes in a large saucepan and cover with water. Bring to a boil. Reduce heat; cover and cook for 15-20 minutes or until tender.

2. Meanwhile, place 1/2 in. of water and Brussels sprouts in a small saucepan; bring to a boil. Reduce heat; cover and cook for 5 minutes. Add garlic; cook 3-5 minutes longer or until tender.

3. Drain potatoes, sprouts and garlic; cool slightly. Place in a food processor; cover and process for 1-2 minutes. Add the remaining ingredients; cover and process just until blended. Transfer to a serving bowl.

Nutrition Facts: 2/3 cup equals 156 calories, 5 g fat (3 g saturated fat), 15 mg cholesterol, 541 mg sodium, 26 g carbohydrate, 2 g fiber, 3 g protein.

MASHED POTATOES 'N' BRUSSELS
SPROUTS NOTES: _____
_____
_____
_____
_____

Honey-Pineapple Sweet Potatoes

Prep: 20 min. • **Bake:** 25 min. • **Yield:** 13 servings.
Pineapple chunks add unexpected yet delicious bursts of tanginess to naturally sweet sweet potatoes. Add pecans, if you'd like, for another layer of flavor that people will love.
—*Paula Mayo, Feedings Hills, Massachusetts*

3 pounds sweet potatoes, peeled and cut into 3/4-inch cubes
1 cup water
1 can (8 ounces) crushed pineapple
1 can (8 ounces) pineapple chunks, drained
1/4 cup honey
1/2 cup coarsely chopped pecans, optional

1. Place sweet potatoes and water in a 2-qt. microwave-safe dish. Cover and microwave on high for 8-10 minutes or until potatoes are tender; drain.

2. Drain crushed pineapple, reserving juice. In a large bowl, combine the crushed pineapple, pineapple chunks and sweet potatoes. Transfer to a 2-1/2-qt. baking dish coated with cooking spray. In a small bowl, combine honey and reserved juice; pour over sweet potatoes.

3. Bake, uncovered, at 350° for 10 minutes. Stir mixture; sprinkle with the pecans if desired. Bake 15-20 minutes longer or until heated through.

Nutrition Facts: 3/4 cup equals 105 calories, trace fat (trace saturated fat), 0 cholesterol, 7 mg sodium, 26 g carbohydrate, 2 g fiber, 1 g protein.
Diabetic Exchange: 2 starch.

EDITOR'S NOTE: This recipe was tested in a 1,100-watt microwave.

HONEY-PINEAPPLE SWEET POTATOES
NOTES:_____
_____
_____
_____

Whipped Potatoes and Carrots

Prep/Total Time: 30 min. • **Yield:** 8 servings.

Root vegetables become special when you whip them together. We love their creamy, slightly chunky consistency and subtle nutmeg seasoning. They're wonderful with roast beef.

—*Kathy Rairigh, Milford, Indiana*

1-1/2 pounds potatoes, peeled and cut into 1-inch cubes	3/4 teaspoon salt
	1/8 teaspoon pepper
1 pound carrots, sliced	Dash ground nutmeg
1/2 cup hot fat-free milk	Minced fresh parsley *or* chives, optional
2 tablespoons butter	

1. Place potatoes in a large saucepan and cover with water. Bring to a boil. Reduce heat; cover and cook for 10 minutes. Add carrots; cover and cook 5-10 minutes longer or until vegetables are tender.

2. Drain and place in a food processor. Add the milk, butter, salt, pepper and nutmeg. Cover and process until blended. Sprinkle with parsley if desired.

Nutrition Facts: 3/4 cup equals 103 calories, 3 g fat (2 g saturated fat), 8 mg cholesterol, 289 mg sodium, 18 g carbohydrate, 2 g fiber, 2 g protein. **Diabetic Exchanges:** 1 starch, 1 vegetable, 1/2 fat.

Potato-Sausage Foil Packs

Prep: 20 min. • **Grill:** 30 min. • **Yield:** 4 servings.

We had these satisfying campfire bundles at a friend's house for dinner and loved the simplicity of this savory meal.

—*Alissa Keith, Lynchburg, Virginia*

1 package (14 ounces) smoked turkey kielbasa, sliced	1 medium onion, chopped
2 large potatoes, cut into wedges	4 teaspoons lemon juice
1 *each* medium green, sweet red and yellow peppers, cut into 1-inch pieces	4 teaspoons olive oil
	1/2 teaspoon garlic powder
	1/2 teaspoon pepper
	1/4 teaspoon salt

1. Divide the kielbasa, potatoes, peppers and onion among four double thicknesses of heavy-duty foil (about 18 in. x 12 in.). Drizzle with lemon juice and oil; sprinkle with garlic powder, pepper and salt.

2. Fold foil around kielbasa mixture and seal tightly. Grill, covered, over medium heat for 30-35 minutes or until the potatoes are tender. Open foil carefully to allow steam to escape.

Nutrition Facts: 1 foil packet equals 349 calories, 10 g fat (2 g saturated fat), 62 mg cholesterol, 1,137 mg sodium, 44 g carbohydrate, 5 g fiber, 21 g protein.

Savory Root Vegetable Soup

Prep: 40 min. • **Cook:** 40 min. • **Yield:** 8 servings (2 quarts).
Instead of the usual side dishes, consider serving a
vegetable-laden soup at Thanksgiving or other holidays.
—*Zan Brock, Jasper, Alabama*

- 4 bacon strips
- 2 celery ribs, chopped
- 1 medium onion, chopped
- 1 medium green pepper, chopped
- 2 medium leeks (white portion only), chopped
- 2 cups frozen shredded hash brown potatoes
- 1 cup cubed peeled sweet potato
- 2 medium parsnips, peeled and chopped
- 2 medium carrots, peeled and chopped
- 2 small turnips, peeled and chopped
- 3 cans (14-1/2 ounces *each*) chicken broth
- 2 tablespoons minced fresh parsley
- 2 teaspoons herbes de Provence
- 1 garlic clove, minced
- 1/2 teaspoon white pepper

SAVORY ROOT VEGETABLE SOUP NOTES:

_____
_____
_____
_____
_____
_____

- 1/2 teaspoon ground coriander
- 1 cup (8 ounces) sour cream
- 1 cup (4 ounces) shredded Swiss cheese

1. In a Dutch oven, cook bacon over medium heat until crisp. Remove to paper towels; drain, reserving drippings. Crumble bacon and set aside. Saute the celery, onion, green pepper and leeks in drippings until tender.

2. Add the hash browns, sweet potato, parsnips, carrots and turnips; cook and stir over medium heat for 10 minutes.

3. Add the broth, parsley, herbes de Provence, garlic, white pepper and coriander; bring to a boil. Reduce heat; cover and simmer for 15-20 minutes or until vegetables are tender. Ladle soup into bowls. Top each serving with sour cream, cheese and crumbled bacon.

Nutrition Facts: 1 cup equals 255 calories, 14 g fat (8 g saturated fat), 43 mg cholesterol, 855 mg sodium, 21 g carbohydrate, 4 g fiber, 9 g protein.

EDITOR'S NOTE: Look for herbes de Provence in the spice aisle.

SQUASH

Acorn Squash with Apricot Sauce

Prep: 10 min. • **Yield:** 55 min. • **Yield:** 4 servings.
With its mild flavor, acorn squash is the perfect base for crunchy walnuts and sweet apricots. I like to double the sauce so I can serve it with my breakfast oatmeal.
—*Judy Parker, Moore, Oklahoma*

- 2 small acorn squash
- 2 tablespoons brown sugar
- 1/4 teaspoon ground cinnamon
- 2 tablespoons butter
- 1 cup orange juice
- 1/2 cup dried apricots, coarsely chopped
- 1/2 cup chopped walnuts, optional

1. Cut squash in half; discard seeds. Cut a thin slice from bottom of squash with a sharp knife to allow it to sit flat. Place hollow side up in a greased 15-in. x 10-in. x 1-in. baking pan; add 1/2 in. of hot water.

2. Combine brown sugar and cinnamon; sprinkle over squash. Dot with butter. Cover and bake at 375° for 55-65 minutes or until tender.

3. Meanwhile, in a small saucepan, combine orange juice and apricots. Bring to a boil. Reduce heat; simmer, uncovered, for 15 minutes or until apricots are tender. Transfer to a blender; cover and process until smooth. Serve with squash; sprinkle with walnuts if desired.

Nutrition Facts: 1 squash half (calculated without walnuts) equals 241 calories, 6 g fat (4 g saturated fat), 15 mg cholesterol, 50 mg sodium, 48 g carbohydrate, 5 g fiber, 3 g protein.

There are two kinds of squash: summer and winter. Summer squash—like zucchini—are most tender and tasty when picked before fully mature. Not so for the hard-rind winter squash, such as acorn and butternut. But both are serious allies for health- and taste-consicous cooks.

SEASON: Year-round; peaks late summer to fall.

AT THE MARKET: Summer varieties, select firm, plump squash with bright, smooth skin; winter varieties, select squash that is heavy for its size. Shells should be a deep color with no cracks or soft spots.

STORAGE: Summer varieties, refrigerate unwashed for up to 4 days; winter varieties, keep unwashed in a cool, dry, well-ventilated area for up to 4 weeks.

ACORN SQUASH WITH APRICOT SAUCE
NOTES:_____
_____
_____
_____
_____

Summer Squash Medley

Prep/Total Time: 20 min. • **Yield:** 2 servings.
This fresh-tasting, colorful side dish would go with any entree, and it's quick and easy to prepare. I came up with this recipe on my own about a year ago. It has a nice combination of flavors.
—*Heather Irwin, Clarksville, Tennessee*

1 medium yellow summer squash, thinly sliced	1 tablespoon butter
1 small zucchini, thinly sliced	1 tablespoon brown sugar
1/3 cup chopped onion	1/4 teaspoon minced garlic
	1/8 teaspoon lemon juice
	1/8 teaspoon salt

1. In a small skillet, saute the yellow squash, zucchini and onion in butter until crisp tender; add the remaining ingredients. Cook and stir until vegetables are tender.

Nutrition Facts: 2/3 cup calculated without crushed red pepper flakes equals equals 61 calories, 3 g fat (trace saturated fat), 0 cholesterol, 403 mg sodium, 9 g carbohydrate, 2 g fiber, 2 g protein. **Diabetic Exchanges:** 2 vegetable, 1/2 fat.

SUMMER SQUASH MEDLEY NOTES:

_____

_____

_____

_____

Zucchini Tomato Frittata

Prep: 20 min. • **Cook:** 15 min. • **Yield:** 4 servings.
Here is a versatile entree packed full of veggies. Egg substitute and low-fat cheese lighten it up, making for a healthy meal.
—*Kim Sosebee, Cleveland, Georgia*

1/3 cup sun-dried tomatoes (not packed in oil)	1/8 teaspoon crushed red pepper flakes
1 cup boiling water	1 cup sliced zucchini
1-1/2 cups egg substitute	1 cup fresh broccoli florets
1/2 cup 2% cottage cheese	1 medium sweet red pepper, chopped
2 green onions, chopped	2 teaspoons canola oil
1/4 cup minced fresh basil *or* 1 tablespoon dried basil	2 tablespoons grated Parmesan cheese

1. Place tomatoes in a small bowl. Cover with boiling water; let stand for 5 minutes. Drain and set aside.

2. In a large bowl, whisk the egg substitute, cottage cheese, onions, basil, pepper flakes and reserved tomatoes; set aside.

3. In a 10-in. ovenproof skillet, saute zucchini, broccoli and red pepper in oil until tender. Reduce heat; top with reserved egg mixture. Cover and cook for 4-6 minutes or until nearly set.

4. Uncover skillet. Sprinkle with Parmesan cheese. Broil 3-4 in. from the heat for 2-3 minutes or until eggs are completely set. Let stand for 5 minutes. Cut into wedges.

Nutrition Facts: 1 wedge equals 138 calories, 4 g fat (1 g saturated fat), 6 mg cholesterol, 484 mg sodium, 11 g carbohydrate, 3 g fiber, 15 g protein. **Diabetic Exchanges:** 2 lean meat, 2 vegetable.

ZUCCHINI TOMATO FRITTATA NOTES:

_____

_____

_____

_____

Cucumber & Squash Salad

Prep/Total Time: 10 min. • **Yield:** 2 servings.
I developed this recipe one summer when I had too many summer squash and needed a different, tasty way to use them.
—*Jacqueline Miller, Wooster, Ohio*

- 1 cup thinly sliced cucumber
- 1 cup thinly sliced yellow summer squash
- 2 tablespoons chopped green onion
- 1 tablespoon shredded Parmesan cheese
- Dash crushed red pepper flakes
- 2 tablespoons prepared Italian salad dressing

1. In a small bowl, combine the first five ingredients. Drizzle with salad dressing; toss to coat.

Nutrition Facts: 3/4 cup equals 86 calories, 6 g fat (1 g saturated fat), 2 mg cholesterol, 298 mg sodium, 6 g carbohydrate, 2 g fiber, 2 g protein. **Diabetic Exchanges:** 1 vegetable, 1 fat.

CUCUMBER & SQUASH SALAD NOTES:

ZUCCHINI CHOCOLATE CAKE NOTES:

Zucchini Chocolate Cake

Prep: 25 min. • **Bake:** 45 min. + cooling • **Yield:** 15 servings.
This moist, chocolatey cake makes good use of summer's bounty of zucchini. Serve it alone or with fresh berries.
—*Weda Mosellie, Phillipsburg, New Jersey*

- 1/2 cup butter, softened
- 1-3/4 cups sugar
- 1/2 cup canola oil
- 2 eggs
- 1 teaspoon vanilla extract
- 1 cup 2% milk
- 1/2 cup buttermilk
- 2-1/2 cups all-purpose flour
- 1/4 cup baking cocoa
- 1 teaspoon baking soda
- 1/2 teaspoon baking powder
- 1/2 teaspoon salt
- 2 cups shredded zucchini
- 1/2 cup semisweet chocolate chips
- Confectioners' sugar

1. In a large bowl, beat the butter, sugar and oil until smooth. Add eggs, one at a time, beating well after each addition. Beat in vanilla.

2. Combine milk and buttermilk. In another bowl, combine the flour, cocoa, baking soda, baking powder and salt; add to batter alternately with milk mixture, beating well after each addition. Fold in zucchini.

3. Transfer to a greased 13-in. x 9-in. baking pan. Sprinkle with chocolate chips. Bake at 325° for 45-50 minutes or until a toothpick inserted near the center comes out clean. Cool on a wire rack. Dust with confectioners' sugar.

Nutrition Facts: 1 piece (calculated without confectioners' sugar) equals 341 calories, 17 g fat (6 g saturated fat), 46 mg cholesterol, 248 mg sodium, 45 g carbohydrate, 1 g fiber, 5 g protein.

Spaghetti Squash with Moroccan Spices

Prep/Total Time: 25 min. • **Yield:** 6 servings.
Here's an easy recipe that's best prepared in the microwave versus a conventional oven. A colorful blend of spices livens up the delicate strands of squash.
—*Lily Julow, Gainesville, Florida*

1 medium spaghetti squash (4 pounds)
2 garlic cloves, minced
2 tablespoons butter
1 teaspoon ground cumin
3/4 teaspoon salt
1/2 teaspoon ground cinnamon
1/8 teaspoon hot pepper sauce
2 tablespoons minced fresh cilantro

1. Cut squash in half lengthwise; discard seeds. Place squash cut side down on a microwave-safe plate. Microwave, uncovered, on high for 15-18 minutes or until tender.

2. In a small skillet, saute garlic in butter for 1 minute. Stir in the cumin, salt, cinnamon and pepper sauce. When squash is cool enough to handle, use a fork to separate strands. Toss with butter mixture and cilantro.

Nutrition Facts: 2/3 cup equals 104 calories, 5 g fat (3 g saturated fat), 10 mg cholesterol, 360 mg sodium, 15 g carbohydrate, 3 g fiber, 2 g protein. **Diabetic Exchanges:** 1 starch, 1/2 fat.

EDITOR'S NOTE: This recipe was tested in a 1,100-watt microwave.

SPAGHETTI SQUASH WITH MOROCCAN SPICES NOTES:_____

Zucchini Tomato Bake

Prep: 30 min. • **Bake:** 25 min. • **Yield:** 6 servings.
Make the most of those bountiful tomatoes and zucchinis. Melted Swiss cheese and sour cream lend a touch of decadence to this healthy and appealing dish.
—*Tina Repak Mirilovich, Johnstown, Pennsylvania*

1 medium onion, chopped
1 tablespoon butter
3 medium zucchini (about 1 pound), shredded and patted dry
3 medium tomatoes, seeded and chopped
1 cup (4 ounces) shredded reduced-fat Swiss cheese, *divided*
1/3 cup reduced-fat sour cream
1 teaspoon paprika
1/2 teaspoon salt
1/2 teaspoon garlic powder
1/4 teaspoon pepper
2 tablespoons shredded Parmesan cheese

1. In a large nonstick skillet, saute onion in butter until tender. Transfer to a large bowl. Add the zucchini, tomatoes, 1/2 cup Swiss cheese, sour cream and seasonings; mix well.

2. Transfer to an 11-in. x 7-in. baking dish coated with cooking spray. Sprinkle with Parmesan cheese and remaining Swiss cheese. Bake, uncovered, at 350° for 25-30 minutes or until vegetables are tender.

Nutrition Facts: 1 serving equals 113 calories, 5 g fat (3 g saturated fat), 18 mg cholesterol, 321 mg sodium, 9 g carbohydrate, 2 g fiber, 9 g protein. **Diabetic Exchanges:** 2 vegetable, 1 lean meat, 1/2 fat.

ZUCCHINI TOMATO BAKE NOTES:

SPAGHETTI SQUASH SUPREME NOTES:

Spaghetti Squash Supreme

Prep: 45 min. • **Bake:** 20 min. • **Yield:** 5 servings.
While dreaming up a healthier pasta dish, I decided to experiment with spaghetti squash. After a few tries, I settled on this delicious casserole bursting with flavor but not fat.
—*Christina Morris, Calabasas, California*

- 1 medium spaghetti squash (4 pounds)
- 1 can (14-1/2 ounces) diced tomatoes, undrained
- 2 tablespoons prepared pesto
- 1/2 teaspoon garlic powder
- 1/2 teaspoon Italian seasoning
- 1/4 cup dry bread crumbs
- 1/4 cup shredded Parmesan cheese
- 1 pound boneless skinless chicken breasts, cut into 1/2-inch cubes
- 1 tablespoon plus 1 teaspoon olive oil, *divided*
- 1/2 pound sliced fresh mushrooms
- 1 medium onion, chopped
- 1 garlic clove, minced
- 1/2 cup chicken broth
- 1/3 cup shredded cheddar cheese

1. Cut squash in half lengthwise; discard seeds. Place squash cut side down on a microwave-safe plate. Microwave, uncovered, on high for 14-16 minutes or until tender.

2. Meanwhile, in a blender, combine the tomatoes, pesto, garlic powder and Italian seasoning. Cover and process until blended; set aside. In a small bowl, combine bread crumbs and Parmesan cheese; set aside.

3. In a large skillet, cook chicken in 1 tablespoon oil until no longer pink; remove and keep warm. In the same skillet, saute mushrooms and onion in remaining oil until tender. Add garlic; cook 1 minute longer. Stir in the broth, chicken and reserved tomato mixture. Bring to a boil. Reduce heat; simmer, uncovered, for 5 minutes.

4. When squash is cool enough to handle, use a fork to separate strands. In a large ovenproof skillet, layer with half of the squash, chicken mixture and reserved crumb mixture. Repeat layers.

5. Bake, uncovered, at 350° for 15 minutes or until heated through. Sprinkle with cheddar cheese. Broil 3-4 in. from the heat for 5-6 minutes or until cheese is melted and golden brown.

Nutrition Facts: 1-1/2 cups equals 348 calories, 14 g fat (5 g saturated fat), 63 mg cholesterol, 493 mg sodium, 32 g carbohydrate, 7 g fiber, 27 g protein.

EDITOR'S NOTE: This recipe was tested in a 1,100-watt microwave.

Creamy Butternut Soup

Prep/Total Time: 30 min. • **Yield:** 10 servings.
Thick and filling, this soup, topped with chives and a drizzle of sour cream, looks as special as it tastes.
—*Amanda Smith, Cincinnati, Ohio*

1 butternut squash, peeled, seeded and cubed (about 6 cups)

5 cups water

3 medium potatoes, peeled and cubed

1 large onion, diced

2 chicken bouillon cubes

2 garlic cloves, minced

Sour cream and chives, optional

1. In a Dutch oven, combine the squash, water, potatoes, onion, bouillon and garlic. Bring to a boil. Reduce heat; cover and simmer for 15-20 minutes or until vegetables are tender.

2. Remove from the heat; cool slightly. In a blender, puree mixture in batches. Return to the pan; heat through. Serve with sour cream and chives if desired.

Nutrition Facts: 1 cup equals 112 calories, trace fat (trace saturated fat), trace cholesterol, 231 mg sodium, 27 g carbohydrate, 4 g fiber, 3 g protein.
Diabetic Exchange: 2 starch.

CREAMY BUTTERNUT SOUP TIP: Dress up individual soup servings with a pretty garnish. Ideas include finely chopped green onions, minced fresh parsley or a dollop of sour cream.
—Taste of Home

Zucchini "Linguine" Salad

Prep: 30 min. + chilling • **Yield:** 6 servings.
I came up with this recipe after seeing a dish with zucchini cut into noodle-like strips and dressed with a creamy sauce.
—*Lily Julow, Gainesville, Florida*

5 medium zucchini

3/4 teaspoon salt, *divided*

1 large sweet red pepper, julienned

1 large tomato, seeded and cut into thin strips

1/2 cup thinly sliced sweet onion

3 tablespoons olive oil

2 tablespoons cider vinegar

1/4 cup minced fresh parsley

1-1/2 teaspoons minced fresh oregano *or* 1/2 teaspoon dried oregano

1/4 teaspoon pepper

Shredded Parmesan cheese, optional

1. Cut the ends off of each zucchini. Using a cheese slicer or vegetable peeler, cut zucchini into thin lengthwise strips. Cut zucchini on all sides, as if peeling a carrot, until the seeds become visible. Discard seeded portion or save for another use. Cut zucchini strips into 1/4 in. widths.

2. Place in a strainer; sprinkle with 1/2 teaspoon salt and gently toss to coat. Let stand for 15 minutes. Gently shake strainer. Drain zucchini on paper towels and pat dry.

3. Transfer to a large bowl; add the red pepper, tomato and onion. In a small bowl, whisk the oil, vinegar, parsley, oregano, pepper and remaining salt. Pour over zucchini mixture and toss to coat. Cover and refrigerate for at least 30 minutes before serving. Sprinkle with cheese if desired.

Nutrition Facts: 3/4 cup equals 100 calories, 7 g fat (1 g saturated fat), 0 cholesterol, 254 mg sodium, 9 g carbohydrate, 3 g fiber, 2 g protein.
Diabetic Exchanges: 1 vegetable, 1 fat.

ZUCCHINI "LINGUINE" SALAD NOTES:

_____
_____
_____
_____

TOMATOES

In terms of popularity, it's no contest. Tomatoes are the rock stars of summer produce. Nothing tops the fresh taste of vine-ripened, homegrown tomatoes, so we've given you plenty of recipes to make the most of these summer beauties.

SEASON: Peaks mid-summer through early fall.

AT THE MARKET: Select tomatoes that are smooth and free of blemishes. Fully ripe tomatoes have a slight softness. Avoid overripe, cracked or bruised tomatoes or ones with green or yellow areas near the stem.

STORAGE: Keep unwashed at room temperature until ripe; store out of direct sunlight; can be refrigerated for up to 3 days.

top
10
heirloom
TOMATOES

THESE "SENIORS" ROCK!

If you crave great taste, heirloom tomatoes belong on your next BLT sandwich. Compared to cross-bred hybrids, heirlooms—open-pollinated veggies that have been grown for generations and whose seeds produce plants identical to their "parents"—flat-out rock when it comes to palate-pleasing flavor. If you want to try to grow your own instead of making a trip to the farmers market, here are some favorites to consider:

AMISH PASTE

Red, meaty and juicy 6- to 8-ounce fruits. Mildly tart flavor is great for sauces or eating straight off the vine. Matures 85 days from transplanting.

BRANDYWINE

Dates back to late 1800s. Produces deep red, 8-ounce to 1-pound fruits with excellent flavor. Matures 80 days from transplanting.

CHEROKEE PURPLE

Reddish-brown fruits weigh up to 12 ounces. These sweeties are meaty, too. Matures 75 to 90 days from transplanting.

AUSTIN'S PEAR RED

Prolific variety yields 2-inch-long, lightbulb-shaped fruits. Known for superior flavor. Matures 80 days from transplanting.

GREEN ZEBRA

Light, citrusy flavor makes quite an impression in mixed salads. Fruit is green with light-green stripes. Matures 75 to 80 days from transplanting.

ITALIAN

Prolific variety produces fruits that weigh more than a pound each. Flavorful, easy to peel and ideal for slicing and canning. Matures 70 to 80 days from transplanting.

MORTGAGE LIFTER (HALLADAY'S)

Grown for generations on a Kentucky farm. Yields 1- to 2-pound flavorful beefsteak fruits; crack-resistant. Ripe 80 to 90 days from transplanting.

NEBRASKA WEDDING

Dates back at least to Great Plains pioneers. Produces tasty, bright orange, 4-inch-diameter fruits. Matures 85 to 90 days from transplanting.

POWERS

More than 100 years old. Produces heavy yields of 3- to 5-ounce oval, yellow paste tomatoes with lots of flavor. Matures 85 to 90 days from transplanting.

TASTY EVERGREEN

Pick this green-flesh heirloom when green, or let it ripen to a mellow yellow. Beefsteak-like fruits offer strong, sweet flavor. Matures 75 days from transplanting.

Gouda Melt with Baguette Slices

Prep/Total Time: 20 min. • **Yield:** 4 servings.
This fun appetizer is guaranteed to wow guests! It takes just moments to whip up this melty delight.
—*Susan Lewis, Reading, Pennsylvania*

1 French bread baguette (4 ounces), sliced
1 round (7 ounces) Gouda cheese
1 plum tomato, seeded and chopped
1 tablespoon minced fresh basil

1. Place baguette slices on an ungreased baking sheet. Broil 3-4 in. from the heat for 1-2 minutes on each side or until toasted.

2. Meanwhile, carefully remove waxed coating from cheese round. Using a 3-in. biscuit cutter, press into the center of cheese, but not all the way through. Scoop out center, leaving a 1/4-in. shell; set shell aside.

3. Place the tomato, basil and removed cheese in a small microwave-safe bowl. Cover and microwave on high for 1 minute or until cheese is melted. Stir until combined; pour into shell. Serve with baguette toasts.

Nutrition Facts: 1 serving equals 303 calories, 17 g fat (9 g saturated fat), 57 mg cholesterol, 578 mg sodium, 24 g carbohydrate, 2 g fiber, 15 g protein.

GOUDA MELT WITH BAGUETTE SLICES NOTES: _____
_____
_____
_____
_____

Gazpacho Salad

Prep/Total Time: 20 min. • **Yield:** 10-12 servings.
Here's a beautiful and tasty way to use garden vegetables. This fresh, colorful salad is great to make ahead and take to a potluck later, after the flavors have had a chance to blend. It's sure to be a success!
—*Florence Jacoby, Granite Falls, Minnesota*

4 tomatoes, diced and seeded
2 cucumbers, peeled and diced
2 green peppers, seeded and diced
1 medium onion, diced
1 can (2-1/4 ounces) sliced ripe olives, drained
1 teaspoon salt
1/2 teaspoon pepper

DRESSING:
1/2 cup olive oil
1/4 cup white vinegar
Juice of 1 lemon (about 1/4 cup)
1 tablespoon chopped fresh parsley
2 garlic cloves, minced
2 teaspoons chopped green onions
1/2 teaspoon salt
1/4 teaspoon ground cumin

1. In a 1-1/2-quart bowl, layer one-third to one-half of the tomatoes, cucumbers, green peppers, onion, olives, salt and pepper. Repeat layers two or three more times.

2. In a small bowl, combine all dressing ingredients. Pour over vegetables. Cover and chill several hours or overnight. Serve with a slotted spoon.

Nutrition Facts: 1 cup equals 116 calories, 10 g fat (1 g saturated fat), 0 cholesterol, 347 mg sodium, 7 g carbohydrate, 2 g fiber, 1 g protein.

GAZPACHO SALAD NOTES: _____
_____
_____
_____
_____

Chicken Bruschetta Sandwiches

Prep/Total Time: 25 min. • **Yield:** 4 servings.
Regular bruschetta can be delightful, but rarely does it make a meal. This appetizer-inspired sandwich, on the other hand, is beautiful and also pleasantly filling.
—*Bette Giles, Dedham, Massachusetts*

2 cups chopped plum tomatoes	4 boneless skinless chicken breast halves (4 ounces *each*)
1/2 cup minced fresh basil	
1/3 cup finely chopped red onion	4 slices Italian bread (1 inch thick), toasted
3/4 cup Italian salad dressing, *divided*	4 slices part-skim mozzarella cheese

1. In a small bowl, combine tomatoes, basil, onion and 1/2 cup dressing; set aside. Flatten chicken to 1/4-in. thickness.

2. Grill chicken, covered, over medium heat for 3-5 minutes on each side or until juices run clear, basting occasionally with remaining dressing. Layer each slice of toast with a chicken breast, cheese slice and tomato mixture.

Nutrition Facts: 1 serving equals 517 calories, 27 g fat (7 g saturated fat), 78 mg cholesterol, 1,233 mg sodium, 31 g carbohydrate, 3 g fiber, 35 g protein.

CHICKEN BRUSCHETTA SANDWICHES
NOTES:_____
_____
_____
_____

Pasta with Mozzarella, Tomatoes and Fresh Basil

Prep: 20 min. + standing • **Cook:** 15 min. • **Yield:** 6 servings.
During the summer season, I like to prepare this pasta salad featuring garden-fresh tomatoes and basil. Fresh mozzarella adds a tasty touch.
—*Ken Churches, San Andreas, California*

12 ounces fresh mozzarella cheese, cubed	1 teaspoon pepper
	1 package (16 ounces) uncooked linguine
6 tablespoons olive oil	1 cup chopped fresh basil leaves
4 teaspoons minced garlic	
1 teaspoon salt	3 medium tomatoes, chopped

1. In a large bowl, combine the cheese, oil, garlic, salt and pepper; let stand at room temperature for 1 hour.

2. Meanwhile, cook linguine according to package directions; drain and rinse in cold water. Add to cheese mixture. Stir in basil and tomatoes. Serve at room temperature or chilled.

Nutrition Facts: 1 cup equals 574 calories, 28 g fat (10 g saturated fat), 45 mg cholesterol, 483 mg sodium, 61 g carbohydrate, 4 g fiber, 21 g protein.

PASTA WITH MOZZARELLA, TOMATOES AND FRESH BASIL NOTES: _____
_____
_____

Open-Faced Chicken Avocado Burgers

Prep: 30 min. • **Cook:** 15 min. • **Yield:** 4 servings.
A creamy avocado spread and thick slices of fresh mozzarella and tomato dress up these chicken patties. They're wonderful with buttered boiled potatoes or a salad.
—*Lisa Hundley, Aberdeen, North Carolina*

1 tablespoon lemon juice
1/4 teaspoon Worcestershire sauce
1/2 medium ripe avocado, peeled
1/2 cup mayonnaise
1/4 cup sour cream
4 green onions, coarsely chopped
1/2 teaspoon salt
1/2 teaspoon cayenne pepper

BURGERS:
1/4 cup shredded Parmesan cheese
2 tablespoons prepared pesto
3 garlic cloves, minced
1/4 teaspoon salt
1 pound ground chicken
4 tablespoons olive oil, *divided*
1/2 pound fresh mozzarella cheese, cut into 4 slices
4 slices Italian bread (3/4 inch thick)
2 cups fresh arugula *or* baby spinach
8 slices tomato
1/4 teaspoon dried basil
1/4 teaspoon pepper

1. In a blender, combine the first eight ingredients; cover and process until smooth. Chill until serving. For burgers, in a small bowl, combine the Parmesan cheese, pesto, garlic and salt. Crumble chicken over mixture and mix well. Shape into four patties.

2. In a large skillet over medium heat, cook burgers in 2 tablespoons oil for 5-7 minutes on each side or until a thermometer reads 165° and juices run clear. Top with cheese; cover and cook 1 minute longer.

3. Meanwhile, brush bread with remaining oil; place on a baking sheet. Broil 3-4 in. from the heat for 1-2 minutes on each side or until toasted.

4. Spread each slice of toast with 2 tablespoons avocado spread (refrigerate remaining spread for another use). Top with arugula, a burger and sliced tomato. Sprinkle with basil and pepper.

Nutrition Facts: 1 burger equals 723 calories, 55 g fat (17 g saturated fat), 136 mg cholesterol, 849 mg sodium, 22 g carbohydrate, 3 g fiber, 35 g protein.

```
OPEN-FACED CHICKEN AVOCADO
BURGERS NOTES: _____
     _____
     _____
X    _____
     _____
     _____
     _____
```

No-Cook Herbed Tomato Sauce

Prep/Total Time: 20 min. + chilling • **Yield:** 3 cups.
This fresh-tasting sauce is wonderful over pasta. It's also a great use of your garden bounty!
—*Taste of Home Test Kitchen*

5 medium tomatoes (about 1-1/2 pounds), chopped
1/4 cup snipped fresh basil
1/2 cup chopped green onions
2 garlic cloves, minced
1 tablespoon olive oil
Salt and pepper to taste
Hot cooked pasta
Grated Parmesan cheese

1. In a large bowl, combine the tomatoes, basil, onions, garlic, oil, salt and pepper. Let stand at room temperature for 30-60 minutes, stirring occasionally. Serve with pasta. Sprinkle with cheese.

Nutrition Facts: 1 serving (sauce only) equals 58 calories, 3 g fat (trace saturated fat), 0 cholesterol, 14 mg sodium, 8 g carbohydrate, 2 g fiber, 1 g protein.

```
NO-COOK HERBED TOMATO SAUCE NOTES:
     _____
     _____
/    _____
     _____
     _____
```

A LITTLE SLICE OF HEAVEN.
Nothing says "summer" like a juicy
slice of tomato. Fresh tomatoes
sliced vertically rather than
horizontally will stay firmer in your
salads and help keep any dressing
from getting watery.

Fresh Mozzarella Sandwiches

Prep/Total Time: 15 min. • **Yield:** 2 servings.
We love this fast, fresh sandwich, especially when it's too warm to turn on the oven to make dinner. We often add avocado to the sandwiches and, in the summer, use fresh Walla Walla onions.
—*Stacey Johnson, Tacoma, Washington*

- 4 slices sourdough bread, toasted
- 2 tablespoons wasabi mayonnaise
- 1/4 pound fresh mozzarella cheese, sliced
- 1 medium tomato, sliced
- 2 thin slices sweet onion
- 4 fresh basil leaves

1. Spread toast with mayonnaise. On two slices, layer the cheese, tomato slices, onion slices and basil; top with remaining toast.

Nutrition Facts: 1 sandwich equals 466 calories, 24 g fat (10 g saturated fat), 50 mg cholesterol, 576 mg sodium, 42 g carbohydrate, 3 g fiber, 18 g protein.

FRESH MOZZARELLA SANDWICHES
NOTES: _____
_____
_____
_____
_____

MOZZARELLA & TOMATO SALAD NOTES:
_____
_____
_____
_____

Mozzarella & Tomato Salad

Prep: 25 min. + chilling • **Yield:** 8 servings.
A splash of lemon and hint of refreshing mint brighten up the medley of red tomatoes, creamy mozzarella and ripe avocados in this colorful, sensational salad.
—*Lynn Scully, Rancho Santa Fe, California*

- 6 plum tomatoes, chopped
- 2 cartons (8 ounces *each*) fresh mozzarella cheese pearls, drained
- 1/3 cup minced fresh basil
- 1 tablespoon minced fresh parsley
- 2 teaspoons minced fresh mint
- 1/4 cup lemon juice
- 1/4 cup olive oil
- 3/4 teaspoon salt
- 1/4 teaspoon pepper
- 2 medium ripe avocados, peeled and chopped

1. In a large bowl, combine the tomatoes, cheese, basil, parsley and mint; set aside.

2. In a small bowl, whisk the lemon juice, oil, salt and pepper. Pour over tomato mixture; toss to coat. Cover and refrigerate for at least 1 hour before serving.

3. Just before serving, stir in the avocados. Serve salad with a slotted spoon.

Nutrition Facts: 3/4 cup equals 305 calories, 26 g fat (10 g saturated fat), 45 mg cholesterol, 309 mg sodium, 8 g carbohydrate, 4 g fiber, 11 g protein.

Delicious Tomato Pie

Prep: 15 min. • **Bake:** 30 min. • **Yield:** 8 servings.
How about pie for dinner? This savory staple is a wonderful
way to accentuate summer's abundance of tomatoes
from the garden or farm stand.
—*Edie DeSpain, Logan, Utah*

1-1/4 pounds plum tomatoes (about 5 large), cut into 1/2-inch slices	1/4 teaspoon pepper
	1/2 cup reduced-fat mayonnaise
1 pastry shell (9 inches), baked	1/2 cup shredded reduced-fat cheddar cheese
1/2 cup thinly sliced green onions	2 bacon strips, cooked and crumbled
2 tablespoons minced fresh basil	2 tablespoons shredded Parmesan cheese
1/4 teaspoon salt	

1. Place half of the tomatoes in pastry shell. Top with onions and remaining tomatoes. Sprinkle with the basil, salt and pepper. Combine mayonnaise and cheddar cheese; spread over tomatoes, leaving 1-1/2 in. around the edge. Sprinkle with bacon and Parmesan cheese.

2. Bake pie at 350° for 30-35 minutes or until the tomatoes are tender.

Nutrition Facts: 1 piece equals 222 calories, 15 g fat (5 g saturated fat), 17 mg cholesterol, 392 mg sodium, 18 g carbohydrate, 1 g fiber, 5 g protein.

DELICIOUS TOMATO PIE TIP:
The best way to cut through the skin
of a tomato is with a serrated knife.
Cut the tomato vertically, from the
stem end to blossom end, for slices
that will be less juicy and hold their
shape better. —Taste of Home

Spaghetti with Checca Sauce

Prep/Total Time: 20 min. • **Yield:** 2 servings.
This appealing, meatless main dish is full of cheesy tomato flavor.
If you want it saucier, add a bit of the reserved pasta water.
—*Angela Strother, Gainesville, Florida*

4 ounces uncooked spaghetti	2 green onions, chopped
2 tablespoons olive oil	2 garlic cloves, minced
2 small tomatoes, quartered	Dash salt and pepper
3/4 cup shredded Parmesan cheese	2 ounces fresh mozzarella cheese, cut into 1/2-inch cubes
5 fresh basil leaves	1/4 cup hot water

1. Cook spaghetti according to package directions. Meanwhile, in a blender, combine the oil, tomatoes, Parmesan cheese, basil, onions, garlic, salt and pepper; cover and process until coarsely chopped.

2. Drain spaghetti and place in a bowl. Add the tomato mixture, mozzarella cheese and water; toss to coat.

Nutrition Facts: 1-1/2 cups equals 564 calories, 29 g fat (11 g saturated fat), 44 mg cholesterol, 638 mg sodium, 50 g carbohydrate, 3 g fiber, 25 g protein.

SPAGHETTI WITH CHECCA SAUCE NOTES:

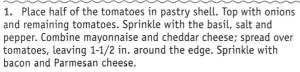

BALSAMIC CHICKEN PASTA SALAD
NOTES:_____
_____
_____
_____

Balsamic Chicken Pasta Salad

Prep/Total Time: 25 min. • **Yield:** 8 servings.
I love all the colors and flavors of this quick and easy dish and serve it often in summer. Everyone loves it! Leftover grilled shrimp makes a tasty substitution.
—*Terri McCarty, Oro Grande, California*

3 cups uncooked bow tie pasta	1/4 cup minced fresh basil
4 cups cubed cooked chicken breast	1/4 cup balsamic vinegar
2 cups chopped tomatoes	2 tablespoons brown sugar
1/2 cup chopped red onion	1 teaspoon minced garlic
4 bacon strips, cooked and crumbled	1/4 teaspoon salt
1/4 cup crumbled Gorgonzola cheese	1/4 teaspoon pepper
1/2 cup olive oil	1/2 cup grated Parmesan cheese

1. Cook pasta according to package directions. Drain and rinse in cold water; transfer to a large bowl. Add the chicken, tomatoes, onion, bacon and Gorgonzola cheese.

2. In a small bowl, whisk the oil, basil, vinegar, brown sugar, garlic, salt and pepper. Drizzle over salad and toss to coat; sprinkle with Parmesan cheese.

Nutrition Facts: 1-1/3 cups equals 408 calories, 20 g fat (5 g saturated fat), 65 mg cholesterol, 323 mg sodium, 28 g carbohydrate, 2 g fiber, 28 g protein.

Bacon & Tomato Spaghetti

Prep/Total Time: 25 min. • **Yield:** 4 servings.
This quick and simple dinner says summer. The refreshing pasta features baby spinach and a tangy balsamic vinaigrette that taste terrific with bacon and cherry tomatoes.
—*Taste of Home Test Kitchen*

8 ounces uncooked spaghetti	3 cups fresh baby spinach
1/2 pound thick-sliced bacon strips, chopped	1/4 cup balsamic vinaigrette
2 cups cherry tomatoes, halved	1/2 teaspoon salt
	1/4 teaspoon pepper
	Grated Parmesan cheese

1. Cook spaghetti according to package directions.

2. Meanwhile, in a large skillet, cook bacon over medium heat until crisp. Using a slotted spoon, remove to paper towels; drain, reserving 2 tablespoons drippings. Saute tomatoes in drippings until tender. Drain spaghetti; stir into skillet. Add the spinach, bacon, vinaigrette, salt and pepper; heat through. Sprinkle with cheese.

Nutrition Facts: 1-1/4 cups equals 409 calories, 18 g fat (5 g saturated fat), 21 mg cholesterol, 833 mg sodium, 49 g carbohydrate, 3 g fiber, 15 g protein.

BACON & TOMATO SPAGHETTI NOTES:
_____
_____
_____
_____

Roasted Tomato Soup with Fresh Basil

Prep: 40 min. • **Cook:** 5 min. • **Yield:** 6 servings.
Roasting really brings out the flavor of the tomatoes in this wonderful soup. It has a slightly chunky texture that indicates it's fresh and homemade.
—*Marie Forte, Raritan, New Jersey*

3-1/2   pounds tomatoes (about 11 medium), halved
   1   small onion, quartered
   2   garlic cloves, peeled and halved
   2   tablespoons olive oil
   2   tablespoons fresh thyme leaves
   1   teaspoon salt
 1/4   teaspoon pepper
  12   fresh basil leaves
Salad croutons and additional fresh basil leaves, optional

1. Place the tomatoes, onion and garlic in a greased 15-in. x 10-in. x 1-in. baking pan; drizzle with oil. Sprinkle with thyme, salt and pepper; toss to coat. Bake at 400° for 25-30 minutes or until tender, stirring once. Cool slightly.

2. In a blender, process tomato mixture and basil in batches until blended. Transfer to a large saucepan and heat through. Garnish each serving with croutons and additional basil if desired.

Nutrition Facts: about 1 cup (calculated without garnish) equals 107 calories, 5 g fat (1 g saturated fat), 0 cholesterol, 411 mg sodium, 15 g carbohydrate, 4 g fiber, 3 g protein. **Diabetic Exchanges:** 3 vegetable, 1 fat.

pineapple salsa
FROM COUNTRY KI...

YELLOW SUMMER SQUASH
relish

savor the
SEASON

CANNING AND
PRESERVING YOUR HARVEST

There's something about canning and preserving the harvest that completes the farm-to-table circle.

Not only do jars of jewel-toned jams and homemade pickles look pretty, canning and preserving is an affordable and healthy way to keep your pantry—and budget—stocked.

From the bare basics to more creative culinary ideas, the recipes featured here let you savor the fruits (and veggies) of your labor all year long.

canning BASICS

TOOLS OF THE TRADE

Everything you see here will get you started canning your garden's bounty using the hot water bath method.

1. **LARGE STOCKPOT:** Choose a stockpot that holds at least 12 quarts and is tall enough to allow the jars to be fully submerged during processing.

2. **LADLE:** Safely pour hot mixtures into canning jars.

3. **JAR FUNNEL:** Place in the mouth of the jar to fill without spilling.

4. **MAGNETIC JAR LIFTER:** Safely lift lids out of hot water with the magnetic end.

5. **BUBBLE REMOVER & HEAD SPACE TOOL:** Slide into the side of filled jar to release any air bubbles and measure head space.

6. **JAR WRENCH:** Turn those stubborn or sticky jar lids effortlessly.

7. **TONGS (WITH COATED HANDLES):** Safely lift foods during canning or cooking.

8. **JAR LIFTER:** Safely remove hot jars from boiling water with one hand.

9. **GLASS CANNING JARS, LIDS AND BANDS:** Fill the glass jars with your yummy creation then seal in the freshness with one-time-use lids and reusable bands.

keys to successful canning:

With a few basic tools, anyone can begin canning. There are two types of canning methods: hot water bath and pressure canning.

This chapter focuses on the hot water bath canning method, which is used to process high-acid foods such as tomatoes, fruits, jams, jellies, pickles and other preserves.

Following the "Keys to Successful Canning" will help you ensure food quality and safety.

• **SELECT FRUITS** and vegetables when they are at the peak of their quality and flavor, and wash them thoroughly before using.

• **FOLLOW DIRECTIONS** for each recipe exactly—don't substitute ingredients or change processing times. Also, prepare only one recipe at a time and do not double recipes.

• **PICK ANY DEEP POT** for a boiling-water canner; just make sure the pot is at least 3 inches deeper than the height of the jars.

Seal the Deal
Canning allows you to savor this year's harvest well into next year.

HOT JARS VS. HOT STERILIZED JARS: Why do some canning recipes call for hot sterilized jars, while others call simply for hot jars?

If the mixture will be processed in the boiling-water canner for 10-plus minutes, jars just need to be hot. If it's less than that, jars need to be sterilized in boiling water for 10 minutes (or 1 more minute for each 1,000 feet of additional altitude).

It's a fact of life that nothing lasts forever. But you can keep on savoring your garden's bounty l-o-n-g after you pull up the last parsnip. How? It all boils down to one simple food-preserving method: canning.

Along with freezing, canning is a successful way to retain virtually all the natural taste and texture of your green-thumb labors. And the process is not difficult. Begin by sterilizing the jars at high temperatures. Then pack the veggies or fruit into bottling jars. Cover the contents with water, syrup or brine and seal while hot to prevent bacteria from entering. Canning really couldn't be much simpler—or the results more delicioius!

PROCESS HEATS UP

Before you start canning, read recipe instructions and gather all equipment and ingredients. Inspect the glass canning jars carefully for any chips, cracks, uneven rims or sharp edges that may prevent sealing or cause breakage. Discard any imperfect jars. Then wash the jars, screw bands and lids in hot soapy water; rinse thoroughly. (You also can use a dishwasher.)

Place the jars in a large kettle. Fill the jars and kettle with hot (not boiling) water that covers the jars by 1 inch; bring to a simmer over medium-low heat. Or, for sterilized jars, after boiling them for 10 minutes, turn heat down so water is at a simmer. Place the lids in a small saucepan of hot water over low heat. Keep jars and lids in the hot water until ready to use. Screw bands just need to be dry and ready to use.

When you're ready to fill the jars, remove them with a jar lifter, emptying water into the kettle. Set jars and lids on a clean kitchen towel.

BRING IT TO A BOIL

1. Add several inches of water to the canner; bring to a simmer. Prepare the recipe as directed. When you're ready to fill the jars, remove them with a jar lifter, emptying water into the kettle or canner. Set jars on a clean kitchen towel, one at a time. Ladle or pour the hot mixture into the prepared jars. Use a ruler to make sure you're leaving the recommended headspace for expansion during processing.

2. Remove air bubbles by sliding a nonmetallic utensil between the food and inside of the jar two or three times. Wipe the threads and rim of the jar with a clean, damp cloth. Place a warm lid on top of each jar with the sealing compound next to the glass. Screw a band onto the jar just until you feel resistance.

3. Immediately after filling each jar, use a jar lifter to place the jar onto the canning rack, making sure the jars are not touching. Using the handles on the rack, lower the filled rack into the canner. Add enough boiling water to the canner to cover jars by 1 to 2 inches. Cover the canner; adjust heat to hold a steady rolling boil. Start counting the processing time when the water returns to a boil. If water level decreases while processing, add more boiling water.

4. When processing time is complete, turn off heat and remove canner lid. Let canner cool 5 minutes before removing jars. Using jar lifter, remove jars and set them upright, 1 to 2 inches apart on a dry towel to cool for 12-24 hours.

5. After jars have cooled, test each lid to determine if it sealed by pressing the center of the lid. Wipe jars to remove any residue. Label and date the jars. Store in a cool, dry, dark place.

6. If the lid is not sealed, do not reprocess. Store the jar in the refrigerator and eat the contents within several days.

- **SUBSTITUTE A CAKE COOLING RACK** if you don't have a rack specifically made for canning. Place it in the canner before you add the canning jars.

- **USE ONLY WHITE VINEGAR** when pickling.

- **USE A CANNING FUNNEL,** which has a wide opening and sits on the inside of the mouth of the jar, allowing you to fill jars cleanly and easily. Wipe the threads and rim of each jar to remove any food that spills.

- **REUSE SCREW BANDS** if they are not warped or rusty. Jar lids are not reusable, however, so use a new one for each of your canned creations.

- **ACCURATELY MEASURE** the head space—the distance between the top of the jar to the food/liquid inside. This is critical because it affects how well the jar seals and preserves its contents. A clear plastic ruler—kept solely for kitchen use—is a big help in determining the correct headspace.

- **REFRIGERATE LEFTOVER PRODUCT** if there's a small amount left that won't completely fill another jar. Use it within several days.

- **USE NONMETALLIC UTENSILS** when removing air bubbles from the jar and measuring head space.

- **STORE HOME-CANNED FOODS** in your cupboard for up to one year.

drying & FREEZING

WHAT'S OLD IS NEW AGAIN!

Drying fruits and vegetables is one of the oldest methods of preserving the harvest.

Luckily for you, it's making a comeback thanks to a renewed interest in do-it-yourself lifestyles and back-to-basics approaches to cooking and eating.

Drying fresh produce, such as green and wax beans, chili peppers and assorted fruits, is simple to do—and easy on the budget, too. In fact, you likely have most of the equipment in your kitchen already.

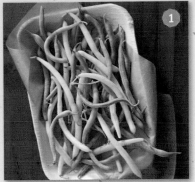

Leather Britches

You bet your britches—drying those extra garden beans is a snap! (And looks pretty nifty, too!)

Tired of steamed green beans? Dry green and wax beansby stringing them together into "leather britches."

PREPARING THE BEANS

STEP 1: Select green beans or wax beans that are fresh and firm. Wash beans and trim off the stem end. Pat beans dry with paper towel.

STRINGING THE BEANS

STEP 2: Hold bean upright. Thread a large darning needle or carpet needle with heavy-duty thread or kite string.

STEP 3: Insert needle and thread through the center of each bean, so both ends of the bean are loose.

SECURING & HANGING LEATHER BRITCHES

STEP 4: Secure the first bean by wrapping the thread around the bean and making a knot. Repeat step 2 until the thread is full. Secure the last bean like the first, cut the thread and. Hang the string of beans in a clean, dry location. Leave for several months or until pods are dried and wrinkled. Once dried, enjoy in soups and stews or keep up as decoration.

Drying Fresh Herbs
Add fresh summer flavor to dishes all year 'round with dried herbs.

Solar drying is suitable in areas with low summer humidity, bright sunshine and good air circulation. The process is slower in humid areas, and mold can be a problem. A small commercial dehydrator is more reliable.

GETTING STARTED

It's important to harvest herbs at the right time. In most cases, leaves provide the herbs' flavors and should be picked before the flowers develop. Harvest them on warm, dry days, in the morning after the dew has evaporated. It's best to pick and prepare one variety of herb for drying at a time.

Discard any damaged or diseased leaves. Strip large-leaved herbs—such as sage and mint—from their stalks. But leave small, feathery herbs—like dill and fennel—on the stalks until drying is complete. Herbs that retain less flavor when dried include basil, chervil, chives and parsley.

DRYING METHODS

Effective drying relies more on abundant dry, fresh air than on heat. A well-ventilated place out of direct sunlight is ideal.

Tarragon, bay, mints, lemon balm, lavender, rosemary and small-leaved herbs such as thyme are well suited to air-drying. Tie sprigs or branches into small bunches to allow adequate aeration. Large, dense bunches can develop mold and discolored leaves.

Hang the bunches up to dry, leaves downward, wrapped loosely in muslin or thin paper bags to

For thousands of years, drying fruits and vegetables was virtually the only way to keep food from spoiling quickly. While it's not nearly as popular today, it's a relatively easy and inexpensive way to preserve produce—especially herbs. It's also an eco-savvy way to embrace a simpler, healthier lifestyle, as dried herbs retain more vitamins and minerals and contain no chemical additives.

Home drying has two principal requirements: correct temperature and adequate ventilation. Food should be laid out on trays or racks, which can be made by stretching muslin, cheesecloth or netting over a wooden frame and fixing it in place. For smaller quantities, use a wire cake rack covered with muslin.

Making a Fragrant Firestarter

To make homemade, fragrant herb fire starters, gather old newspaper and an assortment of herbs. Sage, basil and rosemary work well, but feel free to experiment with your favorites.

Wrap herbs in a sheet of newspaper and secure the ends with raffia or cotton twine.

As you pile the logs, tuck the bundles underneath, allowing the paper ends to stick out. Then, simply light the newspaper ends to start the fire.

As the paper burns, the herbs will ignite, letting the logs catch fire and sending a lovely fragrance through the air.

keep out dust and to catch falling leaves or seeds. Using plastic bags can promote mold development.

Drying time will depend on the size of the branches and humidity. Allow seven to 10 days. The aim is to remove 70 percent of the water content; when crushed, the leaves should sound like crisp cornflakes.

You also can air-dry the seeds of herbs such as fennel, parsley, caraway and coriander. Seed heads ripen unevenly; once most of a head is brown, harvest it with about 2 feet of stem or as long a stem as possible. Bundle four to five stems together, cover the heads with muslin or a paper bag and hang them upside down.

RACK DRYING

You can speed up drying by spacing out individual sprigs or leaves of herbs on a tray. This method is well-suited to large-leaved herbs, such as bay. Place the tray in an airing cupboard, in the warming drawer of an oven or in a warm, airy spot out of direct sunlight. Turn leaves frequently to ensure even drying, which should take two or three days.

OVEN DRYING

The leaves of herbs such as sage, mint, rosemary, thyme and parsley, stripped from their stalks, are well suited to oven drying. Space out leaves on a muslin-covered tray in an oven set to the lowest possible temperature. High temperatures will drive off the fragrant essential oils. Leave the door ajar to allow the moisture to escape.

Turn the leaves over after 30 minutes to ensure even drying; they will be quite dry after about an hour. Leave in the oven until cool.

MICROWAVE DRYING

To dry small quantities of herbs, a microwave oven works quite well. Separate the leaves from the stems, rinse if necessary, and let air dry.

Place a single layer of leaves on a paper towel on a microwave-safe plate. Lay another paper towel on top, and microwave on high for 1 minute. Observe herbs during the drying process, and

stop the microwave if you smell the herbs burning. Continue heating at 30 second intervals, if needed, until the herbs are fully dry.

STORING AND USING

Use the same packing and storing process for all drying methods. Crumble the dried herbs with your fingers (discard the hard leafstalks and midribs) and store in small, airtight containers, preferably made of pottery or opaque glass.

If you use clear glass containers, store them in a dark place so the herbs don't lose their color.

Keep in mind that dried herbs are suitable only for cooked foods, and take note: Drying concentrates the flavors, so you don't need to use as much in recipes. For example, if a recipe calls for 1 tablespoon of fresh herbs, use 1 teaspoon of dried herbs instead.

4

Making A Chili Ristra
Savor the season with an authentic chili ristra.

Chances are, if you've ever traveled out West or eaten at a Mexican or Southwestern restaurant, you've seen a chili ristra. These colorful strings of dried chili peppers originated in New Mexico, where the chili peppers are traditionally harvested and strung into colorful strings called ristras. The chili ristra is allowed to dry in the sun, then hung for use in various spicy dishes throughout the winter.

GETTING STARTED

STEP 1: Select red and green chilis that are ripe (but not overripe), firm and free of blemishes or bruises. Keep the stem intact. Wash and dry the chilis.

MAKING THE RISTRA

STEP 2: Cut a long length of lightweight cotton string, baling wire or twine (approximately 10 feet). Begin making a series of slipknots as pictured.

STEP 3: Begin poking the stems of the peppers through the slipknots. Tighten each knot as you add more peppers. Weave the twine around the stems several times (about every third pepper) and knot twine to make a cluster. Continue the process until you have a "foundation" for your ristra. Cut additional 6-in pieces of twine and attaching more peppers to fill in any gaps.

DRYING THE RISTRA

STEP 4: Once the twine is completely filled in with peppers, hang the completed ristra in full sun, either on a clothesline or from porch rafters where there is good ventilation and light. Good air circulation is key to prevent the chilis from molding. Once dried, use the chilis in sauces and other Southwestern recipes, or simply as kitchen decor.

HOMEMADE DRIED FRUIT
Easy as 1 – 2 – 3!

Dried fruit is a yummy and health-boosting addition to granola, cereal, muffins, yogurt and more. And rumor has it that it tastes even better when you've made it yourself. All you need is your electric oven or a convection oven with a controllable temperature starting at 170 degrees.

Oven drying is the simplest way to dry food, because it requires little to no special equipment. It's also faster and safer than using a sun drying method, especially in cooler regions. Keep in mind, however, that oven drying is for small batches. The average kitchen oven holds approximately 4 to 6 pounds of food at one time.

When it comes to drying produce, patience is key. For the very best quality, prepare produce for drying as soon as possible after harvesting.

PREP

STEP 1: Select fruit that is ripe—but not overripe—and free of bruises. Fresh apples, pears, peaches, berries, cherries, banana and apricots are all good choices. Wash and peel the fruit (blueberries, apricots and cherries work best if dried whole). Remove any pits or cores, then slice the fruit to desired thickness. Keep in mind that thicker slices will take longer to dry, so keep the thickness uniform.

DRYING

STEP 2: Arrange the slices of fruit on nonstick baking sheets—and make sure the pieces aren't touching each other. Preheat the oven to 170°F. Arrange fruit in a single layer on each tray. Put one tray on each oven rack. Be sure to allow 1-1/2 inches on all sides of the tray so air can circulate around the trays while fruit is drying. Keep the oven door open slightly during drying and stir fruit every 30 minutes. Properly dried fruit should be chewy, not squishy or crispy.

ENJOY

STEP 3: Once the fruit is thoroughly dried (it can take anywhere from 4-8 hours depending on the thickness and fruit's water content), remove the trays from the oven and let stand overnight (at least 12 hours) before placing in storage containers.

3

at-a-glance guide to
FREEZING PRODUCE

Have a bumper crop of garden-fresh vegetables and fruits? Lock in peak-season flavor by freezing them. Check out this chart for popular picks that you can enjoy year-round.

PRODUCE	PREPARATION/ STORAGE	BLANCHING TIME	COOKING TIME (FROM FROZEN)
ASPARAGUS	Wash thoroughly, cut off woody parts and grade by thickness. Trim to even lengths; blanch, cool in ice water for 5 minutes and drain. Tie in bundles and store in rigid containers, laying adjacent bundles tips to stalks. Separate layers with parchment paper.	Thin stems: 2 minutes **Thick stems:** 4 minutes	5 to 8 minutes (depending on thickness)
BEANS	Remove tops and tails. Wash and cut into 1-inch pieces. Blanch, cool in ice water for 5 minutes, drain thoroughly and dry. Store in plastic bags.	3 to 4 minutes	5 minutes
BEETS	Freeze only young, small beets about 3 inches across. Wash carefully without breaking skins; boil in water until tender. Cool under cold running water, then rub off skins. Slice or dice, then store in rigid, lined containers with 1/4-inch headspace.		Store for no more than 8 months. Thaw at room temperature in containers and drain.
BROCCOLI	Trim off leaves and woody stems; wash thoroughly in salted water. Divide into sprigs. Blanch, cool in ice water for 5 minutes, drain and dry. Store in cartons, tops to tails, and separate layers with parchment paper.	3 minutes	5 to 8 minutes
BRUSSELS SPROUTS	Choose small, firm heads of uniform size. Remove outer leaves, wash and blanch. Cool in ice water for same amount of time as blanching, then drain and dry. Store in plastic bags.	3 to 4 minutes (depending on size)	8 minutes
CABBAGE (GREEN & RED)	Freeze only young, crisp cabbages. Discard outer leaves. Wash and shred roughly. Blanch, cool, drain and dry. Store in plastic bags.	1-1/2 minutes	8 minutes (use within 6 months)
CARROTS	Use young carrots for best results. Remove tops, trim roots and wash. Peel if necessary. Blanch whole or sliced, cool, drain and dry. Place in rigid containers with 1/4-inch headspace.	**Small, whole:** 5 minutes **Diced, sliced or lengthwise strips:** 2 minutes	8 minutes
CAULIFLOWER	Choose only firm, white cauliflowers. Break into small florets of uniform size, wash and blanch; add several drops of lemon juice to water to preserve color. Cool, drain and dry thoroughly. Store in rigid containers, separating the layers with parchment paper.	3 minutes	8 to 10 minutes (use within 6 months)
PEAS	Shell young garden peas and grade according to size. Blanch, cool quickly in ice water for 5 minutes, drain and dry. Leave sugar snap peas in pods and blanch. Store garden peas in plastic bags; store sugar snap peas in rigid containers with 1/4-inch headspace.	**Garden peas:** 1 to 2 minutes **Sugar snap peas:** 2 to 4 minutes	7 minutes

For more detailed information about freezing and preserving vegetables, visit the website of the National Center for Home Food Preservation at *uga.edu/nchfp*.

PRODUCE	PREPARATION/ STORAGE	BLANCHING TIME	COOKING TIME (FROM FROZEN)
PEPPERS (BELL & SWEET)	Select crisp, tender fruits. Wash, cut in half, remove stems and seeds; if desired, cut into 1/4 inch wide strips or rings. Blanch, cool, drain and seal in plastic bags.	**Halves: 3 minutes Strips or rings: 2 minutes**	Several minutes
SPINACH	Trim stalks, wash thoroughly and drain. Blanch in small portions, cool quickly and squeeze out surplus moisture. Store in rigid containers with 1/4-inch headspace.	2 minutes	7 minutes
SQUASH, WINTER (INCLUDING PUMPKINS)	Wash, peel and cut in half. Scrape out seeds and strings; cut flesh into cubes. Steam, bake or boil until tender. Drain and leave in chunks or mash to a puree. When cool, store in rigid containers, leaving 1-inch headspace.		Thaw at room temperature for about two hours.
SWEET CORN	Freeze only young cobs with pale yellow kernels. Strip off husks and tassels, and trim the stalks close. Blanch a few cobs at a time. Cool, drain and dry. Wrap each cob in aluminum foil, then pack in plastic bags or containers and freeze. Alternatively, scrape the kernels from the blanched cobs and store in rigid containers with 1/4-inch headspace.	**Small: 4 minutes Medium: 6 minutes**	Thaw completely, which takes 3 to 4 hours at room temperature, then boil for 5 to 10 minutes.
TOMATOES	May be frozen whole, but only if used for cooking later. Best frozen as a puree or juice. To freeze whole, wipe small ripe tomatoes and store in plastic bags. To puree, wash and quarter the tomatoes, simmer for 5 minutes and rub through a nylon sieve. Cool and place in rigid containers with 1/4-inch headspace. To prepare juice, wipe and core the tomatoes, cut in quarters and simmer for 10 minutes. Peel and put through a sieve, season with salt and store in rigid containers with 1-inch headspace.		Thaw whole tomatoes in container, slip off skins and use in cooked dishes. Use puree in frozen form in sauces, soups and casseroles. Thaw juice in container and serve chilled.
TURNIPS	May be frozen blanched or cooked and mashed. Trim roots and tops from young turnips. Peel, dice and blanch. Alternatively, cook peeled and quartered turnips until tender, then drain and mash. Cool and store in rigid containers with 1/4-inch headspace.	2 minutes	Cook frozen diced turnips for 8 minutes. Heat partially thawed mashed turnips in a double boiler with butter.
ZUCCHINI	Trim ends from firm young zucchini, wash and cut into 1/4-inch-thick slices. Blanch, cool, drain and dry. Alternatively, fry slices in a little butter and cool quickly. Store in rigid containers, separating the layers with parchment paper and leaving 1/4-inch headspace.	1 minute	Thaw partially and fry in butter.

jams, jellies & SPREADS

WHAT'S THE DIFFERENCE?

Jellies, jams and preserves are all made from fruit mixed with sugar and pectin. So what's the difference, you ask? That depends on the form the fruit is in when it is used in the recipe.

JELLIES: The fruit comes in the form of fruit juice. The finished product is smooth and clear.

JAMS: The fruit comes in the form of fruit pulp or crushed fruit. As a result, the final product isn't as firm as jelly.

PRESERVES: The fruit comes in the form of chunks in a syrup or a jam. The final result is thick, and bits of fruit are visible.

A NOTE ABOUT CANNING & PRESERVING: The processing time listed is for altitudes of 1,000 feet or less. Add 1 minute to the processing time for each 1,000 feet of additional altitude.

Spiced Pear Jam

Prep: 1 hour 40 min. • **Process:** 10 min. • **Yield:** 6 half-pints.
Years ago, my in-laws had three pear trees on their acreage and gave us all the fruit that we wanted to pick. So I canned plenty of pears. Then a neighbor passed along this favorite recipe. I've given many jars of this jam as gifts. My family enjoys it on toast with ham and eggs or on hot rolls with a meat.
—*Karen Bockelman, Portland, Oregon*

8 cups chopped *or* coarsely ground peeled pears (about 5-1/2 pounds)	1 teaspoon ground cinnamon
4 cups sugar	1/4 teaspoon ground cloves

1. Combine all ingredients in a Dutch oven. Simmer, uncovered, for 1-1/2 to 2 hours or until thick, stirring occasionally. Stir more frequently as the mixture thickens.

2. Remove from the heat; skim off foam. Carefully ladle into hot half-pint jars, leaving 1/4-in. headspace. Remove air bubbles; wipe rims and adjust lids. Process for 10 minutes in a boiling-water canner.

Nutrition Facts: 2 tablespoons equals 81 calories, trace fat (trace saturated fat), 0 cholesterol, trace sodium, 21 g carbohydrate, 1 g fiber, trace protein.

EDITOR'S NOTE: This recipe does not require pectin.

SPICED PEAR JAM NOTES: _____
_____
_____
_____
_____
_____

Watermelon Jelly

Prep: 25 min. + standing • **Process:** 10 min. • **Yield:** 5 half-pints.
For a delicious jelly to serve or give as a gift, make this tasty treat. The watermelon is sweet but not too sweet.
—*Taste of Home Test Kitchen*

6 cups seeded chopped watermelon	1/4 cup lemon juice
5 cups sugar	2 to 3 drops red food coloring, optional
1/3 cup white wine vinegar *or* white balsamic vinegar	2 pouches (3 ounces *each*) liquid fruit pectin

1. Place watermelon in a food processor; cover and process until pureed. Line a strainer with four layers of cheesecloth and place over a bowl. Place pureed watermelon in prepared strainer; cover with edges of cheesecloth. Let stand for 10 minutes or until liquid measures 2 cups.

2. Discard the watermelon pulp from cheesecloth; place liquid in a large saucepan. Stir in the sugar, vinegar, lemon juice and food coloring if desired. Bring to a full rolling boil over high heat, stirring constantly. Stir in the pectin. Boil for 1 minute, stirring constantly.

3. Remove from the heat; skim off foam. Ladle hot mixture into hot half-pint jars, leaving 1/4-in. headspace. Remove air bubbles; wipe rims and adjust lids. Process for 10 minutes in a boiling-water canner.

Nutrition Facts: 2 tablespoons equals 106 calories, trace fat (trace saturated fat), 0 cholesterol, 1 mg sodium, 27 g carbohydrate, trace fiber, trace protein.

WATERMELLON JELLY NOTES:
_____
_____
_____
_____

SAVORY JELLIES STAND OUT.
Served with cream cheese and
crackers, spread over a bagel
or used as a glaze for poultry,
jewel-tone herb jellies really know
how to make a delicious name
for themselves. (Pictured here
clockwise: Basil Jelly, Rosemary
Jelly and Mint Jelly.)

Basil Jelly

Prep: 25 min. • **Process:** 15 min. • **Yield:** 6 half-pints.
We grow lots of basil for our local farmers market, and this is a unique way to use it. The jelly is good with cream cheese as an appetizer. I also like to combine a jar with 1 cup of barbecue sauce and simmer mini meatballs or cocktail wieners in the mixture.
—*Sue Gronholz, Beaver Dam, Wisconsin*

4 cups water	3 drops green food coloring, optional
2 cups firmly packed fresh basil leaves, finely chopped	5 cups sugar
1 package (1-3/4 ounces) powdered fruit pectin	

1. In a large saucepan, bring water and basil to a boil. Remove from the heat; cover and let stand for 10 minutes. Strain and discard basil. Return 3-2/3 cups liquid to the pan.

2. Stir in pectin and food coloring if desired. Return to a rolling boil over high heat. Stir in sugar. Boil for 1 minute, stirring constantly. Remove from the heat; skim off foam.

3. Carefully ladle hot mixture into hot half-pint jars, leaving 1/4-in. headspace. Remove air bubbles, wipe rims and adjust lids. Process for 15 minutes in a boiling-water canner.

Nutrition Facts: 2 tablespoons equals 81 calories, trace fat (0 saturated fat), 0 cholesterol, trace sodium, 21 g carbohydrate, trace fiber, trace protein.

Homemade jellies and jams make wonderful gifts for a variety of occasions. Before giving away, put a piece of colorful cloth over the jar and hold in place with a rubber band. Tie a ribbon around the jar, snip off the rubber band and you've got a lovely gift in hand. —Taste of Home

Rosemary Jelly

Prep: 35 min. • **Process:** 10 min. • **Yield:** 3-1/2 pints.
This deliciously different green jelly gets its flavor from an unusual source: savory rosemary. The herb adds a refreshing zip to the otherwise sweet spread.
—*Margaret Dumire, Carroll, Ohio*

1-1/4 cups boiling water	1 pouch (3 ounces) liquid fruit pectin
2 tablespoons minced fresh rosemary	2 to 3 drops green food coloring
3 cups sugar	
1/4 cup cider vinegar	

1. In a large saucepan, combine boiling water and rosemary; cover and let stand for 15 minutes. Strain, reserving liquid. If necessary, add water to measure 1-1/4 cups. Return liquid to pan; add sugar and vinegar. Bring to a full rolling boil over high heat, stirring constantly. Add pectin, stirring until mixture boils. Boil and stir for 1 minute.

2. Remove from the heat; skim off foam. Add food coloring if desired. Carefully ladle hot mixture into hot half-pint jars, leaving 1/4-in. headspace. Remove air bubbles, wipe rims and adjust lids. Process for 10 minutes in a boiling-water canner.

Nutrition Facts: 2 tablespoons equals 42 calories, trace fat (0 saturated fat), 0 cholesterol, trace sodium, 11 g carbohydrate, trace fiber, trace protein.

Mint Jelly

Prep: 20 min. • **Process:** 10 min. • **Yield:** about 6 half-pints.
One whiff is all it takes to tell what we grow on our farm—peppermint! I use fresh mint or mint oil frequently in my cooking and baking. Try this aromatic jelly on lamb or oven-fresh biscuits.
—*Kandy Clarke, Columbia Falls, Montana*

1 cup packed peppermint leaves	1/2 teaspoon butter
2 cups water	2 pouches (3 ounces each) liquid fruit pectin
6-1/2 cups sugar	
1 cup white vinegar	3 to 4 drops green food coloring

1. In a Dutch oven, bring mint and water to a boil. Boil for 1 minute. Remove from the heat and pour though a fine sieve, reserving mint liquid. Discard leaves.

2. Return liquid to pan. Add the sugar, vinegar and butter; bring to a boil, stirring constantly. Quickly add contents of both pectin pouches; bring to a full rolling boil. Boil for 1 minute, stirring constantly. Remove from the heat; skim off foam. Add food coloring.

3. Carefully ladle into hot sterilized half-pint jars, leaving 1/4-in. headspace. Remove air bubbles; wipe rims and adjust lids. Process for 5 minutes in a boiling-water canner.

4. Or cool to room temperature, about 1 hour. Cover and let stand overnight or until set, but not longer than 24 hours. Refrigerate or freeze. (Refrigerate for up to 3 weeks or freeze for up to 12 months.)

Nutrition Facts: 2 tablespoons equals 126 calories, trace fat (trace saturated fat), trace cholesterol, 1 mg sodium, 31 g carbohydrate, trace fiber, trace protein.

JELLY NOTES: _____

_____

_____

_____

_____

_____

_____

Blackberry Apple Jelly

Prep: 45 min. • **Process:** 5 min. • **Yield:** about 9 half-pints.

August is the busiest month of the year on our small farm—that's when we're harvesting sweet corn and pumpkins and pickling cucumbers for our stand. But I always make time to put up this jelly. The apples come from our old-fashioned orchard, while the blackberries grow wild along our creek. No matter how much I make, it's usually gone by January!

—*Liz Endacott, Matsqui, British Columbia*

3 pounds blackberries (about 2-1/2 quarts)
1-1/4 cups water
7 to 8 medium apples
Additional water
Bottled apple juice, optional
1/4 cup bottled lemon juice
8 cups sugar
2 pouches (3 ounces *each*) liquid fruit pectin

1. In a Dutch oven, bring blackberries and water to a boil. Reduce heat; simmer for 5 minutes. Line a strainer with four layers of cheesecloth and place over a bowl. Place berry mixture in strainer; cover with edges of cheesecloth. Let stand for 30 minutes or until strained, reserving juice and discarding pulp.

2. Remove and discard stems and blossom ends from apples (do not pare or core); cut into small pieces. Place in the Dutch oven; add just enough water to cover. Bring to a boil. Reduce heat; simmer for 20 minutes or until apples are tender. Strain through a cheesecloth-lined strainer, reserving juice and discarding pulp.

3. Measure the reserved blackberry and apple juices; return to the pan. If necessary, add water or bottled apple juice to equal 4 cups. Stir in lemon juice, then sugar. Bring to a full rolling boil, stirring constantly. Stir in pectin; return to a full rolling boil. Boil for 1 minute, stirring constantly.

4. Remove from the heat; skim off foam. Carefully ladle hot mixture into hot sterilized half-pint jars, leaving 1/4-in. headspace. Wipe rims and adjust lids. Process for 5 minutes in a boiling-water canner.

Nutrition Facts: 2 tablespoons equals 104 calories, trace fat (trace saturated fat), 0 cholesterol, trace sodium, 27 g carbohydrate, 1 g fiber, trace protein.

Orange Rhubarb Spread

Prep: 5 min. • **Cook:** 20 min. + standing • **Yield:** 5 half-pints.
This tangy spread is easy to make and tastes especially good on hot,
buttered cinnamon toast. The recipe makes enough to have on hand
well beyond the growing season.
—*Betty Nyenhuis, Oostburg, Wisconsin*

- 4 cups diced fresh *or* frozen rhubarb
- 2 cups water
- 1 can (6 ounces) frozen orange juice concentrate, thawed
- 1 package (1-3/4 ounces) powdered fruit pectin
- 4 cups sugar

1. In a large saucepan, bring rhubarb and water to a boil.
Reduce heat; simmer, uncovered, for 7-8 minutes or until
rhubarb is tender. Drain and reserve cooking liquid. Cool
rhubarb and liquid to room temperature.

2. Place the rhubarb in a blender; cover and process until
pureed. Transfer to a 4-cup measuring cup; add enough reserved
cooking liquid to measure 2-1/3 cups. Return to the saucepan.

3. Add orange juice concentrate and pectin; bring to a full
rolling boil, stirring constantly. Stir in sugar. Return to a full
rolling boil; boil and stir for 1 minute. Remove from the heat;
skim off foam.

4. Pour into jars or freezer containers; cool to room
temperature, about 1 hour. Cover and let stand overnight or
until set, but not longer than 24 hours. Refrigerate or freeze.
Refrigerate for up to 3 weeks and freeze for up to 12 months.

Nutrition Facts: 2 tablespoons equals 94 calories, trace fat (trace
saturated fat), 0 cholesterol, 1 mg sodium, 24 g carbohydrate, trace
fiber, trace protein.

ORANGE RHUBARB SPREAD NOTES:

_____
_____
_____
_____
_____

Old-Fashioned Blueberry Jam

Prep: 50 min. • **Process:** 10 min. • **Yield:** 4 half-pints.
This is such an easy jam recipe that comes together very quickly.
It also makes a great gift for friends and family!
—*Kay Laney, North Liberty, Indiana*

- 5 cups fresh *or* frozen blueberries
- 1/4 cup water
- 3 cups sugar
- 1 cup clover honey

1. In a Dutch oven, bring blueberries and water to a boil;
mash and stir for 5 minutes. Add the sugar and clover honey;
boil gently, uncovered, over medium heat for 30 minutes,
stirring frequently.

2. To test for doneness: Remove from heat; spoon about
1 tablespoon of hot jam onto a chilled plate and set plate
in freezer until the jam has cooled to room temperature, 1-2
minutes. When cooled jam holds its shape when mounded with
a spoon, the it has reached its desired thickness. If necessary,
return to heat and repeat test after additional cooking.

3. Skim off any foam. Carefully ladle hot mixture into hot
half-pint jars, leaving 1/4 in. of headspace. Remove air bubbles;
wipe rims and adjust lids. Process for 10 minutes in boiling-
water canner.

Nutrition Facts: 1 tablespoon equals 59 calories, trace fat (trace saturated
fat), 0 cholesterol, trace sodium, 15 g carbohydrate, trace fiber, trace protein.

EDITOR'S NOTE: This recipe does not require packaged pectin.

OLD-FASHIONED BLUEBERRY JAM NOTES:

_____
_____
_____
_____

One day I was in a hurry to make strawberry jam. Instead of mashing the fruit by hand, I put the berries in the blender and gave it a couple of whirls. I had evenly crushed berries in no time.
—Gale S., Pembroke, Ontario

Cherry Almond Preserves

Prep: 30 min. • **Process:** 10 min. • **Yield:** 11 half-pints.
My family likes these preserves on fresh bread, muffins, pancakes and even ice cream—the consistency's similar to a topping.
—Connie Lawrence, Hamilton, Montana

8 cups pitted sour cherries (about 4 pounds)	2 pouches (3 ounces *each*) liquid fruit pectin
1-1/2 cups water	1 teaspoon almond extract
10 cups sugar	

1. In a stock pot, bring the cherries and water to a boil; boil for 15 minutes.

2. Add sugar and bring to a full rolling boil, stirring constantly. Boil for 4 minutes. Stir in pectin; return to a full rolling boil. Boil for 1 minute, stirring constantly. Remove from the heat; stir in extract. Skim off foam.

3. Carefully ladle into hot half-pint jars, leaving 1/4-in. headspace. Remove air bubbles; wipe rims and adjust lids. Process 10 minutes in a boiling-water canner.

Nutrition Facts: 2 tablespoons equals 106 calories, trace fat (trace saturated fat), 0 cholesterol, 2 mg sodium, 27 g carbohydrate, trace fiber, trace protein.

Blushing Peach Jam

Prep: 20 min. • **Process:** 5 min. • **Yield:** 4 pints.
We love this jam so much, we're going to start growing raspberries.
—Cheryl Hall, Osceola, Indiana

2 cups crushed peeled peaches	7 cups sugar
2 cups red raspberries, crushed	2 pouches (3 ounces *each*) liquid fruit pectin
1/4 cup bottled lemon juice	1/8 teaspoon almond extract

1. In a Dutch oven, combine the peaches, raspberries and lemon juice. Stir in sugar. Bring to a full rolling boil, stirring constantly. Stir in pectin; return to a full rolling boil. Boil for 1 minute, stirring constantly.

2. Remove from the heat; skim off foam. Add extract. Carefully ladle hot mixture into hot sterilized pint jars, leaving 1/4-in. headspace. Wipe rims and adjust lids. Process for 5 minutes in a boiling-water canner.

Nutrition Facts: 2 tablespoons equals 89 calories, trace fat (trace saturated fat), 0 cholesterol, trace sodium, 23 g carbohydrate, trace fiber, trace protein.

Cinnamon Plum Jam

Prep: 15 min. • **Process:** 10 min. • **Yield:** 7 half-pints.
When I share this slightly sweet jam with family and friends, it disappears quickly—I've learned to make more than one batch!
—Eloise Neeley, Norton, Ohio

7 cups sugar	juice
5 cups coarsely ground peeled plums (about 2-1/2 pounds)	1 package (1-3/4 ounces) powdered fruit pectin
1/2 cup water	1/2 teaspoon ground cinnamon
1/3 cup bottled lemon	

1. In a Dutch oven, combine sugar, plums, water and lemon juice. Bring to a full rolling boil, stirring constantly. Stir in pectin; return to a full rolling boil. Boil 1 minute, stirring constantly. Remove from the heat; stir in cinnamon. Skim off foam.

2. Carefully ladle hot jam into hot half-pint jars, leaving 1/4-in. headspace. Remove air bubbles; wipe the rims and adjust the lids. Process jam for 10 minutes in a boiling-water canner.

Nutrition Facts: 2 tablespoons equals 110 calories, trace fat (trace saturated fat), 0 cholesterol, trace sodium, 28 g carbohydrate, trace fiber, trace protein.

JAM AND PRESERVES NOTES: _____

WHY SKIM OFF THE FOAM?
The foam that results while making jam is the result of bubbles from the boiling process rising through the viscous jam. Foam left in a jar of jam increases the headspace. That extra head space can increase the chance of the jam molding after prolonged storage. (Pictured here from back: Old Fashioned Blueberry Jam page 217, Cinnamon Plum Jam, Cherry Almond Preserves, Blushing Peach Jam)

Over-the-Top Cherry Jam

Prep: 35 min. • **Process:** 5 min. • **Yield:** 6 half-pints.
We live in Door County, Wisconsin—an area known for its
wonderful tart cherries. This beautiful, sweet jam tastes
especially good on thick slices of toast and English muffins.
—*Karen Haen, Sturgeon Bay, Wisconsin*

2-1/2	pounds fresh tart cherries, pitted	1/2	teaspoon butter
1	package (1-3/4 ounces) powdered fruit pectin	4-3/4	cups sugar

1. In a food processor, cover and process cherries in
batches until finely chopped. Transfer to a Dutch oven;
stir in pectin and butter. Bring to a full rolling boil over
high heat, stirring constantly. Stir in sugar; return to a full
rolling boil. Boil for 1 minute, stirring constantly.

2. Remove from the heat; skim off foam. Ladle hot
mixture into hot sterilized half-pint jars, leaving 1/4-in.
headspace. Remove air bubbles; wipe rims and adjust lids.
Process for 5 minutes in a boiling-water canner.

Nutrition Facts: 2 tablespoons equals 89 calories, trace fat (trace
saturated fat), trace cholesterol, 1 mg sodium, 23 g carbohydrate,
trace fiber, trace protein.

OVER-THE-TOP CHERRY JAM NOTES:
_____
_____
_____
_____

PEAR TOMATO PRESERVES NOTES:
_____
_____
_____
_____

Pear Tomato Preserves

Prep: 1 hour 20 min. • **Process:** 20 min. • **Yield:** 5 half-pints.
I have lived on a farm all my life so I always have had a garden.
I can a lot of my garden-grown fruits and veggies and have
made these wonderful preserves every year.
—*Evelyn Stearns, Alto Pass, Illinois*

4	cups sugar	2	medium lemons, chopped
1	tablespoon ground cinnamon	1	cup water
2	teaspoons ground cloves	2	pounds yellow pear tomatoes, chopped
1	teaspoon ground ginger		

1. In a Dutch oven, combine sugar, cinnamon, cloves, ginger,
lemons and water. Cook over medium heat for 15 minutes,
stirring occasionally. Add the tomatoes. Reduce heat to low;
continue cooking for 45-60 minutes or until tomatoes become
transparent, stirring frequently.

2. Carefully ladle hot mixture into hot half-pint jars, leaving
1/4-in. headspace. Remove air bubbles, wipe rims and adjust
lids. Process for 20 minutes in a boiling-water canner.

Nutrition Facts: 2 tablespoons equals 165 calories, trace fat (trace
saturated fat), 0 cholesterol, 12 mg sodium, 42 g carbohydrate, 1 g fiber,
trace protein.

EDITOR'S NOTE: This recipe does not require packaged pectin.

Cranberry Jam

Prep: 15 min. + freezing • **Cook:** 50 min. + cooling
Yield: 3-4 half-pints.
Although this recipe takes a bit of effort, the mouthwatering results are well worth it. The scarlet red fruits make a lovely spread that has a delicious tart and tangy flavor.
—*Evelyn Gebhardt, Kasilof, Alaska*

7-1/2 cups fresh cranberries	3/4 teaspoon ground allspice
3/4 cup water	1/2 teaspoon ground cinnamon
2 cups sugar	1/4 teaspoon ground nutmeg
1 tablespoon grated orange peel	
2 tablespoons orange juice	

1. In a large covered kettle, simmer cranberries and water for 20-25 minutes, stirring occasionally.

2. Press berries through a strainer; discard skins. Strain mixture through a double layer of cheesecloth (juice will drip through; discard or set aside for another use). Measure 6 cups of the pulp that remains in the cheesecloth and place in the kettle. Add remaining ingredients.

3. Simmer, uncovered, for 30-40 minutes, stirring frequently. Pour into freezer containers. Cool. Refrigerate or freeze.

Nutrition Facts: 2 tablespoons equals 80 calories, trace fat (trace saturated fat), 0 cholesterol, 1 mg sodium, 21 g carbohydrate, 1 g fiber, trace protein.

CRANBERRY JAM NOTES:

CINNAMON BLUEBERRY JAM NOTES:

Cinnamon Blueberry Jam

Prep: 15 min. • **Process:** 10 min. • **Yield:** 4 half-pints.
Watching my grandmother can jars of tomatoes, peaches and pears inspired me to try making jams and jellies myself. This one's a keeper.
—*Barbara Burns, Phillipsburg, New Jersey*

1 pound fresh *or* frozen blueberries (about 1 quart)	1/4 teaspoon ground cinnamon
3-1/2 cups sugar	1/8 teaspoon ground cloves
1 tablespoon bottled lemon juice	1 pouch (3 ounces) liquid fruit pectin

1. Crush blueberries; measure 2-1/2 cups and place in a large saucepan. Add the sugar, lemon juice, cinnamon and cloves; bring to a rolling boil over high heat, stirring constantly. Quickly stir in the pectin. Return to a full rolling boil; boil for 1 minute, stirring constantly.

2. Remove from the heat; skim off foam. Carefully ladle hot mixture into hot half-pint jars, leaving 1/4-in. headspace. Remove air bubbles; wipe rims and adjust lids. Process for 10 minutes in a boiling-water canner.

Nutrition Facts: 2 tablespoons equals 93 calories, trace fat (trace saturated fat), 0 cholesterol, 1 mg sodium, 24 g carbohydrate, trace fiber, trace protein.

RHUBARB MARMALADE NOTES:

_____
_____
_____
_____
_____

Rhubarb Marmalade

Prep: 1-1/4 hours • **Process:** 10 min. • **Yield:** about 8 half-pints.
My daughter makes this marmalade every spring when rhubarb's abundant. Our family enjoys her gift...a refreshing departure in flavor from all the "berry" jams and jellies.
—Leo Nerbonne, Delta Juction, Alaska

| 6 cups chopped fresh _or_ frozen rhubarb | 6 cups sugar |
| 2 medium oranges | |

1. Combine rhubarb and sugar in a Dutch oven. Grind oranges, including the peels, in a food processor; add to rhubarb mixture. Bring to a boil. Reduce heat and simmer, uncovered, stirring often until marmalade sheets from a spoon, about 1 hour.

2. Remove from the heat; skim off foam. Carefully ladle hot mixture into hot half-pint jars, leaving 1/4-in. headspace. Remove air bubbles; wipe rims and adjust lids. Process for 10 minutes in a boiling-water canner.

Nutrition Facts: 2 tablespoons equals 76 calories, trace fat (trace saturated fat), 0 cholesterol, 1 mg sodium, 20 g carbohydrate, trace fiber, trace protein.

EDITOR'S NOTE: If using frozen rhubarb, measure rhubarb while still frozen, then thaw completely. Drain in a colander, but do not press liquid out. This recipe does not require pectin.

Freezer Berry Jam

Prep: 20 min. + standing • **Cook:** 10 min. + cooling
Yield: 3-1/2 pints.
We live on the farm where my husband was raised. Whenever we find wild blueberries nearby, I make this gorgeous ruby-red jam. It's also wonderful as a breakfast sauce.
—Rita Pischke, Whitemouth, Manitoba

4 cups blueberries	3/4 cup water
2 cups raspberries	1 package (1-3/4 ounces) powdered fruit pectin
5 cups sugar	
2 tablespoons lemon juice	

1. In a large bowl, mash the blueberries. Add raspberries and mash. Stir in sugar and lemon juice. Let stand for 10 minutes. In a small saucepan, bring water and pectin to a boil. Boil for 1 minute, stirring constantly. Add to fruit mixture; stir for 3 minutes or until sugar is dissolved.

2. Pour into jars or freezer containers; cool to room temperature, about 30 minutes. Cover and let stand overnight or until set, but not longer than 24 hours. Refrigerate for up to 3 weeks or freeze for up to 1 year.

Nutrition Facts: 2 tablespoons equals 82 calories, trace fat (trace saturated fat), 0 cholesterol, trace sodium, 21 g carbohydrate, 1 g fiber, trace protein.

FREEZER BERRY JAM NOTES: _____
_____
_____
_____
_____
_____

Texas Jalapeno Jelly

Prep: 15 min. • **Process:** 10 min. • **Yield:** 7 half-pints.
A jar of this jelly is always warmly received. I like to add a
Southwestern accent by trimming the lid with a bandanna.
—*Lori McMullen, Victoria, Texas*

- 2 jalapeno peppers, seeded and chopped
- 3 medium green peppers, cut into 1-inch pieces, *divided*
- 1-1/2 cups white vinegar, *divided*
- 6-1/2 cups sugar
- 1/2 to 1 teaspoon cayenne pepper
- 2 pouches (3 ounces *each*) liquid fruit pectin

About 6 drops green food coloring, optional

Cream cheese and crackers, optional

1. In a blender or food processor, place the jalapenos, half of the green peppers and 1/2 cup vinegar; cover and process until pureed. Transfer to a large Dutch oven.

2. Repeat with remaining green peppers and another 1/2 cup vinegar. Add the sugar, cayenne and remaining vinegar to pan. Bring to a rolling boil over high heat, stirring constantly. Quickly stir in pectin. Return to a rolling boil; boil for 1 minute, stirring constantly.

3. Remove from the heat; skim off foam. Add food coloring if desired. Carefully ladle hot mixture into hot half-pint jars, leaving 1/4-in. headspace. Remove air bubbles; wipe rims and adjust lids.

4. Process for 10 minutes in a boiling-water canner. Serve over cream cheese with crackers if desired.

Nutrition Facts: 2 tablespoons equals 92 calories, trace fat (trace saturated fat), 0 cholesterol, 1 mg sodium, 24 g carbohydrate, trace fiber, trace protein.

EDITOR'S NOTE: When cutting hot peppers, disposable gloves are recommended. Avoid touching your face.

pickles & RELISHES

Fresh Tomato Relish

Prep: 30 min. + chilling • **Yield:** about 6 pints.
I usually make a batch as soon as the first tomatoes of the season are ready. It will keep for months in the freezer.
—Lela Baskins, Windsor, Missouri

2	cups white vinegar
1/2	cup sugar
8	cups chopped tomatoes (about 11 large)
1/2	cup chopped onion
1	medium green pepper, diced
1	celery rib, diced
1/4	cup prepared horseradish
2	tablespoons salt
1	tablespoon mustard seed
1-1/2	teaspoons pepper
1/2	teaspoon ground cinnamon
1/2	teaspoon ground cloves

1. In a large saucepan, bring vinegar and sugar to a boil. Remove from the heat; cool completely.

2. In a large bowl, combine remaining ingredients; add vinegar mixture and mix well. Spoon into storage containers, allowing 1/2-in. headspace. Refrigerate up to 2 weeks or freeze up to 12 months. Serve with a slotted spoon.

Nutrition Facts: 2 tablespoons equals 9 calories, trace fat (trace saturated fat), 0 cholesterol, 151 mg sodium, 2 g carbohydrate, trace fiber, trace protein.

Pickling is easy, affordable...and not just for cucumbers anymore!

Here, you'll find a generous selection of recipes for dill and sweet cucumber pickles (as well as some yummy creations that use all that extra summer squash and zucchini you have on hand), pickled vegetables perfect for summer appetizer trays and colorful, tasty relishes to top hot dogs, burgers and sandwiches.

FRESH TOMATO RELISH NOTES:

Spicy Pickled Green Beans

Prep: 20 min. • **Process:** 10 min. • **Yield:** 4 pints.
A coworker brought these pickled beans into work one day...I was
hooked after one bite! And I was thrilled when a jar of my beans
won first place at the local county fair.
—*Jill Darin, Geneseo, Illinois*

1-3/4 pounds fresh green beans, trimmed	4 teaspoons dill seed *or* 4 fresh dill heads
1 teaspoon cayenne pepper	2-1/2 cups water
4 garlic cloves, peeled	2-1/2 cups white vinegar
	1/4 cup canning salt

1. Pack beans into four hot 1-pint jars to within 1/2 in. of the
top. Add the cayenne, garlic and dill seed to jars.

2. In a large saucepan, bring the water, vinegar and salt
to a boil.

3. Carefully ladle hot mixture over beans, leaving 1/2-in.
headspace. Remove air bubbles; wipe rims and adjust lids.
Process for 10 minutes in a boiling-water canner.

Nutrition Facts: 8 green beans equals 9 calories, trace fat (trace saturated
fat), 0 cholesterol, 83 mg sodium, 2 g carbohydrate, 1 g fiber, 1 g protein.
Diabetic Exchange: Free food.

EDITOR'S NOTE: The processing time listed is for altitudes of 1,000 feet
or less. For altitudes up to 3,000 feet, add 5 minutes; 6,000 feet, add 10
minutes; 8,000 feet, add 15 minutes; 10,000 feet, add 20 minutes.

SPICY PICKLED GREEN BEANS NOTES:

Easy Refrigerator Pickles

Prep: 45 min. + chilling • **Yield:** 4-1/2 quarts.
In July, cucumbers are at their peak. Take advantage of garden extras
by whipping up a few jars of pickles. My husband grows cucumbers,
garlic and dill and eagerly waits for me to make these.
—*Angela Lienhard, Blossburg, Pennsylvania*

14 pickling cucumbers	1/2 cup sugar
40 fresh dill sprigs	1/3 cup salt
4 garlic cloves, sliced	1 teaspoon mixed pickling spices
2 quarts water	
1 cup cider vinegar	

1. Cut each cucumber lengthwise into six spears. In a large
bowl, combine the cucumbers, dill and garlic; set aside.

2. In a Dutch oven, combine the remaining ingredients. Bring
to a boil; cook and stir just until sugar is dissolved. Pour over
cucumber mixture; cool.

3. Transfer to jars if desired and cover tightly. Refrigerate for
at least 24 hours. Store in the refrigerator for up to 2 weeks.

Nutrition Facts: 1 pickle equals 4 calories, trace fat (trace saturated fat),
0 cholesterol, 85 mg sodium, 1 g carbohydrate, trace fiber, trace protein.
Diabetic Exchange: Free Food.

EASY REFRIGERATOR PICKLES NOTES:

PICKLED PERFECTION.
When making pickled asparagus, select spears that are fresh and crisp. Remove any soft, spotted or bug-chewed areas. Asparagus that's past its prime won't taste very good, and it won't look as pretty in the jar either. —Taste of Home

Pickled Peppers

Prep: 35 min. • **Process:** 10 min. • **Yield:** about 8 pints.
Making your own pickled peppers is so easy, you will never have to purchase store-bought peppers ever again.
—*Taste of Home Test Kitchen*

4 quarts long red, green *or* yellow peppers (Hungarian, banana, etc.)	4 quarts plus 2 cups water, *divided*
	10 cups white vinegar
	1/4 cup sugar
1-1/2 cups canning salt	2 garlic cloves, peeled

1. Cut 2 small slits in each pepper and place in a large bowl. Dissolve salt in 4 qts. water. Pour salt water over peppers; let stand 12 to 18 hours in a cool place. Drain; rinse and drain thoroughly.

2. In a Dutch oven, combine the vinegar, sugar, garlic and remaining water; bring to a boil and simmer 15 minutes. Remove garlic. Pack peppers into hot pint jars, leaving 1/2-in. headspace. Carefully ladle hot liquid over peppers, leaving 1/2-in. headspace. Remove air bubbles with a non-metallic utensil. Adjust lids. Process 10 minutes in a boiling-water canner.

EDITOR'S NOTE: When cutting hot peppers, disposable gloves are recommended. Avoid touching your face.

PICKLED PEPPERS NOTES:_____
_____
_____
_____
_____
_____
_____
_____
_____
_____

Pickled Asparagus

Prep: 45 min. • **Process:** 20 min. • **Yield:** 8 quarts.
These tangy spears make a great addition to a relish tray.
—*Marie Hattrup, Sparks, Nevada*

9 quarts water, *divided*	1 cup canning salt
16 pounds fresh asparagus, trimmed	1 tablespoon mixed pickling spices
	1 garlic clove, minced
2 quarts white vinegar	

1. In a stockpot, bring 6 qts. of water to a boil. Cook asparagus in batches, uncovered, for 2-1/2 minutes. Remove and rinse in cold water.

2. In a Dutch oven, combine the vinegar, salt, pickling spices, garlic and remaining water; bring to a boil. Pack asparagus in quart jars to within 1/2 in. of top.

3. Carefully ladle hot mixture into hot quart jars, leaving 1/2-in. headspace. Remove air bubbles, wipe rims and adjust lids. Process for 20 minutes in a boiling-water canner.

Nutrition Facts: 1/4 cup equals 7 calories, trace fat (trace saturated fat), 0 cholesterol, 888 mg sodium, 1 g carbohydrate, trace fiber, 1 g protein.

PICKLED ASPARAGUS NOTES: _____
_____
_____
_____
_____
_____
_____
_____
_____
_____
_____

REMEMBER TO TEST THE SEAL: After 12 to 24 hours, test each of the lids to determine if they have sealed by pressing the center of the lid. If the lid is indented, remove the band and try to lift the lid. If the lid is secure, the jar is vacuum-sealed. Wipe the jars to remove any food. Label and date the jars.
If the lid is not sealed, do not reprocess. Store the jar in the refrigerator and eat the contents within several days.

WHITE VS. CIDER VINEGAR.
Vinegar provides the tart, puckery flavor in pickles, but it also acts as an important preservative. You can replace white vinegar with cider vinegar in pickling recipes, as long as the cider vinegar has a 5% (50 grains) acidity level. Look for this on the label. (Pictured here: Pickled Asparagus and Pickled Peppers.)

Pickled Pumpkin

Prep: 15 min. • **Cook:** 1-1/4 hours • **Yield:** 2 cups.
You can enjoy the taste of autumn for weeks at a time!
With just a few basic ingredients, fresh pumpkin turns into
a tasty topping for pork chops or poultry.
—*Myra Innes, Auburn, Kansas*

1 cup water	1/4 cup cider vinegar
1/2 cup sugar	1/2 teaspoon whole
1-3/4 cups cubed peeled pie pumpkin	cloves

1. In a large saucepan, bring water and sugar to a boil; cook and stir for 5 minutes. Add the pumpkin, vinegar and cloves. Reduce heat; simmer, uncovered, for 1 hour and 15 minutes or until pumpkin is tender. Discard cloves. Store in the refrigerator for up to 3 weeks.

Nutrition Facts: 1/4 cup equals 10 calories, trace fat (trace saturated fat), 0 cholesterol, trace sodium, 2 g carbohydrate, trace fiber, trace protein. **Diabetic Exchange:** Free Food.

PICKLED PUMPKIN NOTES: _____
_____
_____
_____
_____

PICKLED PEPPER RELISH NOTES:
_____
_____
_____
_____
_____

Pickled Pepper Relish

Prep: 20 min. + chilling • **Cook:** 10 min. • **Yield:** 1 cup.
Here's an eye-catching medley that's an instant flavor booster. I love it on barbecued beef sandwiches or added to coleslaw or potato salad.
—*Karen Barb, Layton, Utah*

1/4 cup *each* finely chopped green, sweet red and yellow pepper	1/2 cup water
	1/2 teaspoon salt
1 teaspoon finely chopped jalapeno pepper	1 small bay leaf
	1/4 teaspoon ground allspice
2 tablespoons canned chopped green chilies	1/8 teaspoon ground coriander
3 tablespoons finely chopped onion	3 tablespoons white vinegar
	2 tablespoons sugar

1. Place the peppers, chilies and onion in a 2-cup glass container; set aside. In a saucepan, bring water and salt to a boil. Ladle boiling liquid over pepper mixture. Stir in the bay leaf, allspice and coriander. Cover and refrigerate for 12 hours or overnight.

2. In a small saucepan, bring vinegar and sugar to a boil. Reduce heat; simmer, uncovered, for 3-4 minutes or until sugar is dissolved. Drain pepper mixture; discard bay leaf. Transfer to a serving bowl; stir in vinegar mixture. Serve with a slotted spoon.

Nutrition Facts: 1/4 cup equals 36 calories, trace fat (trace saturated fat), 0 cholesterol, 313 mg sodium, 9 g carbohydrate, 1 g fiber, trace protein. **Diabetic Exchange:** 1/2 starch.

EDITOR'S NOTE: We recommend wearing disposable gloves when cutting hot peppers. Avoid touching your face.

Pickled Eggs with Beets

Prep: 10 min. + chilling • **Yield:** 12 servings.

My mother always served pickled eggs at Easter. It was a tradition that my family expected. I made them for my granddaughter the last time she visited, and they were all gone before she left.

—*Mary Banker, Fort Worth, Texas*

2 cans (15 ounces *each*) whole beets	1 cup sugar
12 hard-cooked eggs, peeled	1 cup water
	1 cup cider vinegar

1. Drain beets, reserving 1 cup juice (discard remaining juice or save for another use). Place beets and eggs in a 2-qt. glass jar.

2. In a small saucepan, bring the sugar, water, vinegar and reserved beet juice to a boil. Pour over beets and eggs; cool.

3. Cover mixture tightly and refrigerate for at least 24 hours before serving.

Nutrition Facts: 1 serving equals 168 calories, 5 g fat (2 g saturated fat), 212 mg cholesterol, 200 mg sodium, 23 g carbohydrate, 1 g fiber, 7 g protein.

PICKLED EGGS WITH BEETS NOTES: _____
_____
_____
_____
_____

Garden's Harvest Pickles

Prep: 1 hour + chilling • **Process:** 20 min./batch • **Yield:** 11 pints.

This relish recipe from a friend is similar to giardiniera only sweeter. I have a certain sense of pride when giving jars as gifts knowing all the vegetables were raised in my own garden.

—*Linda Chapman, Meriden, Iowa*

3 large onions, cut into wedges	3 cups cauliflower florets
3 medium green peppers, cut into 1-inch pieces	3 cups cut fresh green beans (2-inch lengths)
3 medium sweet red peppers, cut into 1-inch pieces	3 medium zucchini, cut into 1-inch slices
1/4 cup canning salt	6 cups sugar
6 celery ribs, cut into 2-inch lengths	6 cups white vinegar
6 medium carrots, cut into 1/2-inch slices	1/4 cup mustard seed
	1/4 cup celery seed

1. In a large bowl, combine the onions, peppers and canning salt. Cover and refrigerate overnight.

2. Drain; place mixture in a stockpot. Add the remaining ingredients. Bring to a boil. Reduce heat; simmer, uncovered, for 15-20 minutes or until tender. Carefully ladle hot mixture into hot 1-pint jars, leaving 1/2-in. headspace. Remove air bubbles; wipe rims and adjust lids. Process for 20 minutes in a boiling-water canner.

Nutrition Facts: 1/4 cup equals 30 calories, trace fat (trace saturated fat), 0 cholesterol, 113 mg sodium, 7 g carbohydrate, 1 g fiber, 1 g protein.
Diabetic Exchange: 1/2 starch.

GARDEN'S HARVEST PICKLES NOTES:
_____
_____
_____
_____

EASY DOES IT.
If you plan to prepare a lot
of relish, make the chopping
easier by using a food processor
or a food grinder with a coarse
grinding blade. If using large
zucchini or cucumbers, be sure
to seed them before chopping.
(Pictured here from top:
Eggplant Pepper Relish, Spicy
Corn and Black Bean Relish
and Spicy Zucchini Relish.)

Eggplant Pepper Relish

Prep: 10 min. • **Broil:** 15 min. + standing • **Yield:** 12 servings.
This colorful combination of broiled peppers and eggplant is nicely seasoned with garlic and oregano. Serve it warm or cold, as a side dish, sandwich topper or on toasted bread rounds as an appetizer.
—*Jeanne Vitale, Leola, Pennsylvania*

- 3 medium sweet red peppers, cut in half lengthwise
- 3 medium sweet yellow peppers, cut in half lengthwise
- 1 medium eggplant, cut in half lengthwise
- 2 tablespoons olive oil
- 1 garlic clove, minced
- 1/4 cup minced fresh parsley
- 1 tablespoon minced fresh oregano *or* 1 teaspoon dried oregano
- 3/4 teaspoon salt
- 1/4 teaspoon pepper

1. Place peppers skin side up on an ungreased a broiler pan. Broil for 10-15 minutes or until tender and skin is blistered. Place peppers in a large bowl; cover and let stand for 15-20 minutes. Peel off and discard charred skin.

EGG-CELLENT EGGPLANT.
Young and tender eggplants do not need to be peeled before using. However, larger eggplants, which may be bitter, will taste better if you peel them before adding them to a recipe. —Taste of Home

2. Meanwhile, broil eggplant skin side up for 5-7 minutes or until tender and skin is blistered. Place in a small bowl, cover and let stand for 15-20 minutes. Peel off and discard charred skin. Cut peppers into strips and eggplant into cubes.

3. In a large bowl, combine the oil and garlic. Add peppers, eggplant, parsley, oregano, salt and pepper. Toss to coat. Serve at room temperature.

Nutritional Analysis: 1/3 cup equals 55 calories, 3 g fat (trace saturated fat), 0 cholesterol, 150 mg sodium, 8 g carbohydrate, 2 g fiber, 1 g protein. **Diabetic Exchanges:** 1 vegetable, 1/2 fat.

Spicy Zucchini Relish

Prep: 35 min. + marinating • **Cook:** 40 min. + chilling • **Yield:** 3 cups.
Zucchini creates a nice change of pace from the usual pickle relish, and the assortment of peppers adds a tongue-tingling bite.
—*Amy Martin, Bellefontaine, Ohio*

- 5 cups shredded zucchini
- 1 cup grated onion
- 4-1/2 teaspoons salt
- 1-1/2 teaspoons cornstarch
- 1-1/2 teaspoons ground mustard
- 1-1/2 teaspoons ground turmeric
- 1 teaspoon celery seed
- 3/4 teaspoon pepper
- 3/4 cup white vinegar
- 1/2 cup finely chopped sweet red pepper
- 4-1/2 teaspoons chopped seeded jalapeno pepper
- 1-1/4 teaspoons chopped seeded habanero pepper

1. In a large resealable plastic bag, combine the zucchini, onion and salt. Seal bag and turn to coat; refrigerate for 8 hours or overnight. Rinse with water; drain.

2. In a large saucepan, combine cornstarch, mustard, turmeric, celery seed and pepper. Gradually whisk in vinegar until blended. Stir in peppers and zucchini mixture. Bring to a boil. Reduce heat; simmer, uncovered, for 30 minutes. Cool. Cover and refrigerate for at least 4 hours before serving.

Nutrition Facts: 1 tablespoon equals 5 calories, trace fat (trace saturated fat), 0 cholesterol, 223 mg sodium, 1 g carbohydrate, trace fiber, trace protein.

EDITOR'S NOTE: Wear disposable gloves when cutting hot peppers; the oils can burn skin. Avoid touching your face.

Spicy Corn and Black Bean Relish

Prep: 10 min. + chilling • **Yield:** 6-8 servings.
This relish can be served as a salad or garnish with a Southwestern meal—it's especially good with chicken.
—*Gail Segreto, Elizabeth, Colorado*

- 2-1/2 cups fresh *or* frozen corn, cooked
- 1 can (15 ounces) black beans, rinsed and drained
- 3/4 to 1 cup chopped seeded Anaheim chili peppers
- 1/8 to 1/4 cup chopped seeded jalapeno peppers
- 1/4 cup vinegar
- 2 tablespoons vegetable oil
- 1 tablespoon Dijon mustard
- 1 teaspoon chili powder
- 1 teaspoon ground cumin
- 3/4 teaspoon salt
- 1/2 teaspoon pepper

1. In a large bowl, combine corn, beans and peppers. Combine remaining ingredients in a small bowl; pour over corn mixture and toss to coat. Chill.

Nutrition Facts: 1/8 recipe (calculated without added salt) equals 128 calories, 4 g fat (0 saturated fat), 0 cholesterol, 295 mg sodium, 19 g carbohydrate, 5 g fiber, 5 g protein. **Diabetic Exchanges:** 1 starch, 1 fat.

EDITOR'S NOTE: Wear disposable gloves when cutting hot peppers; the oils can burn skin. Avoid touching your face.

Garden Tomato Relish

Prep: 1-1/2 hours + simmering • **Process:** 20 min.
Yield: 10 pints.

What a great way to use your garden harvest and have a tasty
relish on hand for hot dogs, hamburgers and other dishes.
Why not share a jar with a friend or neighbor?
—*Kelly Martel, Tillsonburg, Ontario*

- 10 pounds tomatoes
- 3 large sweet onions, finely chopped
- 2 medium sweet red peppers, finely chopped
- 2 medium green peppers, finely chopped
- 2 teaspoons mustard seed
- 1 teaspoon celery seed
- 4-1/2 cups white vinegar
- 2-1/2 cups packed brown sugar
- 3 tablespoons canning salt
- 2 teaspoons ground ginger
- 2 teaspoons ground cinnamon
- 1 teaspoon ground allspice
- 1 teaspoon ground cloves
- 1 teaspoon ground nutmeg

1. In a large saucepan, bring 8 cups water to a boil. Add tomatoes, a few at a time; boil for 30 seconds. Drain and immediately place the tomatoes in ice water. Drain and pat dry; peel and finely chop. Place in a stockpot. Add onions and peppers.

2. Place mustard and celery seed on a double thickness of cheesecloth; bring up corners of cloth and tie with string to form a bag. Add spice bag and the remaining ingredients to the pot. Bring to a boil. Reduce heat; cover and simmer for 60-70 minutes or until slightly thickened. Discard spice bag.

3. Carefully ladle relish into hot 1-pint jars, leaving 1/2-in. headspace. Remove air bubbles; wipe rims and adjust lids. Process in boiling-water canner for 20 minutes.

Nutrition Facts: 2 tablespoons equals 20 calories, trace fat (trace saturated fat), 0 cholesterol, 136 mg sodium, 5 g carbohydrate, trace fiber, trace protein.

Spiced Pickled Beets

Prep: 1-1/4 hours • **Process:** 35 min. • **Yield:** 4 pints.
With a spicy, robust flavor, these pickled beets are so delicious,
they are guaranteed to convert any naysayers!
—*Edna Hoffman, Hebron, Indiana*

3 pounds small fresh beets	2 cinnamon sticks (3 inches)
2 cups sugar	1 teaspoon whole cloves
2 cups water	1 teaspoon whole allspice
2 cups cider vinegar	

1. Scrub beets and trim tops to 1 in. Place in a Dutch oven and cover with water. Bring to a boil. Reduce heat; cover and simmer for 25-35 minutes or until tender. Remove from the water; cool. Peel beets and cut into fourths.

2. Place beets in a Dutch oven. Add the sugar, water and vinegar. Place spices on a double thickness of cheesecloth; bring up corners of cloth and tie with string to form a bag. Add to the beet mixture. Bring to a boil. Reduce heat; cover and simmer for 10 minutes. Discard spice bag.

3. Carefully pack beets into hot 1-pint jars to within 1/2 in. of the top. Carefully ladle hot liquid over beets, leaving 1/2-in. headspace. Remove air bubbles; wipe rims and adjust lids. Process for 35 minutes in a boiling-water canner.

Nutrition Facts: 1/4 cup equals 53 calories, trace fat (trace saturated fat), 0 cholesterol, 44 mg sodium, 12 g carbohydrate, 1 g fiber, 1 g protein. **Diabetic Exchanges:** 1 vegetable, 1/2 starch.

SPICED PICKLED BEETS NOTES: _____
_____
_____
_____
_____

Iowa Corn Relish

Prep: 1 hour • **Process:** 20 min. • **Yield:** 5 pints.
I've been making colorful, crunchy corn relish for more
than 30 years, and my family never tires of it. It's excellent
served with roasted turkey, pork or ham.
—*Deanna Ogle, Bellingham, Washington*

20 medium ears sweet corn	1 large sweet red pepper, chopped
2-2/3 cups white vinegar	4-1/2 teaspoons mustard seed
2 cups water	1 tablespoon canning salt
1-1/2 cups sugar	1 teaspoon celery seed
2 medium onions, chopped	1/2 teaspoon ground turmeric
2 celery ribs, chopped	
1 large green pepper, chopped	

1. Place corn in a stockpot; cover with water. Bring to a boil; cover and cook for 3 minutes or until tender. Drain. Cut corn from cobs, making about 10 cups. Return corn to the pan; add remaining ingredients. Bring to a boil. Reduce heat and simmer for 20 minutes.

2. Carefully ladle hot mixture into hot 1-pint jars, leaving 1/2-in. headspace. Remove air bubbles; wipe rims and adjust lids. Process for 20 minutes in a boiling-water canner.

Nutrition Facts: 1/2 cup equals 148 calories, 1 g fat (trace saturated fat), 0 cholesterol, 373 mg sodium, 34 g carbohydrate, 3 g fiber, 3 g protein. **Diabetic Exchange:** 2 starch.

IOWA CORN RELISH NOTES: _____
_____
_____
_____
_____

chutneys, salsas & CONDIMENTS

Presto Black Bean & Corn Salsa

Prep/Total Time: 25 min. • **Yield:** 28 servings (1/4 cup each).
I like to tinker with a variety of foods, including salsa. This chunky version makes a big batch, but it will be gone before you know it!
—*Jan Daniels, Rochester, Minnesota*

- 1 can (15 ounces) black beans, rinsed and drained
- 2 cups fresh *or* frozen corn, thawed
- 5 plum tomatoes, chopped
- 1 large sweet red pepper, chopped
- 1 small green pepper, chopped
- 1 can (4 ounces) chopped green chilies
- 1/4 cup chopped red onion
- 1/4 cup minced fresh cilantro
- 2 tablespoons lime juice
- 2 garlic cloves, minced
- 1 teaspoon sugar
- 1 teaspoon salt
- 1/2 teaspoon ground cumin
- 1 jar (16 ounces) salsa
  Tortilla chips

1. In a large bowl, combine the beans, corn, tomatoes, peppers, chilies, onion, cilantro, lime juice, garlic, sugar, salt and cumin. Stir in salsa until blended. Serve with chips.

Nutrition Facts: 1/4 cup (calculated without chips) equals 35 calories, trace fat (trace saturated fat), 0 cholesterol, 195 mg sodium, 7 g carbohydrate, 1 g fiber, 1 g protein.

Ranked among the top 10 most popular condiments, salsa and chutney add fresh flavor and color to a variety of dishes.

Whether you're cooking up something sweet or savory, mild or spicy, you'll find plenty of options plus a few mustards and sauces to add the perfect sidekick to appetizers, sides and main dishes.

PRESTO BLACK BEAN & CORN SALSA
NOTES:_____
_____
_____
_____
_____

Strawberry Salsa

Prep: 20 min. + chilling • **Yield:** 4 cups.
This fun, fresh-tasting salsa is strawberry-sweet with just a hint of bite. It really adds a punch to fish, chicken or tortilla chips and has wonderful color and eye appeal.
—*Nancy Whitford, Edwards, New York*

- 1-1/2 cups sliced fresh strawberries
- 1-1/2 cups chopped sweet red pepper
- 1 cup chopped green pepper
- 1 cup seeded chopped tomato
- 1/4 cup chopped Anaheim pepper
- 2 tablespoons minced fresh cilantro
- 1/2 teaspoon salt
- 1/2 teaspoon crushed red pepper flakes
- 1/4 teaspoon pepper
- 2 tablespoons plus 2 teaspoons honey
- 2 tablespoons lemon juice

1. In a large bowl, combine the first nine ingredients. In a small bowl, combine honey and lemon juice; gently stir into strawberry mixture. Cover and refrigerate for at least 4 hours. Stir just before serving. Serve with a slotted spoon.

Nutrition Facts: 1/4 cup salsa equals 25 calories, trace fat (trace saturated fat), 0 cholesterol, 76 mg sodium, 6 g carbohydrate, 1 g fiber, 1 g protein. **Diabetic Exchange:** 1/2 starch.

EDITOR'S NOTE: Wear disposable gloves when cutting hot peppers; the oils can burn skin. Avoid touching your face.

STRAWBERRY SALSA NOTES: _____
_____
_____
_____
_____

Mild Tomato Salsa

Prep: 1-1/2 hours • **Process:** 20 min. • **Yield:** 10 pints.
I got this salsa recipe from my sister, and my children and I have been making batches of it ever since. We pair pint jars with packages of tortilla chips for zesty holiday gifts.
—*Pamela Lundstrum, Bird Island, Minnesota*

- 36 medium tomatoes, peeled and quartered
- 4 medium green peppers, chopped
- 3 large onions, chopped
- 2 cans (12 ounces *each*) tomato paste
- 1-3/4 cups white vinegar
- 1/2 cup sugar
- 1 medium sweet red pepper, chopped
- 1 celery rib, chopped
- 15 garlic cloves, minced
- 4 to 5 jalapeno peppers, seeded and chopped
- 1/4 cup canning salt
- 1/4 to 1/2 teaspoon hot pepper sauce

1. In a large kettle, cook tomatoes, uncovered, over medium heat for 20 minutes. Drain, reserving 2 cups liquid. Return tomatoes to the kettle.

2. Stir in the green peppers, onions, tomato paste, vinegar, sugar, red pepper, celery, garlic, jalapenos, canning salt, hot pepper sauce and reserved tomato liquid. Bring to a boil. Reduce heat; simmer, uncovered, for 1 hour, stirring frequently.

3. Ladle hot mixture into hot jars, leaving 1/4-in. headspace. Adjust caps. Process for 20 minutes in a boiling-water bath.

Nutrition Facts: 1 serving (2 tablespoons) equals 14 calories, trace fat (trace saturated fat), 0 cholesterol, 182 mg sodium, 3 g carbohydrate, 1 g fiber, trace protein.

EDITOR'S NOTE: We recommend wearing disposable gloves when cutting hot peppers. Avoid touching your face.

MILD TOMATO SALSA NOTES: _____
_____
_____
_____

> AYE, THERE'S THE RUB.
> Instead of parboiling tomatoes to remove the skins, I rub the tomato all over with the back of a knife. The skin peels right off. I don't have to dirty a pan, wait for water to boil or risk burning my hands.
> —Lauren P., Baton Rouge, Louisiana

Tomato Bounty Salsa

Prep: 1-1/2 hours • **Process:** 20 min. • **Yield:** 9 pints.
I like to make this mild-tasting salsa with yellow tomatoes and use it as as a dip for chips and condiment for meats.
—*Joanne Surfus, Sturgeon Bay, Wisconsin*

9 pounds yellow tomatoes (25 to 30 medium)	3/4 cup white vinegar
4 medium onions, finely chopped	4 jalapeno peppers, seeded and chopped
2 cans (6 ounces *each*) tomato paste	4 garlic cloves, minced
1 large sweet red pepper, finely chopped	3 teaspoons salt
	1/2 teaspoon pepper

1. In a large saucepan, bring 8 cups water to a boil. Add tomatoes; boil for 30 seconds. Drain; immediately place in ice water. Drain and pat dry; peel and finely chop.

2. In a stockpot, combine remaining ingredients. Stir in tomatoes. Bring to a boil over medium-high heat. Reduce heat; simmer, uncovered, for 20 minutes or until desired thickness. Carefully ladle hot mixture into hot 1-pint jars, leaving 1/2-in. headspace. Remove air bubbles; wipe rims and adjust lids. Process for 20 minutes in a boiling-water canner.

Nutrition Facts: 1/4 cup equals 21 calories, trace fat (trace saturated fat), 0 cholesterol, 121 mg sodium, 4 g carbohydrate, 1 g fiber, 1 g protein. **Diabetic Exchange:** 1 vegetable.

Chili Sauce

Prep: 2 hours • **Process:** 15 min. • **Yield:** about 6 pints.
Add a little heat to a variety of dishes with this homemade chili sauce. We love it on nearly everything!
—*Virginia Lanphier, Omaha, Nebraska*

4 quarts chopped peeled tomatoes (about 24 large)	1 cup sugar
2 cups chopped onions	3 tablespoons salt
2 cups chopped sweet red peppers (about 4 medium)	3 tablespoons mixed pickling spices
	1 tablespoon celery seed
1 serrano pepper, finely chopped	1 tablespoon mustard seed
	2-1/2 cups white vinegar

1. In a stockpot, combine tomatoes, onions, peppers, sugar and salt; simmer, uncovered, for 45 minutes.

2. Place pickling spices, celery seed and mustard seed on a double thickness of cheesecloth; bring up corners of cloth and tie with string to form a bag; add to tomato mixture. Cook for 45 minutes or until very thick, stirring frequently.

3. Add vinegar; cook to desired thickness. Discard spice bag. Carefully ladle hot mixture into hot pint jars, leaving 1/2-in. headspace. Adjust caps. Process for 15 minutes in a boiling-water canner.

Nutrition Facts: 1 serving (2 tablespoons) equals 93 calories, 1 g fat (trace saturated fat), 0 cholesterol, 1,196 mg sodium, 22 g carbohydrate, 3 g fiber, 2 g protein.

Jalapeno-Pear Chutney

Prep: 45 min. + simmering • **Process:** 10 min.
Yield: 5 half-pints.
This versatile chutney is a mouthful of flavor. Serve it with your favorite meat entree, as a sandwich spread, over cream cheese.
—*Deb Thomson, Grand Island, Nebraska*

2 pounds pears, peeled and chopped	1 cup packed brown sugar
2 pounds tomatoes, peeled, seeded and chopped	4 teaspoons minced fresh gingerroot
2 cups chopped onions	1 to 2 teaspoons crushed red pepper flakes
1 cup finely chopped seeded jalapeno peppers	1 teaspoon ground mustard
1 cup cider vinegar	

1. In a Dutch oven, combine all ingredients. Bring to a boil. Reduce heat; simmer, uncovered, for 45-60 minutes or until thickened, stirring occasionally.

2. Carefully ladle hot mixture into hot half-pint jars, leaving 1/2-in. headspace. Remove air bubbles; wipe rims and adjust lids. Process for 10 minutes in a boiling-water canner.

Nutrition Facts: 1/4 cup equals 88 calories, trace fat (trace saturated fat), 0 cholesterol, 8 mg sodium, 22 g carbohydrate, 2 g fiber, 1 g protein. **Diabetic Exchanges:** 1 starch.

PUT DOWN THE CHIPS.
Fresh salsas and chutneys kick up the flavor of a wide variety of foods. Try stirring Chili Sauce (top) or Tomato Bounty Salsa (middle) into tomato soup or even mac 'n' cheese. Mix a spoonful of sweet and spicy Jalapeno Pear Chutney (bottom) with some mayonnaise to create a tasty sandwich base.

JALAPENO PEAR CHUTNEY

Raspberry-Onion Jalapeno Chutney

Prep: 45 min. • **Process:** 15 min. • **Yield:** 7 half-pints.
Sweet raspberries and spicy jalapenos come together to create a chutney that's terrific on top of cream cheese or grilled chicken.
—*Jo-Anne Cooper, Camrose, Alberta*

- 4 large onions, chopped
- 2 large red onions, chopped
- 1-1/2 cups packed brown sugar
- 1 cup raisins
- 1-1/4 cups cider vinegar
- 1 cup balsamic vinegar
- 1/2 cup sugar
- 2 jalapeno peppers, seeded and chopped
- 2 tablespoons grated orange peel
- 2 teaspoons canning salt
- 4 cups fresh raspberries

1. In a Dutch oven, bring the first 10 ingredients to a boil. Reduce heat; simmer, uncovered, for 25-30 minutes or until mixture is thickened, stirring occasionally. Stir in raspberries; heat through.

2. Remove from the heat. Ladle hot mixture into hot half-pint jars, leaving 1/2-in. headspace. Remove air bubbles; wipe rims and adjust lids. Process for 15 minutes in a boiling-water canner.

Nutrition Facts: 1/4 cup equals 104 calories, trace fat (trace saturated fat), 0 cholesterol, 178 mg sodium, 26 g carbohydrate, 2 g fiber, 1 g protein.

EDITOR'S NOTE: When cutting hot peppers, disposable gloves are recommended. Avoid touching your face.

Garden Zucchini Chutney

Prep: 20 min. • **Cook:** 50 min. • **Yield:** 4 cups.
At my wits' end with grating zucchini from my garden, I was determined to make something other than zucchini bread. I found this recipe and altered it to our taste.
—*Taren Weyer, Hudson, Wisconsin*

- 6 cups chopped seeded zucchini (about 7 medium)
- 2 medium tart apples, peeled and chopped
- 1-1/2 cups raisins or dried currants
- 1-1/2 cups white vinegar
- 1 cup honey
- 1 medium sweet red pepper, chopped
- 1 small onion, chopped
- 1/3 cup thawed orange juice concentrate
- 2 tablespoons bottled lemon juice

1. In a Dutch oven, bring all ingredients to a boil. Reduce heat; simmer, uncovered, for 45-55 minutes or until thickened.

2. Serve warm or cold. Refrigerate any leftovers.

Nutrition Facts: 2 tablespoons equals 67 calories, trace fat (trace saturated fat), 0 cholesterol, 4 mg sodium, 18 g carbohydrate, 1 g fiber, 1 g protein. **Diabetic Exchange:** 1 starch.

Spicy Chunky Salsa

Prep: 1-1/2 hours • **Process:** 15 min./batch • **Yield:** 8 pints.
Vinegar adds delightful tang to this sweet salsa. You'll love its
taste, but for more heat, leave in some hot pepper seeds.
—*Donna Goutermont, Juneau, Alaska*

  6 pounds tomatoes
  3 large green peppers, chopped
  3 large onions, chopped
  2 cups white vinegar
  1 large sweet red pepper, chopped
  1 can (12 ounces) tomato paste
  4 jalapeno peppers, seeded and chopped
  2 serrano peppers, seeded and chopped
1/2 cup sugar
1/2 cup minced fresh cilantro
1/2 cup bottled lemon juice
  3 garlic cloves, minced
  4 teaspoons ground cumin
  3 teaspoons salt
  2 teaspoons dried oregano
  1 teaspoon hot pepper sauce

1. In a large saucepan, bring 8 cups water to a boil.
Using a slotted spoon, place tomatoes, a few at a time, in
boiling water for 30-60 seconds. Remove each tomato and
immediately plunge in ice water. Drain and pat dry. Peel
and finely chop tomatoes to measure 9 cups. In a stockpot,
combine the tomatoes and remaining ingredients. Bring to
a boil. Reduce heat; simmer, uncovered, for 30 minutes or
until slightly thickened.

2. Carefully ladle hot mixture into hot 1-pint jars, leaving
1/2-in. headspace. Remove air bubbles; wipe rims and adjust
lids. Process for 15 minutes in a boiling-water canner.

Nutrition Facts: 1/4 cup equals 25 calories, trace fat (trace saturated
fat), 0 cholesterol, 117 mg sodium, 6 g carbohydrate, 1 g fiber, 1 g
protein. **Diabetic Exchange:** 1/2 starch.

EDITOR'S NOTE: When cutting hot peppers, disposable gloves are
recommended. Avoid touching your face.

CREATIVE CONDIMENTS.
Want to add a little kick to your
scrambled eggs? Try topping
them with a spoonful of Curry
Ketchup with a Kick (Pictured
top right). Jazz up egg salad
by replacing regular yellow
mustard with Spicy Mustard
(middle) and perk up grilled
pork chops with Raspberry
Barbecue Sauce (bottom).

Curry Ketchup with a Kick

Prep: 10 min. • **Cook:** 25 min. + chilling • **Yield:** 2 cups.
Turn up the heat on ordinary ketchup with this spicy version that stars curry. Delicious on brats and grilled sausages, it can be served warm or cold.
—*Alexandra Williams, Pfofeld, Germany*

- 1 bottle (20 ounces) ketchup
- 1 cup water
- 1/2 cup curry powder
- 1-1/2 teaspoons paprika
- 1-1/2 teaspoons Worcestershire sauce

1. In a large saucepan, combine all ingredients. Bring to a boil. Reduce heat; cover and simmer for 20-25 minutes or until thickened, stirring occasionally. Cover and refrigerate for at least 8 hours.

Nutrition Facts: 1 tablespoon equals 24 calories, trace fat (trace saturated fat), 0 cholesterol, 241 mg sodium, 6 g carbohydrate, 1 g fiber, trace protein.

CURRY KETCHUP WITH A KICK NOTES: _____
_____
_____
_____

Spicy Mustard

Prep: 15 min. • **Cook:** 5 min. + standing • **Yield:** 1-1/2 cups.
When I make this mustard, I add fresh horseradish from our garden and vinegar seasoned with homegrown tarragon. It adds a little extra zip to burgers and sandwiches.
—*Joyce Lonsdale, Unionville, Pennsylvania*

- 1/2 cup tarragon *or* cider vinegar
- 1/2 cup water
- 1/4 cup olive oil
- 1 to 2 tablespoons grated horseradish
- 1/2 teaspoon bottled lemon juice
- 1 cup ground mustard
- 1/2 cup sugar
- 1/2 teaspoon salt

1. In a blender or food processor, combine all ingredients; cover and process for 1 minute. Scrape down the sides of the container and process for 30 seconds.

2. Transfer to a small saucepan and let stand for 10 minutes. Cook over low heat until bubbly, stirring constantly. Cool completely. If a thinner mustard is desired, stir in an additional 1-2 tablespoons water. Pour into small containers with tight-fitting lids. Store in the refrigerator.

Nutrition Facts: 1 tablespoon equals 67 calories, 4 g fat (trace saturated fat), 0 cholesterol, 54 mg sodium, 6 g carbohydrate, 1 g fiber, 2 g protein.

SPICY MUSTARD NOTES: _____
_____
_____
_____

RASPBERRY BARBECUE SAUCE TIP:
Barbecue sauce and slowly cooked ribs is a near perfect, heaven-made match. But don't let ribs have all the fun! Slather that thick and sassy sauce on burgers and hot dogs, use it in place of pizza sauce, stir a spoonful or two into a pot of baked beans or use it as a dipping sauce for some oven-baked sweet potato fries. Yum! —Taste of Home

Raspberry Barbecue Sauce

Prep: 40 min. + cooling • **Yield:** 4 servings.
Raspberries replace the traditional tomatoes in this unique barbecue sauce. Red pepper flakes add a little kick to the thick ruby-red sauce. This is great over chicken breasts or pork tenderloin. Brush on the sauce near the end of the grilling time.
—*Garnet Pirre, Helena, Montana*

- 3 garlic cloves, peeled
- 1/4 teaspoon olive oil
- 1-1/4 cups fresh raspberries
- 3 tablespoons brown sugar
- 1 tablespoon balsamic vinegar
- 1 tablespoon light corn syrup
- 1 teaspoon molasses
- 1/2 teaspoon bottled lemon juice
- 1/4 to 1/2 teaspoon crushed red pepper flakes
- 1/8 teaspoon salt
- 1/8 teaspoon pepper
- Dash onion powder

1. Place garlic on a double thickness of heavy-duty foil; drizzle with oil. Wrap foil around garlic. Bake at 425° for 15-20 minutes. Cool for 10-15 minutes.

2. Place softened garlic in a small saucepan. Add remaining ingredients. Cook over medium-low heat for 15-20 minutes until sauce is thickened and bubbly. Remove from the heat; cool slightly.

3. Transfer to a food processor; cover and process until smooth. Strain seeds. Store in the refrigerator.

Nutritional Analysis: 1 serving (2 tablespoons) equals 83 calories, trace fat (trace saturated fat), 0 cholesterol, 86 mg sodium, 21 g carbohydrate, 3 g fiber, 1 g protein. **Diabetic Exchange:** 1-1/2 fruit.

RASPBERRY BARBECUE SAUCE NOTES: _____
_____
_____
_____

sweet treats & BEVERAGES

Blueberry Preserves

Prep: 30 min. • **Process:** 5 min. • **Yield:** 3 half-pints.
Juicy blueberries swimming in a sweet jelly taste terrific over vanilla ice cream. We also enjoy it on top of waffles and pancakes.
—*Shannon Arthur, Lucasville, Ohio*

- 5 cups fresh blueberries
- 2-1/4 cups sugar
- 2 teaspoons cider vinegar
- 1/2 teaspoon ground allspice
- 1/2 teaspoon ground cinnamon
- 1/4 teaspoon ground cloves

1. In a large saucepan, combine all the ingredients. Bring to a boil; cook for 15-18 minutes or until mixture is thickened, stirring frequently.

2. Remove from the heat; skim off foam. Ladle hot mixture into hot sterilized half-pint jars, leaving 1/4-in. headspace. Remove air bubbles; wipe rims and adjust lids. Process for 5 minutes in a boiling-water canner.

Nutrition Facts: 2 tablespoons equals 90 calories, trace fat (trace saturated fat), 0 cholesterol, trace sodium, 23 g carbohydrate, 1 g fiber, trace protein.

EDITOR'S NOTE: The processing time listed is for altitudes of 1,000 feet or less. Add 1 minute to the processing time for each 1,000 feet of additional altitude.

There's always room for dessert—especially when it means a bowl of homemade ice cream topped with a luscious fresh fruit sauce or a big slice of a freshly baked cherry pie!

So loosen that belt a notch or two, and get ready to dig into some of the freshest, most decadent creations that ever met your taste buds.

BLUEBERRY PRESERVES NOTES:

_____

_____

_____

_____

_____

Strawberry Sundae Sauce

Prep: 25 min. + standing • **Yield:** 8 cups.
My husband and kids simply love this recipe over their
ice cream! It may also be used in banana splits.
—*Peggy Townsend, Florence, Colorado*

2 quarts fresh strawberries	1/3 cup chocolate syrup
6 cups sugar	1/3 cup raspberry liqueur, optional
1 pouch (3 ounces) liquid fruit pectin	Vanilla ice cream

1. Wash and mash strawberries, measuring out enough mashed berries to make 4 cups. In a Dutch oven, combine the strawberries and sugar. Bring to a full rolling boil over high heat, stirring constantly. Stir in pectin. Boil 1 minute longer, stirring constantly.

2. Remove from the heat. Stir in syrup and liqueur if desired. Skim off foam. Pour into jars or freezer containers, leaving a 1/2-in. headspace. Cool to room temperature, about 1 hour. Cover and let stand overnight or until set. Refrigerate for up to 3 weeks or freeze for up to 1 year. Serve with ice cream.

Nutrition Facts: 1/4 cup (calculated without liqueur and ice cream) equals 174 calories, trace fat (trace saturated fat), 0 cholesterol, 3 mg sodium, 43 g carbohydrate, 1 g fiber, trace protein.

STRAWBERRY SUNDAE SAUCE NOTES:

_____

_____

_____

_____

Strawberry Mango Sorbet

Prep: 20 min. + freezing • **Yield:** 1 quart.
This is fresh, really simple and will keep in a freezer container—that
is if you don't eat it all the first day.
—*Sandra Vachon, Saint-Constant, Quebec*

3/4 cup sugar	1-1/2 cups fresh strawberries, halved
1-1/2 cups water	1/4 cup lime juice
1-1/2 cups chopped peeled mangoes	

1. In a small saucepan, bring sugar and water to a boil. Cook and stir until sugar is dissolved; set aside to cool.

2. In a food processor, cover and process mangoes and strawberries until pureed. Transfer to a large bowl; stir in sugar syrup and lime juice.

3. Pour into a 13-in. x 9-in. dish; cover and freeze for 45 minutes or until edges begin to firm. Stir and return to freezer. Freeze 2 hours longer or until firm.

4. Just before serving, transfer to a food processor; cover and process for 2-3 minutes or until smooth.

Nutrition Facts: 1/2 cup equals 103 calories, trace fat (trace saturated fat), 0 cholesterol, 1 mg sodium, 27 g carbohydrate, 1 g fiber, trace protein.
Diabetic Exchanges: 1-1/2 starch, 1/2 fruit.

STRAWBERRY MANGO SORBET NOTES:

_____

_____

_____

_____

Pound Cake with Brandied Peach Sauce

Prep/Total Time: 30 min. • **Yield:** 6 servings.
This peach sauce is so quick and elegant, you'll want to
serve it over pound cake, shortcake, ice cream,
waffles or whatever your palate desires.
—*Suzy Horvath, Gladstone, Oregon*

1 cup water
3 tablespoons brandy *or* apricot nectar
2 tablespoons sugar
2 tablespoons peach preserves
Dash salt
3 cups sliced peeled peaches (about 5 medium)
   or frozen unsweetened sliced peaches
1 cup heavy whipping cream
4-1/2 teaspoons confectioners' sugar
2-1/4 teaspoons vanilla extract, *divided*
6 slices pound cake

1. In a large saucepan, combine the water, brandy, sugar, peach preserves and salt. Bring to a boil; reduce heat. Add peaches; cook and stir for 3-4 minutes or until tender.

2. With a slotted spoon, remove peaches to a bowl; set aside. Bring sauce mixture to a boil; cook and stir until reduced to 1/2 cup.

3. Meanwhile, in a small bowl, beat cream until it begins to thicken. Add confectioners' sugar and 1/4 teaspoon vanilla; beat until stiff peaks form.

4. Add the reduced sauce and remaining vanilla to the peaches; stir gently to combine. Serve with pound cake and whipped cream.

Nutrition Facts: 1 slice with 1/3 cup sauce and 1/3 cup whipped cream equals 346 calories, 21 g fat (13 g saturated fat), 121 mg cholesterol, 159 mg sodium, 34 g carbohydrate, 1 g fiber, 3 g protein.

Apple Dessert Sauce

Prep/Total Time: 10 min. • **Yield:** 1-3/4 cups.

Spooned over vanilla ice cream, this sauce gives you the taste of warm apple pie without all the fuss. The recipe is so easy, even kids can make it.

—Jacqueline Graves, Cumming, Georgia

3/4 cup chopped peeled tart apple	1 cup (8 ounces) sour cream
1 tablespoon water	1/4 teaspoon ground cinnamon
1 cup packed brown sugar	Vanilla ice cream

1. In a 1-qt. microwave-safe dish, combine apple and water. Cover and microwave on high for 1 minute. Stir in brown sugar. Cover and cook 1 minute longer.

2. Stir in sour cream and cinnamon. Cover and cook at 50% power for 1-1/2 to 1-3/4 minutes or until brown sugar is melted, stirring once. Stir until blended. Serve warm with ice cream.

Nutrition Facts: 1/4 cup equals 193 calories, 6 g fat (4 g saturated fat), 23 mg cholesterol, 24 mg sodium, 33 g carbohydrate, trace fiber, 1 g protein.

EDITOR'S NOTE: This recipe was tested in a 1,100-watt microwave.

APPLE DESSERT SAUCE NOTES: _____
_____
_____
_____

Rhubarb Sauce

Prep/Total Time: 20 min. • **Yield:** 1-1/4 cups.

Celebrate spring with the sweet-tart taste of rhubarb in my simple sauce. I serve it on toast, English muffins and pancakes, but it's just as good drizzled on pound cake or ice cream.

—Jackie Hutshing, Sonoma, California

1/3 cup sugar	1/8 teaspoon ground nutmeg
1/4 cup water	Pound cake *or* vanilla ice cream
2-1/4 cups sliced fresh *or* frozen rhubarb	
1 teaspoon grated lemon peel	

1. In a small saucepan, bring sugar and water to a boil. Add rhubarb; cook and stir for 5-10 minutes or until rhubarb is tender and mixture is slightly thickened. Remove from the heat; stir in lemon peel and nutmeg.

2. Serve warm or chilled over pound cake or ice cream. Refrigerate leftovers.

Nutrition Facts: 1/4 cup (calculated without cake or ice cream) equals 64 calories, trace fat (trace saturated fat), 0 cholesterol, 2 mg sodium, 16 g carbohydrate, 1 g fiber, 1 g protein. **Diabetic Exchange:** 1 starch.

EDITOR'S NOTE: If using frozen rhubarb, measure rhubarb while still frozen, then thaw completely. Drain in a colander, but do not press liquid out.

RHUBARB SAUCE NOTES: _____
_____
_____
_____

SORBET, ICE CREAM & FROZEN YOGURT.
Unlike its "cousins" ice cream
and frozen yogurt, sorbet's base
is fruit juice, not milk. Because
it contains no dairy, it's a great
alternative for people who are
sensitive to dairy products.
—Taste of Home

Mint Watermelon Sorbet

Prep: 20 min. + freezing • **Yield:** 7 servings.
You'll have a taste of summer with this refreshing sorbet.
Watermelon, mint and lime juice are the predominant
flavors that give it just the right amount of zip.
It would be perfect on a hot afternoon.
—*Taste of Home Test Kitchen*

1/2 cup sugar	1 tablespoon minced fresh mint
1/2 cup water	
4 cups cubed seedless watermelon	1 tablespoon honey
	2 teaspoons lime juice
2 tablespoons orange juice	

1. In a small saucepan, bring sugar and water to a
boil, stirring constantly until sugar is dissolved; set
aside. In a blender, process watermelon in batches
until smooth. Transfer to a large bowl; stir in the sugar
syrup, orange juice, mint, honey and lime juice.

2. Pour mixture into a 13-in. x 9-in. dish; cover and
freeze for 8 hours or until firm. Just before serving,
transfer to a food processor; cover and process in
batches until smooth.

Nutrition Facts: 1/2 cup equals 90 calories, trace fat (0 saturated
fat), 0 cholesterol, 3 mg sodium, 25 g carbohydrate, 1 g fiber,
trace protein. **Diabetic Exchanges:** 1 starch, 1/2 fruit.

FROZEN TREATS NOTES: _____
_____
_____
_____
_____
_____
_____
_____
_____
_____
_____

Blueberry Ice Cream

Prep: 15 min. + chilling • **Process:** 20 min./batch + freezing
Yield: about 1-3/4 quarts.
The wild blueberries on our property spark recipe ideas. When
my daughter and I made this ice cream at a Girl Guide meeting,
it was well-received. Even today, our 10 children, 19 grandkids
and four great-grandchildren think it tastes great.
—*Alma Mosher, Mohannes, New Brunswick*

4 cups fresh or frozen blueberries	2 tablespoons water
	4 cups half-and-half cream
2 cups sugar	

1. In a large saucepan, combine the blueberries,
sugar and water. Bring to a boil. Reduce heat; simmer,
uncovered, until sugar is dissolved and berries are
softened. Strain mixture; discard seeds and skins. Stir in
the cream. Cover and refrigerate overnight.

2. Fill cylinder of ice cream freezer two-thirds
full; freeze according to manufacturer's directions.
Refrigerate remaining mixture until ready to freeze.
When ice cream is frozen, transfer to a freezer container;
freeze for 2-4 hours before serving.

Nutrition Facts: 1 serving (1/2 cup) equals 226 calories, 7 g fat
(5 g saturated fat), 34 mg cholesterol, 35 mg sodium, 37 g
carbohydrate, 1 g fiber, 3 g protein.

Blackberry Frozen Yogurt

Prep: 30 min. + freezing • **Yield:** 8 servings.
I pair sun-ripened blackberries with a tangy vanilla yogurt to
churn out this creamy purple delight. You could also use fresh
boysenberries, raspberries or strawberries.
—*Rebecca Baird, Salt Lake City, Utah*

5 cups fresh *or* frozen blackberries	2 teaspoons vanilla extract
1/3 cup water	4 cups (32 ounces) fat-free frozen vanilla yogurt
2 tablespoons lemon juice	
1 cup sugar	

1. In a food processor, puree blackberries, water and
lemon juice. Strain blackberries, reserving juice and
pulp. Discard seeds. Return pureed blackberries to food
processor; add sugar and vanilla. Cover and process until
smooth.

2. In a large bowl, combine yogurt and blackberry
mixture. Fill cylinder of ice cream freezer two-thirds
full; freeze according to the manufacturer's directions.
Refrigerate remaining mixture until ready to freeze.
When yogurt is frozen, transfer to a freezer container;
freeze for 2-4 hours before serving.

Nutritional Analysis: 1 serving (3/4 cup) equals 200 calories,
2 g fat (1 g saturated fat), 7 mg cholesterol, 80 mg sodium,
41 g carbohydrate, 3 g fiber, 6 g protein.

A TASTY TRIO.
Because of it's high milk
and air content, ice cream is
the creamiest when stacked
against frozen yogurts or
sorbets. Because it lacks dairy,
sorbets will have an icier
texture and more tart flavor
than its frosty counterparts.
(Pictured here clockwise from
top: Blueberry Ice Cream,
Blackberry Frozen Yogurt and
Mint Watermelon Sorbet.)

Rhubarb Ice Cream

Prep: 40 min. + freezing • **Yield:** 2-3/4 cups.
Always refreshing, this rich-tasting ice cream is
great on a spring or summer evening.
—*Rachel Garcia, Honolulu, Hawaii.*

3 cups sliced fresh *or* frozen rhubarb	1 teaspoon lemon juice
2 cups sugar	1 cup heavy whipping cream

1. Place rhubarb in an ungreased 13-in. x 9-in. baking
dish. Sprinkle with sugar; toss to coat. Cover and bake
at 375° for 30-40 minutes or until tender, stirring
occasionally. Cool slightly. Process in batches in a blender
or food processor. Transfer to a bowl; cover and refrigerate
until chilled.

2. Stir in lemon juice. In a bowl, beat cream until stiff
peaks form. Gradually fold into the rhubarb mixture.
Transfer to a shallow 2-qt. freezer container. Freeze,
uncovered, for 1 hour, stirring every 15 minutes. Cover and
freeze overnight.

Nutrition Facts: 1 serving (1/2 cup) equals 489 calories, 18 g fat (11 g
saturated fat), 65 mg cholesterol, 22 mg sodium, 85 g carbohydrate,
1 g fiber, 2 g protein.

RHUBARB ICE CREAM NOTES: _____
_____
_____
_____
_____
_____

Raspberry-Lemon Spritzer

Prep/Total Time: 15 min. • **Yield:** 2 servings.
This is my favorite summer refreshment. It isn't too
sweet, and the color is spectacular.
—*Margie Williams, Mt. Juliet, Tennessee*

1/2 cup fresh *or* frozen raspberries, thawed	1/4 cup lemon juice
1/3 cup sugar	Ice cubes
2-1/2 cups club soda, chilled	2 lemon slices

1. Place the raspberries and sugar in a food processor; cover
and process until pureed. Strain; reserving the juice and
discarding seeds.

2. In a small pitcher, combine the club soda, lemon juice and
raspberry juice. Serve in tall glasses over ice. Garnish with
lemon slices.

Nutrition Facts: 1-1/2 cups equals 148 calories, trace fat (0 saturated fat),
0 cholesterol, 66 mg sodium, 39 g carbohydrate, trace fiber, trace protein.

RASPBERRY-LEMON SPRITZER NOTES:
_____
_____
_____
_____
_____

Red Carpet-tini

Prep/Total Time: 5 min. • **Yield:** 1 serving.
Bubbly Champagne gets a fruity punch with pomegranate juice and raspberry and orange liqueur.
—*Taste of Home Test Kitchen*

Ice cubes
1 ounce raspberry liqueur
1/2 ounce orange liqueur
1/2 ounce pomegranate juice
3 fresh raspberries
1/2 cup chilled Champagne

1. Fill a mixing glass or tumbler one-third full with ice. Add the raspberry liqueur, orange liqueur and pomegranate juice; stir until condensation forms on outside of glass.

2. Place raspberries in a chilled champagne flute or cocktail glass; strain liqueur mixture into glass. Top with champagne.

Nutrition Facts: 1 serving equals 243 calories, 0 fat (0 saturated fat), 0 cholesterol, 2 mg sodium, 20 g carbohydrate, 0 fiber, trace protein.

RED CARPET-TINI NOTES: _____
_____
_____
_____

APPLE PIE FILLING NOTES:
_____
_____
_____
_____

Apple Pie Filling

Prep: 35 min. + freezing • **Cook:** 10 min. + cooling
Yield: 5-1/2 quarts (enough for about five 9-inch pies).
My family is always delighted to see an oven-fresh apple pie cooling on the counter. What a convenience to have jars of this canned homemade pie filling on hand so I can treat them to pies year-round.
—*Laurie Mace, Los Osos, California*

18 cups sliced peeled tart apples (about 6 pounds)
3 tablespoons lemon juice
4-1/2 cups sugar
1 cup cornstarch
2 teaspoons ground cinnamon
1 teaspoon salt
1/4 teaspoon ground nutmeg
10 cups water

1. In a large bowl, toss apples with lemon juice; set aside. In a Dutch oven over medium heat, combine the sugar, cornstarch, cinnamon, salt and nutmeg. Add water; bring to a boil. Boil for 2 minutes, stirring constantly. Add apples; return to a boil. Reduce heat; cover and simmer until the apples are tender, about 6-8 minutes. Cool for 30 minutes.

2. Ladle into freezer containers, leaving 1/2-in. headspace. Cool at room temperature no longer than 1-1/2 hours. Seal and freeze; store up to 12 months.

Nutrition Facts: 1 serving (1 each) equals 128 calories, trace fat (trace saturated fat), 0 cholesterol, 60 mg sodium, 33 g carbohydrate, 1 g fiber, trace protein.

General Index

Alphabetical Index

Tips & Charts By Season